Banging My Head Against the Wall

A Comedy Writer's Guide to Seeing Stars

ANDY COWAN

Foreword by Jay Leno

not for sale on ebay — Love, Andy

Black Rose Writing | Texas

ISBN: 978-1-68433-013-3
PUBLISHED BY BLACK ROSE WRITING
www.blackrosewriting.com

Printed in the United States of America
Suggested Retail Price (SRP) $22.95

Banging Your Head Banging Your Head is printed in EB Garamond

For my parents, Audrey and Raymond

Acknowledgments

Thanks to Reagan Rothe and *Black Rose Writing* for believing in this work.

Thanks to producer Paul Solomon for hearing my persistent knocking and opening the door to *The Merv Griffin Show*. Thanks to Merv and producer Peter Barsocchini for keeping the faith. Thanks to director, Dick Carson, first assistant director, Kevin McCarthy and Mort Lindsey and his orchestra for keeping the performer in me afloat. Talent coordinators Karen Gruber, John Scura, Ray Richmond, Lisa Dee, Chris Bavelles, producer Les Sinclair, researchers Carole Dixon and Reva Solomon, stage managers Dave Fraser, John Lauderdale, Ray Sneath, photographer Mark Edward Harris, production manager Mark Fogelman, production assistants Stefanie Berger, Wendy Dawson, Andrew Goldsmith and audience coordinator Lee Valentine – thanks for making my first showbiz gig feel like a family. Cheers to fellow talent coordinator and writer, David Williger, for the ride we shared to our first sitcom.

Thanks to Harry Bliss, Brian Crane, Fred Crippen, Brandon Fall, David King, Dan McConnell, Dan Piraro, Dan Povenmire, Hilary Price, Alex Schumacher and Steve Smallwood for artfully enriching my words.

Thanks to Nina Beck, Barry Cogert, Steve Crum, Jonathan Daddis, Ric Dante, Larry Feldman, Johnny Hatton, Josh Heffernan, Martin McSweeney, Joel Minamide, Marty Rifkin, Jack Sheldon, Mel Steinberg, Jeff Stern and Ken Treseder for your music to my ears.

Andy Ackerman, Reza Ahmadi, Louie Anderson, Ed Asner, Richard Axelrod, Robert E. Ball Jr., Ally Balson, Michael Balson, Professor Iran Berlow, Fahimeh Betts, Aaron Bilgrad, Jenny Birchfield-Eick, Perry Block, Henry Bolton, Arthur Booth, Barbara Bowman, Richard Brassaw, Pierre Brogan, James Burrows, Rob Burnett, Al Burton, Randall Caldwell, Glen Carliss, Peter Casey, Matt Casper, Ernie Chambers, Ed Chuk, Ted Collins, Al Cowan, Lorraine Cowan,

Tim Crescenti, Dottie Dartland Zicklin, Mitchel Delevie, Diane Eaton, Brittani Ebert, Diane English, Kevin Fagan, Janet Falciglia, Harold Federman, Ruth Federman, Alan Feiman, Joe Fisch, Greg Fitzsimmons, Jan Goldsmith, Elaine Goldstein, Sid Goldstein, Alan Gottlieb, Lori Gottlieb, Dennis Green, Hilary Green, Sonny Grosso, Paul Gilbert, Cathy Guisewite, Gary Gurner, Michael Harrison, Clay Heery, Sally Hellström, Mark Hetelson, Holly Hines, Thom Hinkle, Larry Hoffman, Robert Ingram, Ellen Isaacoff, Lizzy Isaacoff, Ted Isaacoff, Christa Jackson, Keith Johnson, Brian Kahn, Stefanie Kahn, Mitch Kaplan, Sam Kass, Tracy Katsky, Bruce Kirschbaum, Scott Kopoian, Ben Kurland, Renee Kurland, Amy Lago, Morgan Langley, Howard Lapides, Richard Lawit, David Lee, Joelle Lennox, Ken Levine, Richard Lewis, Abby Mannix, Chris May, Doug May, Mike McCaul, Nicola McGillicuddy, Mark Miller, Alan Minsky, David Misch, Kevin Morrow, Kevin Mulholland, Stephen Nathan, Trevor Oliver, Jerry Packer, Glenn Padnick, Scott Page, Dr. Shirley Pakdaman, Rosemond Perdue, Dr. Drew Pinsky, Jeanna Polley, Eric Poticha, Cindy Rappoport, Rich Reinhart, Cindi Rice, Alice Robin, Leo Robin, Gregg Rogell, Sy Rosen, Hank Rosenfeld, Richard Rubin, Art Rutter, Barry Schwam, Sidney Schwartzberg, Brad Shairson, Grover Silcox, Gary Silow, Brad Simpson, Andrew Singer, Michael Smerconish, Kingsley Smith, Dennis Snee, David Spancer, Elliot Stahler, Tammy Stockfish, Fred Stoller, Bart Tessler, Jeff Topper, Lou Wallach, Coco Weaver, Ben Wolfinsohn, Jay Wolpert and Rob Young – thanks for your support.

Thank you to David Angell, Glen Charles, Les Charles, Larry David and Jerry Seinfeld for allowing me into the worlds of two revered comedies, and Jason Alexander for championing *Howie* and doing the opposite of not guesting on my talk show pilot. Thanks to Tracy Columbus for opening the way to Larry. Thanks to Jeff Wayne and Brad Dickson for their contributions to the Lewis project, and to Jerry Lewis for the fire that was still in his belly. Thanks to David Steinberg and Robyn Todd for literally opening their door to me and *The Lost Sessions*, and to co-creator Rich Ross for his counsel. And thank you to Jay Leno for your foreword thinking!

Banging My Headlines

"Andy Cowan lives the life we generally leave unexamined. He examines. Then he re-examines. Then he postulates, examines again and finally writes about it. The result is insanely wise, madly funny and completely endearing. Read this book. Laugh, enjoy and discuss."

– Jason Alexander

"Wonderfully written, *Banging My Head* is a creative tour de force and personal journey of admirable determination that shines a light on what it takes to keep going in Hollywood even when you feel like doing "the opposite." After absorbing the wealth of funny, smart and painstakingly rendered projects Andy has generated over the years, you'll understand how the arbiters of what gets on the air don't always represent a meritocracy."

– Dan Piraro, Creator, award-winning King Features panel, *Bizarro*

"Andy Cowan's career is a ballad of talent and tenacity in equal measure. *Banging My Head Against the Wall* offers an unflinching and entertaining account of the show business roller coaster, which for Andy always seems to flicker between sky-scraping exhilaration and deep nausea."

– Rob Burnett, Executive Producer/Head Writer, *Late Show with David Letterman*

"After reading this lovingly executed groundswell of creativity, you too will know Andy remains one of the industry's sharpest comedy minds. This is the first book I've ever recommended that doesn't have recipes in it."

– Louie Anderson

"Andy Cowan's time has finally come."

– David Steinberg

"Andy Cowan lives in a different universe than we do. Fortunately, it's a much funnier and more entertaining place and this book is our ticket in."

– Bart Tessler, EVP News and Talk Programming, *Westwood One*

"Boomers will get a bang out of classic Hollywood and *Seinfeld* fans of all ages will savor a season's worth of inspired new episodes that never were. I thoroughly enjoyed this front row seat to Andy Cowan's life story. Can't wait for the sequel."

– Hank Rosenfeld, co-author of *The Wicked Wit of the West*, with Marx Brothers screenwriter, Irving Brecher

Crafting a blurb for a gifted writer like Andy Cowan is intimidating stuff – kinda like being asked to take batting practice for Pete Rose or to tap out a few keys in front of Billy Joel. *Banging My Head* clearly displays Andy's gifts."

– Michael Smerconish, *SiriusXM, CNN*

"Andy Cowan's unique mind operates at the turbulent intersection between the generations, the centuries, the down-to-earth, and the absurd. He is a largely unsung genius and potential cultural hero to the gigantic but quietly suffering population of neurotics that drag their sorry asses amongst the rest of us who are perfect."

– Michael Harrison, Publisher, *Talkers Magazine*

"It's my job to know Funny, so I know Funny. Andy Cowan is Funny."

– Amy Lago, Comics Editor, *Washington Post Writers Group*

Banging My Head Against the Wall

Against the Wall

A Comedy Writer's Guide to Seeing Stars

Contents

Foreword

I'm glad Andy Cowan is writing this book. If there's one person who never gets enough credit for discovering new comedians, it's Merv Griffin. Where Johnny's *Tonight Show* was tense and scary and could put you either in show business or out of show business, *The Merv Griffin Show* was relaxed and fun. And if you didn't do that great, Merv would say, "Get another set together. We'll try it another time." There wasn't the intense pressure like there was on other shows. Consequently, many comics were a lot looser their first couple of times with Merv than they ever were with Johnny. Many comics did Merv's show first. When they landed on Johnny's later in their career, they would credit *The Tonight Show* with their first late night appearance.

Though Merv's was considered the "safer" show, he didn't always use safe comics, taking chances with Richard Pryor, Andy Kaufman, George Carlin, Dick Gregory, Moms Mabley and Brother Theodore – performers his audience might not always "get." But Merv thought it was important that their voices be heard.

We always got to see Merv before the show, and he'd always try to share some innocuous piece of show business gossip to make you feel like an insider: "Zsa Zsa was here and she said *this*!" We'd always smile, because Merv's references were never our references. It was Old Hollywood versus new Hollywood.

This truly was the Golden Age of Television, because one appearance on a "Merv" or a "Johnny" would equal ten appearances on a talk show today. And audiences were more susceptible back then. When Johnny Carson jokingly referred to a toilet paper shortage, people ran out and bought toilet paper. When Merv held up some product, a million of them were sold the next day. This was the era of "As Seen on TV."

When you were a young writer pre-interviewing everybody from Andy

Kaufman to Orson Welles, performing comedy *and* singing on national television for the first time, it was more than just TV. It was "Showbiz University." Andy Cowan really makes you understand tenacity and what it's like to have your first job in show business – including the methods behind the comedy, and his later trips to *Cheers*, *Seinfeld*, Jerry Lewis and "six minutes of fame." We get bumps in the road after an early gutsy mission to *SNL*, and 'the opposite,' a theme from his life he applied to none other than George Costanza! Throw in personal observations from tons of actual celebrities – none named Kardashian – and there's more than enough here for Merv to go, "Oooooooooooh."

~Jay Leno

Climbing the Walls

1984 – Andy and Merv

I used to rush home from junior high school, hop on the couch and flip on *The Merv Griffin Show*. These were the black-and-white, smoke-filled New York swinging sixties, with a young Richie Pryor and other adult revelers granting this kid a virtual seat on their couch.

Twenty years later, I met the wizard of "Ahhhhs" behind the curtain, now in vibrant color, and in front of the curtain on their actual couch. The show and yours truly had moved to Los Angeles. I was in the middle of my first Hollywood job that began in 1981, talent coordinator (pre-interviewing the stars in this book) and writer on Merv's talkfest. It was a veritable showbiz university for a kid who, returning to junior high in suburban Philadelphia, had his earliest major encounter with stars when a bully on the bus broke his hand on a future talent coordinator's head. When I eyed his bandaged fingers the next day, I realized I'd won the fight! An apt metaphor for Hollywood – getting pummeled one day and triumphing the next.

So what was I, Andy Cowan, doing on the couch, the one not overseen by a shrink, that is? It was my fifth comedy performance on the show; this time I'd be doing panel. I was about to be interviewed by my boss on national television based on notes I'd prepared for him as a talent coordinator. Was I nervous? Not after the one appearance out of five in which I preemptively downed half a beta blocker (prescribed for stage fright) to curb the butterflies. In retrospect, the edge I might have gained from adding to my butterfly collection wouldn't have killed me.

Merv: How does it feel being interviewed by your employer?

Andy: I'm just wondering. Out here, can I call you Merv, or do I still have to call you Your Excellency?

Audible laughter (talk show spackle) from the boss and audience. That was a relief. Attempting scary pursuits towards the goal of creative fulfillment, the dangling carrot that never fully lands in your lap, was always a bit easier when I imagined that others in my shoes might chicken out. So the pursuit, regardless of the outcome, was already a victory.

An early lesson was when I pushed my twin sister, Ellen, to join me in making a beeline to childhood idol Jack Benny backstage at a Temple University Music Festival concert in 1974. For those of you born during the forty-some years since, Benny was an iconic and lovable comedy star who turned pausing before reacting into an art form, and influenced Johnny Carson, Bill Cosby (before the accusations gave us pause), Steve Martin and countless other comedy icons. Most people didn't brave the restricted area backstage, but we did. From our cheap seats, like his eternally thirty-nine-year-old character, he'd appeared ageless, proficient enough on the violin to be both good and intentionally bad while he accompanied the grand symphony orchestra. As he approached us backstage, he appeared to be pushing eighty. Trembling, I geared up for the best Jack Benny impression my classmates ever heard, the one ingrained in me since my ears first heard him utter, "Oh, Rochester!"

Andy: Well! ... Finally... I get to see... the real... Jack Benny.

He offered up that generous laugh of his and I was elated – I'd wished. Seemingly not hearing or acknowledging my channeling of him, he took in the smattering of others around us. Oh... *well...* indeed. My sister, overcome from being within close proximity to our idol, tearfully requested a hug. After welcoming her embrace and kiss on the cheek, he turned to me...

Jack: Do you want to kiss me too?

He then grabbed the hand of the young female with him, literally skipped in the air, entered his limo, and died four months later, the only time Joanna Carson saw her husband, Johnny, cry.[1]

1964 – Twelve-year-old's signed Carson drawing

A year later I reported, wrote and – when there was no news – concocted multiple segments every weekday for WLYH-TV's newscast in Lebanon, Pennsylvania, not exactly a hotbed of activity. It was the year I graduated from Boston University with a master's in broadcasting, and here I was broadcasting! They eventually moved my beat to the "big" city, Lancaster, Pennsylvania. When Amish Country marked a step up, you knew you weren't in a top ten market. But my "Action News" '75 Gremlin felt top-tier next to the horse-drawn buggies. I shot, voiced and edited my pieces with a then state-of-the-art fairly portable color (!) video camera all by my lonesome, and even stuck my head in front of the lens once or twice. At night, I'd drive up to WHUM radio in Reading, Pennsylvania, pre-screen the late-night talk show callers and voice the classified ads, before collapsing in my motel room and driving back to Lebanon/Lancaster the next day to do it all over again. It was the summer Captain & Tennille's *Love Will Keep Us Together* blared over WHUM's bathroom speakers... *I will, I will, I will, I will...* do my best to ignore... the "itch." I wasn't yet sure what would relieve it. But conveying straight information minus my skewed take on it didn't stop me from scratching.

On my old manual typewriter whose broken carriage "return" no longer did, I wrote my first spec sitcom script in '76 for a show from MTM Productions, heralded for nurturing quality writing. The producers wound up sending my suburban Philly address an encouraging pass. (I'd work with them in Los Angeles a decade later.) In November, the itching overpowered my lifelong public speaking phobia just enough for me to set foot on the stage of the Philadelphia comedy club, Grandma Minnie's. The mike remained in the stand for fear my shaky hand that removed it would sabotage my fake calm. If this first attempt at stand-up bombed, I'd pack it in and at least know I gave it a shot. Strangers *laughed*. I was hooked – into stomaching random future bombing in continued search of another fix, the elusive perfect set.

Over the next year I became a growing minnow in the Philly stand-up pond, as the early comedy club boom began to rumble, and worked two music clubs with a long history. Frantically reviewing my material as my neighbor drove me to

Center City during a blizzard, I was the last-minute warm-up act replacement for Yvonne "If I Can't Have You" Elliman at the Bijou, where Bette Midler, Barry Manilow and slews of other future stars had performed. During fair weather, I headlined at The Main Point, a celebrated coffeehouse that once opened its doors to Martin Mull, Elton John and Bruce Springsteen. Then one November I noticed in the *Philadelphia Inquirer* that Lorne Michaels was scouting for new talent on *SNL* behind and in front of the camera. It was still the "not ready for prime time" era. Why not me? I wasn't ready for prime time!

Following the most audacious train ride of my life, I hooked up with an old college buddy in New York who worked inside NBC at 30 Rock, and we dialed Lorne's office. Choosing the alias of "Sandy Troy," my pal's childhood friend, we told Lorne's secretary that I was a producer in from L.A. who wanted to meet with him. Hard as it still is to believe, she set an appointment for that evening at 6 p.m. My cohort needed to leave the building for the rest of the day, so I chose to anxiously await this sham killing the hours in NBC restrooms and stairwells, rather than exit the premises and risk not getting back in. It may have been long before 9/11, but the front desk still needed to see ID, and my driver's license didn't say "Sandy Troy." Somewhere in town that day, although it didn't run by 30 Rock, I remember spotting remnants of a big Veteran's Day Parade, fantasizing that the revelry somehow represented The Big Apple shouting, "Go get 'em, Andy!" Uh, Sandy. Shortly before six, I almost blew my cover when Michaels' secretary addressed me as Mr. Troy and I forgot to respond. Finally, Lorne walked out of his office, extended his hand and uttered words still deposited in my memory bank: "Hello, Sandy. What is this all about, and it better be important."

As I shuffled into his office, I sensed there were others in the room but didn't dare give any of them eye contact. Launching into my carefully rehearsed bits and impressions through the fog of adrenaline coupled with abject terror, I remember Lorne occasionally nodding as I wondered if and when he'd kick me out. I steamrolled through and finally revealed my true identity: I'm not Sandy Troy. I'm Andy Cowan! I'd taken a train up from Philly, I'd do anything for the show, perform, write, sweep floors, anything!

Dan: That was a good Tom Snyder.

Dan Aykroyd was in the room. Jean Doumanian, who later had a short run producing the show and some of Woody Allen's films, was in the room. Talent coordinator, Barbara Burns, was in the room. They were all cordial and probably smelled a phony from the get-go. Barbara agreed to eventually check out my video from The Main Point, which included one of my favorite bits, a parody of a *60 Minutes* popular segment at the time, "Point/Counterpoint," with Jack Kilpatrick and Shana Alexander, the predecessors to Andy Rooney's few minutes. (I'd get lucky with Andy years later.)

A Philly TV station reported on my adventure:

Laughter. Coast to coast on the NBC hit, Saturday Night Live. But if you're a young comedian, SNL isn't necessarily a laughing matter. Because if you're Andy Cowan, would-be comedian, Saturday Night Live is a dream.

Barbara Burns kept in touch. And *SNL* ultimately offered... *nada*. Dan's "Jane, you ignorant slut" to Jane Curtin later became one of the show's signatures, an offshoot of Point/Counterpoint I chalked up to parallel development.

Pretty soon Andy Cowan has to make a couple of the decisions all young stand-up comedians have to make. First, he has to decide whether or not to stay in the business. Then he has to decide whether to stay in Philadelphia or leave and go to New York or Los Angeles. And those are tough decisions. And that's no joke.

Nearly twenty years later in L.A., I walked up to Lorne Michaels at a party and asked if he remembered the time a guy arranged a phony meeting with him back in the '70s. Nope. Maybe it happened so often, they were all blurs. It wouldn't be the last time I'd try hitching my wagon to his universe.

My other out-of-body *SNL* experience occurred during executive producer Dick Ebersol's reign in 1983, after my trusty and still awe-inspiring VCR recorded the show while I was out. (In my '84 *Television Quarterly* piece, "Confessions of a VCR Junkie," I marveled over the time machine H. G. Wells never imagined, and how I was now the TV programming head of my own network whose target audience numbered just one.) It was a new *SNL* episode but part of it sounded unsettlingly familiar. "Perfectly Frank" featured that week's guest host, actor and future director Betty Thomas, as a psychologist railing against advertisers who slip pictures of Coke or other fleeting subliminal messages into programming, brainwashing the audience into craving the product moments later.[2] Defending the practice, advertising exec Joe Piscopo subliminally slips in, "I want you" ... "I love you" ... "Fondle me" ... "Pelvic thrust" ... before she eventually peels a banana and succumbs, as did moderator and SNL cast member Gary Kroeger, to Piscopo's charms. The sketch landed reasonably well, however over the top the performances seem now. Three years later when Lorne was back in charge, comedian Kevin Nealon (not long after my two-time interviewee's appearances on the Griffin show) would introduce Mr. Subliminal in his very first *SNL* sketch.[3] Playing an ad man, he slipped in fast patter meant to be subliminally absorbed by his boss, Jon Lovitz – who winds up giving him a raise. He also wins over the boss's initially disinterested secretary, Victoria Jackson...

Mr. Subliminal: Maybe we can just be friends – hot sex! And leave it at that...

By sketch's end, he subliminally maneuvers her into paying for dinner, wearing a push-up bra and heading back to his place for some hot sex.

KN: It was nerve-wracking; it's like having two conversations at once. I remember seconds before going out, coming out of commercial, Lorne taps me on the shoulder – keep in mind, my first sketch ever – and says, 'Are you sure this is what you want?'[4]

A naturally funny performer, Nealon turned it over the years into a recurring character all his own, the one among his arsenal he would have brought back for the 2015 SNL 40th anniversary special.[5] So why my out-of-body experience when Piscopo first performed his version in '83? The original premise sprang from my yellowed notes of stand-up comedy ideas, which I feverishly rummaged through drawers to dig out as the show continued playing...

Taking advantage of subliminal advertising in our normal everyday conversation... "How are you, nice weather we're having ... Gotobedwithme ... Folks are fine, uh-huh..." And it works on woman's subconscious and she responds.

Every word of the initial sketch had come from one of several I'd written with another comedy writer a few years earlier, save for "*The A-Team*," a show not yet on the air when we'd referenced an earlier dumb TV show as a punchline at the same point in the sketch, and our subliminal "oral sex" mention prior to the banana peel, removed by Standards and Practices.[6] Even the female character's last name, a former girlfriend's I used in scripts at the time, hadn't changed. After fast-forwarding to the credits at the end of *SNL* that November of '83, I learned the writer with whom I'd collaborated on *my* idea was now on *their staff.* When I bumped into him backstage at the Griffin show with another comic a year or so later, he showed nary a hint of discomfort or remorse. I felt like saying, "How are you... *apologizeandpaymeyouthief...* nice weather we're having." But feeling embarrassed for the both of us, I decided to let it go. Till now.

. . . . . .

Pursuing the Griffin gig, as with most showbiz jobs worth pursuing, was a lengthy process of persistence just short of becoming a pest, not sounding desperate for a break even though you were, and not letting the lack of progress convince your inner demons there won't be a breakthrough one day. They should just keep the

"H" in the Hollywood Sign, knock down "ollywood" and replace it with "urryupandwait." Hungry though I was for a way in, I hadn't originally set out for the show, per se, focusing on writing spec sitcom scripts for *Taxi* and my own stand-up. But being a part of this Hollywood institution was always enticing. In November of 1980, associate producer Paul Solomon sent me a hand-written note:

Andy – If you're still out there wanting a job here, call me next week and let me know. No promises, but something may come up.

The next week I sent him a sample interview, *Taxi* script, and cassette of comedy bits, including an impression of mine that always scored in clubs, *Merv Griffin*. A little over three months later, their offer came my way. I felt like Robert Redford's character in *The Candidate*, after the endless job of campaigning for the job was over: *What do we do now?* Still in my twenties, I couldn't help but be a little anxious about ingratiating myself into the high-profile worlds of public figures, including a host who'd been at it for nearly twenty years. Something that dawns on you later after you're comfortable in your own skin: They're all just people whose goals are to be comfortable in theirs.

I would speak to guests' handlers, but more often the celebrities themselves, as was the case with the fifty no longer with us featured in a later chapter. After spotting my initials on an upcoming guest's name card in the office of producer, Peter Barsocchini, I'd figure out potential questions that could hopefully bear fruit. Herein are their chitchat tidbits, which I'd committed to notes with the help of my seemingly advanced IBM Selectric. Not yet omnipresent PCs and the internet would have been welcome substitutes for correction tape and articles hot off last week's presses!

• • • • •

One of my favorite long-defunct conceptual bits I used to do for college audiences involved the typewriter. I aimed for an economy of words in the setup, to spell out the premise without overstaying its welcome...

Repopulating the world is a big job. That's why God made sex fun, so we'd be sure to get the job done. Why couldn't he have made other big jobs fun? Like... term papers?

Cute typewriter. What's your name? ... "Olivetti" ... (manufactured till the mid '90s) Hi, Olive ... Where are you from? ... Oh, Italy, of course. Mucho bello ... You've got beautiful i's ... j's ... semicolons ... How's about a little... touch-typing back at my place? CHH-CHH (moaning) Uhhh! ... CHH-CHH! ... Ahh! ... CHH-CHH ... Olive? ... I want to go to desk with you! ... I'm taking out my paper... I'm sticking it in... Okay, gently ... CHH-CHH. CHH-CHH ... Tabulate! Tabulate! ... DING! ... CHH-CHH. CHH-CHH. Ooh, that felt good, backspace. DING! ... CHH-CHH-CHH-CHH. CHH-CHH-CHH-CHH ... I'm coming!! To the bibliography!! CHH-CHHCHH-CHH-CHH-CHH-CHH-CHH-CHH-CHH. DING! ... Z-Z-Z-Z-Z-Z-Z-Z.

It didn't really transition to word processors, so I eventually updated it to other applications that made for less tactile "big jobs" like...

Doing the laundry:

Cute washer... May... Tag. Where are you from, May? ... Sears? Love their catalogues... You've got a nice set of knobs... I wouldn't mind getting dirty for you... (water running) SHHHHHHH ... Ooh, you're wet ... SHHHHHHH ... You're hot... I'm sticking in my load ... SLOSH, SLOSH, SLOSH ... Be gentle! ... with my knits... SLOSH, SLOSH, SLOSH, SLOSH ... Circulate! Circulate!! ... I'm coming ... to the spin cycle!

Or grocery shopping:

Where are you from? ... Oh, outside and somebody rolled you back in? No wonder you're hot. I mean from the sun, not that you're not hot anyway ... How's about you and me takin' a spin around this meat market? ... Ahh... You feel so good. But I want to move forward in our relationship, we just keep going in circles; oh, it's that damn crooked wheel, there we go ... Ready to stick my cucumber... AHH ... in you? ... Banana ... AHH ... Salami ... AHH ... Meatballs ... AHH ... I'm coming ... to the checkout counter!

My other favorite conceptual stand-up bit I first did in the late '70s recognized the very early days of computers sharing our personal information. Other comics started calling me "A. Cooag," which I considered a badge of honor...

FOCUS Entertainment

Andy Cowan, left, and Ben Kurland ham it up at the Comedy Store.

Got my usual supply of junk mail today – addressed to ("reading" while nearly shouting) **A. COWAN** *... * **A. COOAG***... * **A. CACA***... Interspersed throughout the mail, in (demonstrating with sweeping hand gesture and booming voice) BOLD-FACED TYPE... is your name! Really gives it that... personal touch...*

"Dear (hand gesture/booming voice) **A. COOAG** *... We're sure you,* **A. COOAG***... would be happy to win your very own private island! ... Yes, you would be a very happy* **PENNSYLVANIAN***."*

I'm starting to wonder – how much do these people know about me?

"Yes, we're sure you would be a very happy and excited **FORMER BEDWETTER** *indeed!* (Not true, but anything for a laugh!) *Yes, you and other* **JEWS** *like you..."* (This usually scored decent albeit slightly nervous laughter.)

Any day, I'm expecting to pick up my mail: "Dear Premature Ejaculator:"

Anything (if "clever" took priority over "edgy") for a laugh! Such was the misplaced thinking shortly after my arrival in Los Angeles when, desperate for a stand-up hook, I was introduced on a Marina del Rey venue stage with a hydraulic system raising it fourteen feet into the air. And there I stood... in my pajamas. Hanging around after the show in this get-up made me feel like Hugh Hefner minus the harem, namely an idiot. It was Andy PJ Cowan's first and final performance.

·　·　·　·　·

It felt good to finally be on the inside of show business. As I strode down that long hall to the morning Griffin show staff meetings, I'd welcome the big names as the producer's vote of confidence, even when they entailed more work. But some of the lesser names required more digging to make them interesting. The authors with esoteric subjects conjured up nightmarish memories of pop quizzes on a subject you'd yet to study. After cramming, I pretended to ask knowledgeable questions of a "world-renowned authority on economics and business, and the author of an important new book (HOLD UP – we not only skimmed books, we cued Merv in the intros when to lift them) *Get Really Rich in the Coming Super Metals Boom.*" *Bizarro* (see **Tooning In**) book cover cartoon panel idea I pitched decades later to Dan Piraro: *Making You Rich in These Economic Times*, by William You.

Two days later, I was surprised to receive a copy of the author's publicist's letter to the head of *Merv Griffin Productions...*

Gordon McLendon was quite pleased with the interview. We both were impressed with the background research of Andrew Cowan. Strategic metals is a difficult subject, but the questions asked and the remarks made were by far some of the best in the entire book tour. Merv was better informed than some of the hosts of financial shows!

I was a kid again back in day camp, the time I got an A for swimming for what I believe to this day was fake paddling in the pool.

In my later years on the job, I'd occasionally notice a lighter load of interviews for the week ahead and figure, "Ahh, they value my contributions so much, they're granting me a well-deserved rest." Other times I'd think – Wait a minute. I always interviewed Leonard Nimoy before. Why aren't they giving him to me now? In '82, I'd asked him the critical question – were movie "ears" different from TV "ears?" His ears on *Star Trek*, the series, could be reused for two or three days, unlike his feature film ears that had to withstand big screen scrutiny. Nimoy lived long and prospered with or without super metals.

The other talent coordinators and I would meet with Merv shortly before each show, he'd quickly absorb everyone's transcripts and later make the guests feel at home, no matter who was sitting across from him. He would lean in and gaze at them with such concentration that audiences figured they must be as interesting as Merv thought they were. Viewers related with what appeared to be genuine warmth, and it was a large part of his offstage persona as well. Sure, he could be reserved at times, but no celebrity was "on" 24/7. After lavishing non-stop attention upon the guests, he couldn't help but seem more removed off-camera. I figured highly visible personalities like Merv also instinctively pulled back to keep the hangers-on who might be currying favors at bay.

The camera was able to pick up on his joie de vivre. Looking back in 2015, Leno remembered...

Jay: He was really a kind man, and I liked him for that. I never heard any drunken, mean, spiteful stories about Merv Griffin. There are a lot of hosts where you hear – Oh, this guy was really ugly behind the scenes. No, Merv was beautiful behind the scenes as well. He sure loved his sweets and candy. Trying to hide his weight was the funniest thing in the world. He'd just keep getting bigger and bigger.

As I wrote his only child, Tony (always down to earth and unaffected) after Merv's death in 2007, his dad loved life and life loved him right back.

In '82, not long after *The Waltons* ended its run, Tony's sudden snicker punctured the relative silence during one of Merv's pre-show notes-reading sessions. Merv's son had picked up the latest *People* from the coffee table, featuring "John-Boy's triplets," Richard Thomas cradling all three infants. And all three had little moles drawn on their cheeks, a la their proud papa's mole, courtesy of... yours truly.

Merv had a healthy sense of humor, himself. One time, he promised us he'd slip an assortment of bleep-worthy curse words throughout the show without getting bleeped.

Merv: Fuck-get about it!

The talent coordinators stifling their laughter in the back of the studio didn't forget about it.

In one of my first meetings with him, I pushed myself to do the Merv impression. Rather than face him, I turned the other way...

One of Hollywoooood's most <u>handsome</u>... leading men izzzzz with us today... Annnnnd one of its <u>awl</u>-tiime...<u>competent</u> actors. TV fans <u>know</u> him as not only a <u>classic</u>... entertainer... buhhhht awwwl-so annnn... <u>exceptional</u> talent... This man does it awwwl, annnnnnnnnnnnnnnnd... <u>awlways</u> with <u>great</u> style...

Wait a beat. Then insert name humorously non-worthy of aforesaid big build-up. In '81, my punchline was the schlocky late-night TV commercial car salesman...

<u>*Cal Worthington*</u> *is with us.*

A dark-haired Jay Leno was among the future comic kingpins I pre-interviewed (ten times) on the Griffin show. It became the first talk show he guest-hosted in 1986 – the day the Space Shuttle Challenger exploded. Because it wasn't airing until months later, nobody could reference it. In 2015, I asked Jay if he remembered being nervous at all.

Jay: No, not particularly. It was Merv!

Jay didn't recall being all that different from his hosting persona on *The Tonight Show*, other than a younger version of his future self. I can still picture him as a guest in his leather jacket, wheeling his motorcycle onto the stage, a pit stop prior to riding it all the way down to Daytona Beach, Florida, for Harley Week. If ever a visitor came prepared, it was Leno. All Merv had to do was ask, "How's the family?" And Jay could tap into how his folks think just because he's in show business, he must know everybody in show business. Or how his dad went overboard saving receipts. Or how his mom used Jay's hot tub for boiling potatoes. Already one of the hardest working comedians, he would humorously harp on traveling with carefully constructed use of the language drawing you in. From a 1983 Leno intro I wrote, Merv noted that Jay had been on the road for 138 days:

He makes Charles Kuralt (veteran CBS On the Road correspondent) look like a shut-in.

Jay also poked fun at TV and commercials, which he had plenty of time to watch on the road. And he could always extract a comedic spin off the latest news.

Merv: Are you excited about the Olympics coming to L.A.?

Jay: I saw a sign the other day – "Baskin-Robbins, the official ice cream of the U.S. Olympic Team." No wonder we're not winning any events. The Russians are out there doing sit-ups, and our guys are wolfing down Rocky Road.

A young Billy Crystal told me he could spend a segment on how he would have rather captured a big audience off mixed reviews for his recently canceled (after two episodes) *The Billy Crystal Comedy Hour* than what he got, no audience off great reviews. A sign Bill Maher wasn't yet a household name: I phonetically spelled it "Marr" to ensure Merv pronounced it correctly. In '85, the twenty-nine-year-old was playing slick lawyer, Marty Lang, a small role in Geena Davis' NBC series, *Sara*. Joy Behar debuted on Merv's show that same year.

When they opened with stand-up, I'd include their "tag" or last bit that signaled the band it was time for the music to kick back in. Garry Shandling's tag in '82: "They showed the wedding films in reverse, with the couples walking away from each other." Playing comedy *Jeopardy* (the cash cow Merv's wife invented in 1963) I can surmise the bit: What is divorce? Arsenio's tag in '82: "Thank you and goodnight." Okay, that one has me stumped. Along with performing their sets, some also sat on the panel where the pre-interviews simply functioned as lead-ins to additional comedy "hunks" they'd weave into their patter.

At a 1980 L.A. college gig, my kind of audience, I was feeling pretty good about my own stand-up set until I first watched the young guy following me who effortlessly commanded the stage. Whatever "it" was, this Jerry Seinfeld guy had it. He told me he wasn't ready yet, after I wondered if he was planning on trying out for Carson. About a year later, some two months before I would pre-interview him the first of six times for Merv's show, he earned Johnny's coveted A-OK signal at the end of his first *Tonight Show* set, took a bow and was on his way. Revisiting his Merv notes from an '81 show we did in Vegas (when he was all of 27), you notice how he could smoothly veer from the question, like a politician, into a response barely related to it...

Merv: Are you one for the excitement, the gambling?

Jerry: Well, I don't know about those guys that sit at the crap tables. They seem so suspicious of everybody. It's like the kind of guy who, when you drive with him, he steps on the brake on his side of the car too. Why are these people doing that? When someone does that to me, I just speed up and start swerving around the road. I figure if he's got the brake, I don't have to worry about it.

As Jerry's panel shots continued over the years, as was the case with Leno, Merv didn't need to read the material to rest assured that the leanest of set-ups would lead to pay dirt...

Merv: Feeling good?

Jerry: I have a bit on how this is life right now. And you have to feel good right now.

While an occasional lead-in could still elicit a spelled-out reply...

Merv: How's the career going?

Jerry: (joke) It's going well. I just took birthday parties off my business card.

By now, I'll bet he's also taken off bar mitzvahs.

Among the myriad other performers I pre-interviewed who were on the cusp of huge fame...

George Clooney:

My next guest is a fine young actor who's begun co-starring this season in NBC's hit series, The Facts of Life...

Only twenty-four, he'd moved to Los Angeles from Kentucky a mere four years earlier.

GC: If someone says they're a producer in Kentucky, you're impressed. L.A. is very phony. When I first came here, I met the head of ABC casting on the beach and I didn't believe him. He later called me in to do a scene, and he put me under contract for five months.

Mel Gibson:

My next guest has lived and worked much of his young life in Australia, where he was heralded by the Australian Film Institute as Best Actor in 1979...

His Australian accent was heavy considering he'd lived in the states until he was nearly thirteen.

MG: An accent was required to be understood and accepted in my profession. After enough elocution exercises, my American accent was beaten out of me... When they greet you over there, it's not just "Hello, how are you?" It's "How are you, you old bastard?" Less bullshit.

Tom Cruise:

Joining me now is a gifted young actor rapidly building a repertoire of memorable screen roles in such films as Taps, The Outsiders, and two brand new motion pictures – Risky Business and All the Right Moves... He's making all the right moves...

He was only three years into his career at twenty-one, after passing on college to pursue acting on the strength of one role – Nathan Detroit in his high school production of *Guys & Dolls.*

TC: It was great having all sisters. It's really helped me to appreciate and understand women. I don't feel threatened by smart and strong women. If I'd grown up with all brothers, everything about girls would have been such a mystery.

The Opposite

In 1994 I was fortunate enough to cross paths with Jerry Seinfeld yet again. My manager at the time, Tracy Columbus, had opened the door in late '92 to Larry David, to whom I began doggedly faxing story ideas for *Seinfeld*, his co-creation with Jerry about a lot more than nothing. The chemistry among the principles and natural rhythms in those early years of the show were electrifying to me. You felt like you were palling around with living and breathing, organically funny characters. Larry was receptive enough to my various pitches addressing each of the four leads to keep the door open for more. I came close with a story about George's discovering a lost large bra in a dryer and trying to find the woman this "glass slipper" fit (with reservations after Kramer and the woman's phone voice lead George to think it could be a grandmother's bra). After a lot of back and forth, he remarked in June of '93, "Boy, you're really persevering on this thing," still calling it a funny idea and an A story. In the end he went with another bra story and the season couldn't accommodate two, but he invited me to keep pitching. If this were baseball, my arm would be sore.

As an afterthought, I tossed him a nugget I'd often reflected on in my own life: What if I'd done the complete opposite of whatever I'd done up till then? Would I have been better off? He didn't curb his enthusiasm – sorry – for that one, but I had to figure out three other quirky enough stories that went in a direction he could sign off on, something he volunteered was "hard." One of the others made him laugh: Kramer putting a sock down his pants to make him look more endowed (off-camera but alluded to). Women artificially enhance up north, why can't guys down south? Echoing again that it was funny and made him laugh, he agreed that maybe it could work if I found a different place to go with it. As for George's opposite story, there were so many funny things in there, he said, that he wasn't worried; the ending would find itself. I wondered how he might feel if one of the others accidentally stumbled upon the opposite and found it worked for them too. "That's not bad," Larry replied, likening it to a new Zen-type philosophy.

He finally suggested taking one last crack at all the stories, the heavy lifting, he noted, on a show like *Seinfeld*. The writing that followed it sort of took care of itself. Calling each of them so far "good and funny," he also called getting all of them right and a solo writing credit a long shot, but said he wanted to reward me for my hard work. He threw in, "I can still give you the money if that's what you want. I'm right now prepared to give you the money if you want it," which I answered with, "I feel like you're (original host of *Let's Make a Deal*) Monty Hall." Short of a mercy chuckle, he added that he couldn't guarantee the show would get made.

Ending our conversation days before the show won its first (and puzzlingly last) Emmy for best comedy, he promised, "Something's gonna happen. It won't be for naught, all this work." Months later I was given the green light to deliver a freelance episode, incorporating "the opposite" among my three other stories. I finished and dated the cover January 17, 1994, hours before the big Northridge earthquake hit. Had I labored a bit more dotting a few i's, a bookshelf might have toppled over me. With the *Seinfeld* stage seriously damaged, the whole town shifted into recovery mode. Two weeks later, I sent the script to a founding partner of the show's production company, their president of television, whom I'd first met when he headed up Embassy TV...

January 31, 1994

Mr. Glenn Padnick
Castle Rock Entertainment
335 North Maple Drive
Beverly Hills, CA 90210-3867

Dear Glenn:

I had a good meeting with Larry David shortly before the holidays, at which time he told me to go ahead with the script and that one of the final nine of the season would be mine. I wound up selling him on several other stories along with the main one he already "loves." After the holidays, I pitched the tentative beats to him over the phone, and about a week later, two hours before the quake hit, I finished the enclosed. He finally got the script after a mail mix-up (due to the quake) last week.

Best,

Andy Cowan

In March, Larry called with his verdict...

LD: I think you did a really good job. And in a very short amount of time too. There are a couple things that aren't working with the other stories. But that's not because of the writing. The writing is really very good. You should be very happy with the job you did.

After telling him I was very happy to hear him say that, he countered, "I'm not just saying that." Knowing he of all people wouldn't just be saying that was why, I reminded him, I was very happy to hear him say that. He thought the way I'd handled the George story was "great," the first scene in the coffee shop, in particular, was "really funny." He "didn't quite buy" the Jerry or Kramer stories, but "absolved" me from doing any further work on the script. Acknowledging how much time I'd put into it, he suggested I prepare myself for it to dramatically change and not get too attached to my words. Anticipating the loose ends he'd have to tie up, he guessed he might also take a writing credit. Sharing a writing credit with Larry David wasn't a terrible thing, especially since most outside scripts never got shot, let alone made into a season finale. But I still felt obligated to gently recall his mentioning the one way to receive sole credit was after getting approval on all the stories, as I had before going off to script. But with this now being the last show of the season, Larry said the other stories would need to change. And George couldn't still be living with his folks the following season; Larry needed a reason to get him out. I'd had George move out in my draft too, but whatever Larry thought was fair in the end was okay by me.

He called me after the table read with "some news to tell" me. I could sense a little tension in his voice. First, it had gotten a great response. Secondly, he was putting his name on it along with Jerry's. If I had strong objections, he suggested I go to arbitration with the Guild. I wasn't about to do that and relayed how much I was looking forward to seeing the show. He added that he would give me sole credit, but it didn't seem right. I wasn't talking about that, I snuck in, adding that it was now a third versus a half, but that was okay, and I still felt honored being associated with the show. (And sharing it with Jerry wasn't too shabby either!) Larry replied, "I see what you mean. I think you do have a point and do owe you somewhat of an apology." He hadn't anticipated Jerry's helping him, but it was the end of the season and Larry's comment about feeling a little tired was easy to understand. Curious and a little squeamish raising the question, I asked how they handle such credits – alphabetically? No, it would be Larry David & Jerry Seinfeld and Andy Cowan. I wondered aloud if the industry would look at that as less than a third. He responded that a third was a lot to ask considering my involvement didn't equate with a third of the show. I was up for doing the rewrite, but that, he replied, wasn't how it worked on this show versus the others. I nonetheless stressed it was a positive experience. Larry didn't want it to be messy. I assured him it wouldn't. He said I was a nice guy, and that he was a nice guy, and didn't see why we should have a problem. I didn't either and told him this was starting to sound like dialogue from the show. Another sign of Larry's best intentions: he later reversed the order of the credits, with my name first. The opposite!

My first draft had fate written all over it, before Larry's and Jerry's input was written all over it. Insightful writers with complementary sensibilities, they were obviously attuned to one another and naturally trusted each other's rhythms. In my version, George also lamented his lackluster life to Jerry at Monk's Café, after barely being able to cover the check. His system was in desperate need of failure antibodies. He was jobless. He was woman-less. He has no future. He doesn't even have a present. And who does he have to blame? Himself. Every conscious decision he made to get to this time and this place was a blueprint for disaster. His life is the complete opposite of what he wants it to be. He should have done the complete opposite of whatever he's done up till now. Even the puniest rat finally learns when there's no cheese at the end of the maze. Well damn it, he can learn too. It's time he tried a completely different maze!

I too had him switch from his usual tuna to chicken salad, and eventually approach an attractive woman after Jerry goads him, guessing George would now do the opposite of what he'd normally do (wimp out) and wimp *in*. It all starts working for him. Instead of inching closer to her on his folks' couch, he inches farther. After she wonders if she should leave, he chokes... sure. She'd rather not and inches closer; he inches still farther. Instead of bathing himself in cologne, he didn't use one drop. Instead of wearing socks without holes in them, he wore socks *with* holes in them. She liked his manly scent and tickled three of his toes. Instead of forcing himself to cuddle after the big moment, he made himself a chicken salad sandwich. (The old George would've made a tuna.) After telling her he's out of work with absolutely no job prospects, she admired his honesty, insisted on paying for dinner, and turned him on to an uncle who might throw him a job as a furrier, the opposite of a smart career move (something Elaine compares to being a cholesterol salesman). George's opposite approach to both landing and keeping the job (not shaving, dressing down, telling a customer she looks horrendous in a sable – which, coming from Mr. Fashion Plate, is high praise – prompting her to buy it) unexpectedly wins him success and a ticket back into his own apartment.

Meanwhile Jerry favors his right side, what George contends is Jerry's "good" side (and Elaine claims is Jerry's "bad" side) when dating a waitress he meets out of uniform (noting how much better a woman can look with a tad more makeup minus the hair bun) who luckily doesn't remember having already met Jerry's left side at Monk's before he deservedly left her a lousy tip. Her lack of eye contact on the job might have something to do with her amnesia, part of why he'd left her chump change to begin with. Elaine memorizes only the book jacket of a highbrow work she gives her erudite boyfriend – in case he later wants to have an intelligent conversation with her about it – and pretends to know the meanings of fancy words he tosses her way. Jerry, also hiding his unfamiliarity with the guy's lexicon, later leads the boyfriend to a false deduction that Elaine is a floozy. And Kramer fears he's losing his sex drive – *Hustler* doesn't do it for him anymore. As a kid, Mrs. Butterworth used to be enough. He's melting! After vitamin supplement megadoses don't seem to help, he discovers an unexpected side benefit – vastly improved memory – and tests it out counting cards at an Atlantic City blackjack table with George, who does the opposite and queasily hits on 18 – drawing a two... and further annoying the players... hits on 20 – drawing an ace.

On a double dinner date with the waitress, Elaine and her elitist beau, Jerry goes overboard using fancy words and defending their waitress's lousy service. But he eventually gets called out by his date who recognizes Jerry's swirl – not the hair swirl on his good side, the swirl in his signature on the gift card he winds up giving her with the fur George gave Jerry for pushing him to the wall and doing the opposite, the fur the uncle gave George after George said he didn't want a bonus (the opposite). The swirl on the "y" in "Jerry," the one on the receipt with that crummy tip he'd left her at Monk's! She'd know that swirl anywhere – for a week it's burned an afterimage on her retina. Fur or no fur, when a guy doesn't even leave a poor working girl a lousy fifteen percent tip, it says an awful lot about him. Jerry insists he's sorry, he'd really like to see her again and is very attracted to her. After that doesn't work, he tells her he's not sorry, wouldn't like to see her again, and isn't very attracted to her. This time the opposite strikes out.

Kramer's fear he's losing his sex drive is finally squelched after a cabbie who barely speaks English takes Kramer and the gang in the wrong/opposite direction and into a metaphor for sex, the Lincoln Tunnel. In a final word of dialogue, the cabbie parrots back a surprisingly erudite description of the loose type of woman he guesses a newly recharged Kramer is now looking for – "Meretricious?" The erudite boyfriend mistakenly associated the same word with Elaine after Jerry – thinking it must mean something to do with "merit," not a prostitute – doubled down with "that's an understatement." After the boyfriend dropped some million-dollar words to George in his quest for a fur that's, among other things, "meretricious," George did the opposite of hating to admit his ignorance and asked, what the hell is "meretricious?" Elaine insisted the sleazy fur-trimmed negligee her guy presents her, an offshoot of her previous comparatively innocent flirtations and Jerry's lesser vocabulary, wasn't her style. "Your friend, Jerry, and I know all about your style," he responds. That's the end of erudite boyfriend.

Ultimately George's opposite system becomes too effective. The more distant he is, the more worshipful is his new girlfriend to the point where he finally pleads, "I am not kidding. This is for real. I need... my... space!" – attracting her even more. After he finally acts clingy, the opposite of the opposite, he's dumped and again hates his space. Jerry hates his space too. The waitress won't talk to him and Elaine won't talk to him.

Years later I was surprised to catch this brief interchange from the languid pilot for *Seinfeld*, originally entitled *The Seinfeld Chronicles*, implying George followed the opposite of the opposite. After advising Jerry to never do what his instincts tell him about cleaning the bathroom before a lady visits (but the opposite) because filth is good, George sarcastically answers Jerry's question about whether he operates that way: "Yeah, I wish."[1]

The fact "The Opposite" became a season finale that needed to address the following season's arc made it change significantly, I didn't join the staff until that next season, and Jerry and Larry rewrote even the staffers. (My tombstone will read: "To be rewritten over my dead body.") But with all their changes, the main theme survived. "The Opposite" turned into a top ten *Seinfeld* episode where George's opposite epiphany lands him the girl and the big job with the Yankees, along with 30.1 million viewers, at the top of the ratings. Jerry planned to submit it for Emmy consideration but after the Writers Guild deemed me "half" of the writers represented on the script versus the TV Academy's "third," the Academy concurred, and I could now let the show submit it on my behalf, freeing him to submit another episode. Glenn Padnick predicted a near lock for a writing nod. After its editing nomination (and eventual win) Larry, who was nominated for "The Puffy Shirt," even admitted his surprise "The Opposite" hadn't landed one for writing.

At a 1999 Writers Guild forum five years later I didn't attend, an audience member told Larry how much he enjoyed that episode. He replied, "That's one of my favorite shows. I love that show." I was happy to learn he credited me and my idea, in answer to whether he'd set out for George to join the Yankees or whether the engine that helped get George there originated as a separate idea unto itself.

LD: I was a Yankees fan when I was five years old. When Steinbrenner took over the team, I absolutely detested him. And I thought, well, boy, what a good way to get even with this guy. George needed a job. He'd been out of work for a year, living with his parents. He had to go back to work next season. He couldn't live with his parents for another year; that wouldn't be funny. So... it came down to that. I did the voice for the rehearsal, but we were casting... And Jerry said to me, "You should just do it."... The most fun I had during the whole run of the series was not only writing Steinbrenner but doing his voice. It was just a blast.[2]

In 2011, the comedy website, *Splitsider*, rated it the series' number one *Seinfeld* episode.[3] In a case of life imitating art, it helped foster the discussion and application of the opposite into various walks of life worldwide. In his 1999 book, *Seinfeld and Philosophy: A Book about Everything and Nothing*, Professor William Irwin examined the philosophical ramifications behind George's tactic. In 2013, Rob Asghar advised a new generation of *Forbes* readers to mark the episode's approaching twentieth anniversary by applying the "miracle" of the "Opposite Principle" in their own lives. He predicted...

Fifty years from now, sociologists will be studying Seinfeld for insights into human nature, because it frankly explains the idiosyncrasies of the species more crisply and sensibly than most peer-reviewed social-science studies.[4]

Global strategy consulting firm founder Cesare R. Mainardi drew from it in his 2015 *The Wall Street Journal* "The Experts" column...

There's a classic episode of "Seinfeld" where George Costanza does the opposite of all his natural instincts and completely transforms his life. I never thought I'd be giving advice based on a TV sitcom – but George might actually have been onto something. Look at some of the world's most successful companies, legendary organizations like Apple, IKEA, Haier, Natura and Toyota. Surprisingly, the secret to their success lies in doing the opposite of what most companies do... It may be time to pull a corporate George Costanza – and "do the opposite" when it comes to key strategic decisions.[5]

In his 2018 Sunday "Inside View" piece, "George's Investment Strategy," the business bible's columnist and seasoned venture capitalist, Andy Kessler, proposed...

How do you know what's right? It almost always feels wrong. There's an old saying on Wall Street: "Your hand should be shaking when you place your order." You can learn from George Costanza of "Seinfeld." [6]

On a 2010 episode of *Jeopardy*, Merv's answer and question game show based on its own opposite hook, categories included: *My Name is George, I'm Unemployed and I Live with My Parents.* Jon Stewart equated another George's 2007 State of The Union Address on balancing the budget and curbing global climate change with Costanza's opposite scheme. In targeting the opposite of Obama's policies in 2012, Romney referenced it before he did the opposite of win.[7] Donald Trump's unconventional approach to campaigning was likened by MSNBC host Steve Kornacki in 2015 to "that old *Seinfeld* episode where George started doing the exact opposite of every instinct he had, everything he thought he was supposed to do, and suddenly his life turned around."

In *Morning Drive*, a memoir about his terrestrial radio days, CNN anchor and author/columnist Michael Smerconish wrote about his own inner George Costanza and the opposite of sticking to conservative talking points. Calling "The Opposite" one of the all-time great *Seinfeld* episodes on his SiriusXM radio show in March of 2016 and Trump "George Costanza," Smerconish acknowledged the comparison and me on his CNN show.[8] He devoted a Sunday *Philadelphia Inquirer* column to my takes on the Trump/Costanza method of running for president.[9] And he interviewed me on his radio show about the Donald potentially becoming my epitaph.[10] After I apologized to America, *TV Guide*'s TV Insider website announced, "*Seinfeld* Writer Apologizes if Donald Trump is Imitating George Costanza's *The Opposite* Episode." In a later year-end *Inquirer* Sunday column reflecting on 2016, Smerconish cited the "one column I wrote that sums up Trump's success and the year in general... In every instance imaginable, Trump has done the opposite of what is expected of a presidential candidate, making him the George Costanza of the 2016 cycle... inspired by a Philly guy, comedian Andy Cowan." After referencing the column in a CNN commentary, Smerconish added that former Trump campaign manager Corey Lewandowski arrived on the CNN election night set "more dour than you'd expect... and noted that many had ridiculed his candidate, one going so far as to compare him to Costanza... The following week, Lewandowski gave a speech at the Oxford Union in the United Kingdom... repeated the Costanza affront... citing me...as its originator."

At his final thank-you rally in December of 2016, President-elect Trump told the crowd, "They're saying as president he shouldn't do rallies, but I think we should. We've done everything the opposite." A year later CNN Politics Reporter and Editor-at-Large, Chris Cillizza, recalled George's decision to do the opposite of every natural instinct he has, and how the "driving force of Trump's presidency is to simply do the opposite – of what past presidents would have done...of what political conventional wisdom suggests and of what politeness dictates."

"What would have been the opposite for Andy Cowan?" Smerconish asked me on his radio program. Aside from a more traditional line of work, settling down and having kids, I would have done the opposite of mindlessly wiping my dipsticks all those decades *after*... not just before... checking my oil. What was I thinking? They were going back to where the rest of the oil was. What a waste of oil.

I clung to the dream I might land on *Seinfeld* the next season, but my first draft of "The Opposite" was a hot commodity elsewhere. Larry couldn't guarantee that a spot on staff would open up and suggested I take the bird in the hand from *Murphy Brown* creator, Diane English, who'd asked my agent how the *Seinfeld* assignment came about, along with the question, "How old is he?" Still in my early forties, three or four years Diane's junior, I'd passed for younger than my years ever since junior high school. Taking advantage or not knowing the mileage on my odometer, my agent informed her I was in my early to mid-thirties. The heck with seven to ten extra years of accumulated wisdom. Hollywood wasn't attracted to laugh lines on a writer's face, just the ones on the page. I was offered "story editor" on her new bicycle messenger CBS sitcom, *Double Rush*, on the lot where *Seinfeld* also filmed, featuring such up-and-comers as David Arquette, Adam Goldberg and D.L. Hughley.

Months later in October, the reprieve from the governor came in – Larry reported that I could finally join the *Seinfeld* staff in what was already its sixth season as "program consultant!" One tiny hitch: I had to break my contract with Diane and rumor had it she could be tough. Thankfully she couldn't have been more gracious about my situation. As I later told Jerry, I felt like I was back in camp and moving to a better bunk. I followed up with a phone call to Larry at which point he tossed me: "What if Castle Rock (*Seinfeld*'s production company) doesn't have the money?" *Huh?* "You gave me the greenlight. The dominoes have already fallen!" As my heart continued pounding, I heard that unmistakable chuckle you can often catch in the background of a *Seinfeld* episode. Relieved, I asked him, "Now do you know why I find it easy writing for George?" The canny curmudgeon after whom George was modeled replied, "You *are* George."

With no room left in their regular offices, I was tickled to receive my own dressing room/bathroom/office on the lot, surrounded by continually revolving guest stars' names from other sitcoms on the dressing room doors around me. Florence Henderson popped up and out as quickly as a *Brady Bunch* opening. I'd meet in the main office for a catered lunch each day, where Larry and the others would often muse over minutiae unrelated to the show, akin to a *Seinfeld* episode. The New York penchant for cutting through B.S. with surgical precision was a part of Larry's refreshingly non-showbiz vibe. I also sensed his underlying identification with the underdog, having fought the good fights on his way up the mountaintop. Underneath the gruff exterior, I detected empathy and a good heart. You always took notice of his ruminations, part and parcel of the kind of material he sought for the show. If it reminded him of anything else on television, it was dead on arrival. This was the year *Friends* first hit the airwaves, a show he suspected was something of a *Seinfeld* wannabe before earning its own identity. It was also the year of *Pulp Fiction* – the Tarantino flick that married criminal behavior with intermittent chatter about minutiae that Jerry appreciated and recognized bore some ironic similarity to the tone of the show bearing his name.

It was gratifying to hear Jerry laugh at "edible underwear," a joke of mine off another writer's comment that you stood a better chance getting something on the air if the story pitched involved either food or clothing. I'd included underwear in an earlier *Seinfeld* spec script, with this hunk replicating the sample stand-up bit he was still doing at the top of the show...

I think you'll agree that we all share the same secret world of clothing – the world of underwear. It's the underworld of clothing, not always a pretty world, which is why it's a good thing it's covered up. Even though very few people get to see our underwear, one of the cardinal rules of the underwear world is the changing of the underwear. Just like the changing of the guard, it must happen every day. What's strange is the more visible the clothing, the less this rule applies. The jeans that go over your underwear you can wear twenty days in a row. The even more visible coat that goes over the jeans that go over the underwear you can wear for an entire season. Which means clothes should either be seen, but not washed. Or washed, but not seen.

I was always impressed by Jerry's ongoing calm at the center of what was then the number one show on television. As for Larry, I suspected my east coast/neurotic nature was cut from the same cloth and craved a mutual connection with a guy whose enthusiasm-curbing proclivities left him naturally wary. Many years later, I semi-amused myself with this rationalization: Maybe I didn't last longer there, because he was self-loathing and I reminded him of the man in the mirror!

•   •   •   •   •

Larry invited us into the editing room to catch the piecing together of the show, and also offered me a chance to do Steinbrenner's voice, before bringing his own unique spin to what became an ongoing character. After I'd absorbed the Yankee owner's voice clips ad nauseam, my audition sounded more like the guy, himself...

http://bit.ly/AndySteinbrenner

At least my vocal cords got to share a half-minute screen time with Julia Louis-Dreyfus, as the radio deejay whose contest enabled her to snag Mr. Pitt a Woody Woodpecker balloon-holding spot in the Macy's Thanksgiving Day Parade.[11] (Add to that my brief Willard Scott.) At a pre-show crew dinner table one night, I felt I'd come a long way – but not really – when Julia happened to grab the seat next to me, and I was once again a teenager trying to keep cool around the cutest and most popular girl in school.

1995 class picture (Andy one from left in back)

Seinfeld
100th
Episode
January 10, 1995

Showbiz crushes came with the territory.

Sheena Easton performed *Morning Train* for her American television debut on the Griffin show, along with a number on me. During a pre-interview for a follow-up appearance, I asked her about the type of guy she was looking for now that her career was flourishing, but I'd posed her the question for my own selfish reasons.

Sheena: Now if I broadcast that to the entire nation, there won't be any mystery left, will there? Let's just say a cross between Dustin Hoffman and Harrison Ford, with the sense of humor of John Cleese.

My chances were as dead as the parrot in the Monty Python sketch.

•   •   •   •   •

A sketch I wrote several years ago, "Moral Bankruptcy," imagined a John Cleese type as moral bankruptcy attorney, Nick Isaacs, greeting his client, Mr. Devlin...

Nick: Ah, Mr. Devlin. Take a seat.

Client grabs the seat and starts walking out with it.

Nick: Please return the seat.

Client obliges and sits down.

Nick: That chair is expensive.

Client: I'm too lazy to steal cheap chairs.

Nick (jotting down) Under my nose no less. Morally bankrupt indeed. But stealing chairs, whether they're cheap or expensive, requires a certain amount of effort. I don't immediately jump to "lazy."

Client: I don't immediately jump to let an old lady have my seat. Too lazy.

Nick: So, you eventually jump?

Client: The old lady. If she's got a purse.

Nick: By "old lady," you don't mean...

Client: My old lady.

Nick: (jotting down) Morally... bankrupt. Now, if you're declaring moral bankruptcy, we need to know – have you any assets?

Client: Besides occasionally not cheating on my wife and sometimes picking up after the dog but only after it's hardened, no.

Nick: (jotting down) Only... after... it's hardened. How often don't you cheat on your wife?

Client: Maybe... once or twice a month.

Nick: So you feel obliged to remain faithful to your wife once or twice a month?

Client: I have 29 mistresses. In the months with 30 days, I'm faithful to my wife one day. In the months with 31 days, I'm faithful to my wife two days.

Nick: Do you have corroborating records?

Client: (hands over big manila envelope) Would 29 time-and-day-stamped pictures of me in different motel beds with each mistress count?

Nick: That should help. Still, the court may look at the fact you have allegiance to your wife up to 24 days out of the year as a hidden asset.

Client: Stringing her along to make her think I still love her to avoid alimony should count for something.

Nick: Does she know you have mistresses?

Client: No.

Nick: She'd be hurt if she knew?

Client: I'd be hurt if she knew.

Nick: (quickly slipping in) Emotionally?

Client: Physically.

Nick: (jotting down) Good answer. Tell me, how do you deal with February?

Client: In non-leap years, I have sex with 27 of my mistresses. In leap years, 28.

Nick: So, you refrain from having sex with one or two of your mistresses in February, but never your wife? That's thoughtful.

Client: No, it isn't.

Nick: Relax. The moral bankruptcy code in California allows you to hold onto some assets. This is about eliminating your outstanding moral debts to society and getting a fresh start. Now, getting back to your dog...

Client: I never pick up after him when it's somebody else's lawn. Hard or soft.

Nick: But you're a dog person?

Client: I like how his barking annoys the neighbors.

Nick's secretary pops in over the intercom.

Secretary (V.O.): Sorry to bother you. Your wife is on line six.

Nick: Excuse me. (takes call) Hello, love... No, that's okay... Be home by six... Okay, honey... Me too...

Client: Tell her I said hi.

Nick: Oh... Mr. Devlin says... (then, fearing worst, to client) How do you know my wife?

Client: Just being friendly.

Nick: (a beat) The court shouldn't hold that against you.

As Nick wraps up call, we...

FADE OUT.

I might as well have been in a sketch around the same time, when I entered a West Los Angeles shopping center elevator containing one lone passenger – Dustin Hoffman. Part of me had the squirm-worthy urge to imitate my trapped one-man audience as I collectively rattled off his famous movie lines... "Are you seducing me, Mrs. Robinson?" ... "I'm walkin' here!" ... "Don't you touch that ice cream!" ... I made do with: "I enjoy your work!"

·   ·   ·   ·   ·

A memorable *Seinfeld* episode in its final season featured a sketch-like and surreal (a more prevalent tone post-Larry) main plot, one that undoubtedly reflected Jerry's nostalgia for his Merv days. In "The Merv Griffin Show," written by Bruce Eric Kaplan, Kramer discovered the old Griffin show set in a Manhattan dumpster and procures it to recreate the show in his own apartment. As funny as it was, the fact Merv had wrapped eleven years earlier, nearly three thousand miles away no less, made it even funnier to me.

Larry was interested in six of my stories prior to my joining the *Seinfeld* staff, adding that it was hard enough coming up with *one* decent story. Upon settling there four months later, I learned another writer had incorporated one of the stories into the main plot of a script of his and Jerry, to Larry's disappointment, passed on it. After reading the script, I could see why.

By the end of *Seinfeld* season six, following an assortment of story pitches to Larry and sometimes Jerry that were given the initial green lights, I poured myself into multiple outlines and first draft scripts that never found their way onto the air. One was about George's discomfort addressing his new girlfriend, "Gerri," two years before the final season when he was uncomfortable dating a girl who looked like Jerry.[12] I had him hit on a plan (after a *Gigi* subplot made him realize G's can sound like Zh's) for faking a speech impediment. That way he could pronounce all words that began with J or G "Zh," leading to "Zherri," something a lot more feminine. One of the writers later informed Larry that she'd heard another sitcom was planning a story involving names. After I learned about it, it struck me as a case of apples vs. oranges (if not an entirely different food group) but I continued with other stories, creatively feeling at the top of my game. Being in the writers' table-free zone of penning scripts on my own helped, versus the typical multicam sitcom method of rewriting first drafts with a group of disparate personalities sharing different tastes and agendas. Table writing, to my way of thinking, prized pitching and performing jokes over the purity and magic of the writing process – ad-libbing in the privacy of your own head.

The jokes were incidental on *Seinfeld*. Again, the stories took center stage, with four (although Larry once told me it could be as few as two) servicing each of the four main characters. Some others I'd thrown against the wall...

Jerry avoids any and all moments of silence with his latest girlfriend to avoid her increasingly annoying and invasive, "What are you thinking about?"

Combing through old photos, George's new lady friend makes a crack about how goofy he looked as a little kid, prompting him to poke fun at *her* goofy young likeness, what turns out to be a recent picture of her young daughter. Backpedaling, he goes overboard convincing her camera-unfriendly little girl how lovely she is – enough to support her stage mother's goal of pushing the kid into acting and linking her up with Jerry's agent. The kid would remain off camera, so our imaginations fill in the rest, as with the ugly baby in "The Hamptons."

Kramer tracks down the perpetrator of a loose button on his new shirt, "Inspector #5," per the title on the tiny slip of paper in his shirt pocket. Either this guy's an incompetent, or inspectors 1 through 4 blew it big time.

Elaine dreads visiting a cousin who's always rubbed her success in Elaine's face, a world- class "I, I, me-er," who turns out to be surprisingly nice and caring – and down on her luck. The "down-er" she is, the "up-er" Elaine is, who enjoys her cousin's new appreciation of Elaine's relative success until cuz's luck starts turning around again, courtesy of Kramer, and the I, I, me-er returns with a vengeance. (This story had an opposite mini-theme.)

After George tells his new girlfriend he's out of change at a wishing well, she calls him cheap after detecting telltale jingling from his pocket. George's goal: to guilt-trip her into thinking he's anything but cheap... that the jingling came from keys to the new car he bought her... *Jerry's* new car, which George promises Jerry she'll be too guilt-ridden to accept this early in their relationship.

Despite his agent's trademark "I hear you" in response to Jerry's plea that he find him better gigs, Jerry suspects his agent never hears a word anyone says, and further proves he's a non-listener with the help of George and Kramer. After the agent *hears* Jerry's strictly sarcastic wisecrack about how he wouldn't mind what sounds like the worst gig possible, thinking it too will go in the guy's one ear and out the other, the agent takes the remark literally, leading to Jerry's worst booking ever.

Kramer gets a cold and loves it, the most orgasmic sneezing he's ever had, olfactory orgasm. Welcoming drafty open windows to keep it alive, he winds up giving it to Elaine before reaching simultaneous olfactory orgasm with her. (The unexpected glories of sneezing found its way onto a *3rd Rock from the Sun* episode a year later.[13]) Jerry catches their colds, and courtesy of his stuffy nose, unintentionally incriminates himself in answer to his girlfriend's father's question about what Jerry and she did last night: "Dinner." (As Larry's famous episode, "The Contest," implied but never spelled out "masturbation," my goal was for Jerry and the others, based on the old man's chilly reactions, to deduce without spelling out that a stuffed up "dinner" sounded like "didder," as in "did her" as in had sex with her.) And before George's platonic girlfriend he wishes wasn't platonic heads off on her Club Med vacation and risks meeting somebody, he tries to cross the platonic border with her, barely hiding the fact Kramer's pesky germ made him sick too.

As Elaine and another job seeker await interviews, an assistant returns with two coffees, forgetting who wanted which: "One cream and sugar, one black?" As the interviewer enters, Elaine responds, "I'm black." She later gleefully informs the regulars she got the job, but eventually comes to realize they hired her, because they must think she's black. Elaine supports the higher ground here, feeling like an honorary black person, but resents the company's tokenism. "I want to be accepted because of my qualifications, not because I'm black!" "You're *not* black." Considering the preferential treatment she perceives, she's not anxious to let them know otherwise. (Another twist on mistaken racial identity – Elaine thinking her white boyfriend is black while he thinks she's Hispanic – was in the final season's "The Wizard," written by Steve Lookner.)

Jerry leaves a waitress at Monk's a huge tip to make up for the one a guy steals from another table, a guy who'd kindly offered Jerry his table, so Jerry feels guilty ratting on him. Disabusing her of the notion his big tip means he's interested in her, Jerry starts leaving other waitresses equally big tips, triggering annoyingly attentive behavior from all. (Like your sandwich cut horizontally, or diagonally? With or without the crust?) Before they start to equate big tips with normal service and expect even bigger tips for exceptional service he doesn't want, Jerry falls short of blowing the whistle on the kind crook that started him on the road to over-tipping when he keeps popping back into Jerry's life with other unexpected good deeds. George offers to shake his head over Jerry's soup. He's already losing his hair. What's one more? Then Jerry can tell her there's a hair in his soup and can tip her a normal fifteen percent. What about the next time Jerry orders *hair-free* soup? Fifteen. The fact Jerry isn't charging her for the therapy he'll need from his hairy soup trauma, reasons George, is bonus enough.

Elaine raves about Paul, a new guy in her life none of the others have ever seen her with. "That's because I... don't... like... being with him." She connects really well with the guy over the phone but it's never the same in person. It might be because he sounds like a Paul but looks like a "Todd." So, she prefers the inside Paul but not the outside Paul? Elaine wonders why she can't just enjoy the audio portion of the relationship, avoiding opportunities to meet up with him in the flesh whenever possible.

Somebody Jerry isn't crazy about who's holding out hope for something big, like a new job, tells him, "Wish me a good thought, I need the light. Send me the white light." Coerced into it, Jerry half-heartedly says okay. But he feels hypocritical sending white light to a gal he doesn't care for, when there are so many worthier people, and it's not like he sends white light to them, so why do it for her? He makes a feeble attempt to send some light but can't bring himself to pull it off. She could wind up with the job, thanking Jerry for his white light, and now he wonders if his feeble attempt worked. He's concerned he used up white light on her, rather than saving it for when it's really needed, and one night asks the powers that be for the light back. Could the woman suffer repercussions without the white light? Could Jerry be concerned about pulling a fast one with the forces of nature after Kramer reminds him he'd sent the white light under false pretenses? To con the universe is the biggest con of them all!

Jerry wonders if a prim and proper woman he's started dating might have another side to her personality, as he suspects that the items around her house... the bananas she never eats... the cucumbers she never eats... the jumbo hot dogs she never eats... are phallic substitutes.

Elaine has been faking laughs in response to her unfunny new boyfriend who thinks he's funny, and she's afraid she'll eventually be found out, because with real laughing the eyes crinkle; fake laughing: nary a crinkle. Jerry would weigh in on the irony that Elaine's dating an unfunny guy after dating him. Laughing about it at work, Mr. Pitt tells her to laugh again... Mr. P: "No, no, no, Elaine. You're snorting! I want you to laugh, damn it!" Elaine nervously tests out her laugh on Jerry and the others, with Pitt now wanting her to laugh at his bon mots at an important cocktail party, before she winds up accidentally laughing at one of his serious remarks and undermines a potential business deal.

Kramer follows up his coffee table book on coffee tables with a new idea for a book – *CliffsNotesNotes*. *CliffsNotes* on *CliffsNotes*. For people too lazy to read the *CliffsNotes*. i.e.) *Crime and Punishment* – it's about crime. And it's about punishment.

George gets an unsuspecting Newman to dress up like George and accompany him on what is actually a secret blind date. George's goal: to present a lesser version of himself, so the woman can initially think the less good-looking guy (Newman) matches the description George had given her over the phone and is disappointed, until she's relieved to discover that George turns out to be

George. A George line I'd always wanted to use: "Blind people have it made. They don't care about a person's looks. All they're looking for is a decent voice. There are tons of decent voices!" Jerry: "*Looking* for?"

Another story about looking better by comparison... George will only take dates to movies featuring less good-looking actors, why he suspects Jerry's latest movie date didn't go that well. G: You took her to a Tom Cruise movie? J: Yeah, so what? G: No wonder she was less enthralled with you. She spends two hours looking at Tom Cruise. Then the first guy she looks at after that... is you. J: And what exactly are you driving at? G: You should always take them to see movie stars less good looking than you. J: *Less* good looking. G: That's right. Until they really get to know you and fall under your spell. Too bad that new Godzilla remake isn't out yet. J: Godzilla? There's no movie star better looking than Godzilla that's less good looking than me? G: King Kong.

A story off a facial mannerism I'd noticed among politicians (also touching on the opposite): Jerry dates an inappropriate smiler, a woman with the disconcerting habit of smiling when relaying depressing or sad information, constantly throwing him off as to how he should react.

George has an unbelievably rare "perfect" first date. They shared the same wavelengths. Why isn't he basking in the glow? Now this woman will need an even more perfect date to make her feel as euphoric as she did on a measly "perfect" date. He peaked too early! The Orson Welles Syndrome: This date was George's *Citizen Kane*. If the next one is *The Magnificent Ambersons*, she'll still be disappointed. And before you know it... it'll be down to an acting gig in *The Muppet Movie*. Welles – One day, boy genius. Next day, bit player to a Styrofoam pig. George's new goal is to raise the bar the next time and make that date an even more impossible act to follow, which – however stressful – works, raising the bar yet again. His first date was *The Godfather*. The second date was *The Godfather II*. Let the anticlimax begin – we all know what happened with

The Godfather III. George is the pusher; his date is the addict, needing stronger and stronger evenings to keep from crashing. And how will "real George," if he ever shows that side to her, ever be able to compete with "perfect George?"

Elaine meets a guy who's very affectionate, but less so on the second date. She thinks she knows why. Alluding to all this without spelling it out – she first met him before her period, when her breasts were bigger. The PMS makes her more irritable, and he was still more affectionate? He only likes her when she's bigger! Jerry says maybe the guy wants what he can't have and prefers her bitchier side. (The opposite) George concurs, which Elaine, getting in George's face, doesn't appreciate. G: "I prefer your less bitchy side." Elaine lays a little bitchiness on the guy during a normal time of the month, but he's still not as affectionate as when she was bigger, making her as bitchy as she is during PMS, minus her bigger size and his monthly display of affection. She finally dumps him to dump the bitch she's turned into.

In the world of handshakes, when you're on the receiving end of a dead fish, you can't help but offer a dead fish back. Jerry's weak handshake from a new potential manager he was out to impress makes him want to keep bumping into him again towards the hope of initiating a stronger handshake back.

· · · · ·

Larry had liked the dead fish for a B story but thought it might be too similar to an open-lipped kiss beat they'd once done, something I didn't understand at the time. Years later, I included it as a B story for Brad Garrett about his police commissioner in an *Everybody Loves Raymond* spec...

Robert: Shake my hand.

Ray: This isn't going to legally bind me to you in any way, is it?

Robert: Will you please shake my hand?

Ray: Okay.

They shake.

Robert: Was it solid?

Ray: Was what solid?

Robert: The shake! Was it solid?

Ray: Yeah. I guess.

Robert: Very solid?

Ray: I don't know about "very." I reserve the use of "very" for important occasions. Notice I didn't say "very" important occasions.

Robert: All right, all right. Answer me this. Was it firm?

Ray: Yeah. It was firm. For a girl.

Robert: Raymond! Was it firm?

Ray: All right, all right. It was reasonably firm.

Robert: Reasonably? What's that supposed to mean?

Ray: Firm. Without the reasonably. Are you happy now?

Robert: I knew it. His handshake was the dead fish!

I was happy to learn that Romano called the *script* "very solid." The A story involved Doris Roberts' character spoiling a newly arrived neighborhood family's kid – who reminded Robert, and a slightly threatened Ray, of Raymond as a kid. I'd landed it Ray's way after *Seinfeld* wrapped in '98 and he weighed in at *Entertainment Weekly* with his vote for the show's best episode...

RR: The one where George reverses whatever his instinct is because nothing ever works. It was super-neurotic and hit a level of loserdom I can relate to.[14]

Ray passed along the *Raymond* spec to creator Phil Rosenthal, and seemed to sincerely suggest I keep in touch, according to his cordial assistant, Christy, even though they were fully staffed. She felt it said a lot that Ray had read it, because specs rarely got to him even for staffing until the last phase. Meanwhile their one female writer left the show, and they weren't about to replace her with a guy. Seven months later, Christy notified me they'd hired two new writers, something she hadn't known was in the works, but still suggested I keep in touch because they'd hopefully be doing another season. On a Canadian movie set three months later, Ray made sure she called me back. Unfortunately, there were still no openings. As for the script supervisor's "well-written and funny" report on my spec, he added that didn't necessarily mean a busy guy like Phil had had the time to read it.

· · · · ·

Other *Seinfeld* pitches...

A one-floor elevator rider, the lazy jerk who gets on an elevator to ride up one measly floor, impacts a story in two unexpected ways.

Kramer's lifelong phobia about Sundays and that sickening feeling that school is the next day makes him realize one seventh of his life will continue to be ruined unless he finally does something about it. So he develops his own system of time, Kramer Time – a six-day week, minus Sundays, with each day 28 hours long.

George asks out a cute psychic who tells him he'll have a very successful future. How can she not want to go out with a guy with a very successful future? Plus, the pressure isn't on him to have a successful future. It's on her! If he's a failure in the future, it'll mean she's a failure as a psychic. He can't lose! There's your success right there. George's confidence in her prediction starts dwindling as he notices how her everyday short-term predictions (how long it'll take to get home, how George will react to a movie she recommends, etc.) fall short.

Speaking of the future, Jerry and George discover a "life loophole" in realizing that nothing ever turns out the way you picture it will beforehand: For something to not turn out a certain way you'd rather not have it turn out, all you need do is *imagine* it turning out that way... and it won't. All test out this theory, involving scenes which depict the way their imaginations conjure up worst-case scenarios – how they hope upcoming events don't turn out – followed by later scenes showing how they actually turn out. With Jerry and a club gig he's not looking forward to, Elaine and a dreaded chore Mr. Pitt is unloading on her, Kramer and an upcoming visit to the proctologist, anticipating the worst precedes realities more tolerable by comparison. But with George and a job interview he's dreading, conjuring up the worst foreshadows an event that turns out even worse than he'd imagined.

As Pitt pages her for yet another menial task, Elaine moans about how she's sicker of her job than ever and feels like quitting. George notes if she quits, she can't collect unemployment; if she's fired, that's another story. Jerry: "He knows of what he speaks." Elaine decides not to return Pitt's page. Whatever inventive method of slacking off backfires and even wins her praise. (Again, the opposite!) As when he complains about the crumbs she's dropping on the floor, before bending down to pick up some and coming across a treasured cufflink he'd thought he'd lost. Mr. P: "If I hadn't been looking for crumbs, I would have never found this. Thank you, Elaine!" Elaine can do no wrong until Pitt renders guilt by association and fires her for a slight that her friend Kramer committed. Faking remorse, Elaine can barely contain her glee – until Pitt apologizes and welcomes her back, just as she's about to sign up for unemployment.

Larry had called the getting fired to collect unemployment story "beautiful" when I'd pitched it months earlier for George (at a time I didn't need another George story). Liking elements of the Elaine story, Larry said she shouldn't remain fired unless it was the last show of the season, which would have made for two season finales in a row with my name on it, the mentioning of which probably didn't help my chances.

Glenn Padnick read my collection of first drafts and was equally at a loss as to why they hadn't made the cut. I was a kid in the candy store and couldn't quite taste the candy. Plus, it was dark chocolate, my kind of candy! Larry told me, "I'm sure you look at what gets on the show and think your stuff is just as good." I nodded. He added that it was a very quirky process as to what does get on. One day he bellowed at me, "Stop working so hard!" Talk about the opposite.

Ten years earlier Larry had quit *SNL* midseason as a writer after his own frustration in landing just one of his sketches on the air, shortly before the closing credits no less. He returned a few days later as if the quitting had never taken place, and eventually turned that into grist for an early *Seinfeld* episode, "The Revenge." As for me, starting late in the season made it more challenging getting stuff on. Had Larry hired me in June versus mid-October, he conceded he would have had more time to sit down and help chart out an episode or two with me, as he had with the other writers. As the season was winding down, I took what I could get. After he asked us for notions on what might wind up getting stuck up one's posterior, I suggested uncooked pasta. In what became "The Fusilli Jerry" (an outside script rewrite Larry initially divided between me and fellow staffer, Sam Kass) Frank Costanza had a "million-to-one" encounter with uncooked fusilli. You're welcome, America. At the sixth season wrap party, Jerry thanked me for the "great job", but I had no illusions that it didn't mark a wrap for me, and as it turned out, three additional staff writers.

1995 – *Seinfeld* wrap party

At a New Year's Eve party later that year, I relived the glory and pain. A woman literally bowed down to me after hearing I'd written for the show, then rose and knocked her head into my soon-to-be bloody lip. My ego swelled for a second; my lip swelled for an evening.

3 Cheers, 5 Mervs, 12 Icons, 6 Minutes

Adecade before the show that was allegedly about nothing, I and my one other early writing partner, fellow Griffin show talent coordinator Dave Williger, did *the opposite.* Rather than follow conventional wisdom and submit our *Cheers* spec script to other shows that wouldn't be as prone to prejudice against it, we asked a lawyer friend to help land it on the pile at *Cheers,* where everybody may know your name but most didn't know ours. Months later, after figuring it was turned down or never read, we were shocked to get the thumbs up from producer David Angell, a respected writer and true gentleman, and the chance to pen the first of three Shelley Long era episodes (and contribute to another story about Cliff growing a potato that looked like Nixon[1]). Servicing a new character, "Woody," before Woody Harrelson ironically secured the role, we also worked with producers Peter Casey and David Lee, and *Cheers* co-creators and class acts, Glen and Les Charles. When I reminded Glen that he'd written me nearly ten years earlier back in Philly about my first spec script, *Phyllis,* the Cloris Leachman sitcom on which they were producers, he cracked, "So you're the one who watched that show." Angell later co-created *Frasier* along with Casey and Lee, and tragically joined his wife, Lynn, on a trip they'd arranged to Los Angeles for the Emmys, placing them on the first plane to strike the World Trade Center on 9/11.

· · · · ·

The entertainment world had to gingerly broach humor in the weeks following that harrowing event, when *Time* and *Vanity Fair* were proclaiming the end of the age of irony. *The Hollywood Reporter* columnist and friend, Ray Richmond (who'd also worked on the Griffin show) enabled me to help with host Ellen DeGeneres' Emmy monologue rescheduled to October. Preferring not to focus on the somber mood in the room, nor the serious implication behind the separate New York feed for those who were scared of flying to L.A., she told me she would affirm up front that it was indeed a different show but wanted to keep things light and fun. By the same token, she didn't want to commit to anything too ridiculous, because it was hard to laugh at anything overly out there. One of mine she "loved" ...

It's ironic. If I'm funny tonight, you'll say, why wasn't she more serious? And if I'm serious, you'll say, why wasn't she funnier? But since the age of irony is over, it's not ironic. Which is really ironic.

Conveying the right tone was challenging. Up for an Emmy herself, she reasoned the winners wanted to feel good about winning although it was tricky. With that in mind, she liked the punchline to this one if the celebration setup were tweaked, but still wasn't sure the audience would laugh, or feel uncomfortable...

Just a reminder... if you win an Emmy tonight, keep your celebrating to a minimum. And if you lose an Emmy tonight, you're free to look as miserable you are.

Another one referenced the change in wardrobe, a safer subject...

It's so nice to see people in business attire instead of tuxes. Makes sense. It's show <u>business</u>. Not show-fancy-stuff-I'm-wearing-to-try-to-compensate-for-the-fact-I-never-went-to-my-high-school-prom-because-I-was-such-a-nerd-and-good-thing-nerds-become-the-cool-people-when-they-grow-up-and-the-cool-kids-become-nerds... figuratively speaking that is.

It was all scrapped. The already postponed event was cancelled for the first time in Emmy history, hours before air time, as U.S. and British forces attacked the Taliban in Afghanistan. Ellen would host with new material the next month and slay it with the joke:

What would bug the Taliban more than seeing a gay woman in a suit surrounded by Jews?[2]

• • • • •

Ted Danson happened to be my guest on Merv's show during the rehearsals of our first *Cheers* episode, "The Barstoolie," where Cliff's father is wanted for mail fraud and Diane befriends Sam's surprisingly cultured girlfriend to his dismay. During our pre-interview, Danson admitted that being a chauvinist pig was wonderful to try on if you don't get stuck in it. Outrageously skinny back in prep school, and brought up to be sensitive and sweet, he noted that playing Sam was a great way to bring him in touch with his maleness. Upon meeting him at his dressing room door, I was greeted with our script he'd signed along with the other cast members, including Shelly Long's "Let love and light prevail." It was a heady moment that deflated a little, after I first learned how much a freelancer's initial draft changes by the time the staff sinks their teeth into it. As Ted himself volunteered, it happened all the time. Still, the basic story and intermittent chunks of our dialogue survived, as did our names on the cover. Our second big episode, "The Cape Cad," followed the '86-'87 season premiere, "The Proposal," in which Diane rebuffed Sam's offer before changing her mind in ours. But Sam would now be headed to the Cape with another lady and rubbing Diane's nose in it, till she unexpectedly checks out to visit her sick grandmother and he maintains the charade she's still with him for a spying Diane, who knows she left. One of my favorite gags about his looking forward to ordering "some of that fish head soup" survived from our outline to first draft to shooting script:

Diane: Bouillabaisse.

Sam: No, I mean it.[3]

A fair share of other gags survived as well, as was also the case in our third episode, "Norm's First Hurrah." In one of the last episodes featuring Shelley Long, Diane tried to entice Norm to achieve at his new job after the gang surprised him with an office-warming plant in his cubby hole/office shared by an obnoxious co-worker.

After Merv learned I was doing double duty on the first *Cheers* script (the more you do, the more you can do) he called me into his office. The bottom line: He wanted to be made aware of such extracurricular pursuits in the future. I also think he felt writing for a prestigious show like *Cheers* reflected well on his staff. Another reason he couldn't exactly balk: I was being paid Writers Guild minimums for the script, while my title on the Griffin show was "talent coordinator." That way they could pay us considerably less than WGA minimums for writing the week's monologue jokes (as Dave Williger and I had individually begun doing before joining the Guild) along with the interviews. I guess the joke was on us.

Dave and I also went on to pen an episode for the syndicated series about a small record label, *Throb*, starring Diana Canova, Jonathan Prince and Jane Leeves pre-*Frasier*, and were story editors on George Segal's first sitcom in '87 on CBS, *Take Five*, from Ron Howard and Brian Grazer's Imagine Entertainment. A plaque where it filmed at Radford Studios commemorated the classic that ended its run ten years earlier on the very same stage, *The Mary Tyler Moore Show*. Consulting on our writing staff was a guy who'd matched wits with Carl Reiner, Mel Brooks and Neil Simon as head writer on Sid Caesar's influential *Your Show of Shows*, and much later was a story editor on *All in the Family*, Mel Tolkin. Comedy writers in their forties can start to feel the pangs of ageism and underemployment, but here was a guy in his seventies! Segal, then in his fifties, felt it was good to have some gray hair among the youthful staff.[4] CBS yanked the show in its youth – after a mere two episodes aired. *Night Court* subsequently offered Dave and me a gig, but I preferred to wait for *Family Ties*, a less "zany" show I bonded with more that was expressing interest short of an immediate job offer. Dave transitioned from comedy writing to developing game shows. The produced *Cheers* scripts with our names on them now represented a defunct writing team. If I wanted to move forward in the sitcom jungle, I needed to reinvent myself and begin anew on spec scripts showcasing my name alone.

While on the Griffin Show in '83, one extracurricular pursuit I'd kept to myself was testing the waters at *The Tonight Show*. Dropping off a sample pack of material for Carson's long-time head writer Ray Siller over at NBC, I felt a little guilty "cheating" on Merv, while also knowing the vibe under Johnny wouldn't feel as inclusive. As a former Carson writer who'd previously worked for Merv told me, don't expect to ever see Johnny and don't expect stroking when your material's good. I'd pretty much surmised by then that if you were looking for effusive praise in show business, not getting fired was about as effusive as it got. Your thirteen-week contract was generally picked up for another thirteen at *The Tonight Show* unless you hadn't bothered showing up. After that, Johnny could be very unpredictable about deciding they needed new blood, and he might not even look at your material. But once you made it over the hump and survived the initial hot seat, it was civil service time and you could crank it out for years. Though the desk bit/sketch position didn't ultimately open up and they weren't looking for monologue writers, it was fun to give "Tea-Time Movie" along with some of their other staples my own spin...

Hi, feature film freaks. Art Fern here with today's feature film find... Audrey Meadows, Sally Fields, Rosemary Woods, Burt Parks, and Wallop the Wonder Larvae in "The Three Stooges Slap the Three Faces of Eve."

As for the monologue, today's late-night hosts appear less concerned with maintaining the illusion of a conversation with the audience, as Carson did so well, than steamrolling into the material. Curiously America's top monologist would often hammer what sounded like the wrong syllable. When reporting about a "com*pu*ter virus," Johnny's version became "computer *vi*rus." "Thanks to the _pri_vacy act" turned into "Thanks to the privacy _act_."

Merv's "monologues" were more like audience icebreakers at the top of each show. The first line or two out of the guy you're used to seeing on television, now standing in front of you in the flesh, couldn't help but elicit some kind of response. After Williger left for the game show world, I continued these relatively stress-free writing assignments on my own...

Applause is society's way of saying it's okay to touch yourself in public.

Welcome to Hollywood, where one day you're a nobody, and the next day you're a nobody with an agent.

Welcome to Hollywood, the town where the sun always rises. As long as the son has a father in the business.

Welcome to Los Angeles, also known as never-never land. Thanks to the smog, birds fly right by and never never land.

Did you hear? There was a _major_ accident in Hollywood today. Carly Simon's teeth ran into Brooke Shield's eyebrows.

Today we're changing this to The "Mervyn" Griffin Show, because Reverend Jerry Falwell is here and "Merv" is a four-letter word.

Don Rickles is here. Don didn't want you to know this, but he's donated his tongue to science, so that another loudmouth can live on.

Charles Nelson Reilly is here. Not many know he has a stepbrother – Charles Half Nelson Reilly.

Joyce Brothers is on the show. Do you realize if she married Norman Cousins and later became a nun, she'd be Sister Brothers Cousins?

Welcome to the show where Hollywood celebrities tell me their deepest, darkest secrets... during the commercial breaks.

As for my no longer secret side gig, the night of the filming on the Paramount lot and that magical *Cheers* set was a sensory overload of pleasures: Our being introduced in the audience by co-creator and pioneering director, Jim Burrows...watching the majesty of four cameras following the performers in a finely calibrated waltz... and hearing out of the blue from one of the Charles brothers' assistants who happened to be reading the coffee table-sized new 52nd anniversary edition of *Variety*:

Hey, Andy, I liked your article.

What article?

To my surprise, there was "Remarkable...Unforgettable... and the Butler Did It," my piece on how movie reviewers spill too many of the story plot beans, akin to the way movie previews often do today. I'd been driven to write it after discovering in a review of *Terms of Endearment* that Debra Winger's character got cancer. This was well into the story, when I would have grown attached to the poor girl and been shocked at this turn of events, if it weren't for the loudmouth critic who made sure I wasn't. (If you still haven't seen the movie – my loud mouth apologizes.)

After getting passed on by a bunch of periodicals, I thought one Griffin show guest might at least connect with its message – Jack Valenti, president of the

Motion Picture Association of America. This influential leader who'd created the movie rating system also worked with Lyndon Johnson and was in that historic picture aboard Air Force One when LBJ first took the presidential oath. Valenti was nice enough to send me back a note:

Your article is right on, but no publisher will run it and bite the hand that feeds him.

Here I was, temporarily ignoring the filming of my first sitcom episode, *Cheers* no less, feeling especially triumphant as I scanned the article I'd mistakenly figured *Variety*, among the others, had rejected. (As with our *Cheers* spec script, not hearing back right away doesn't necessarily mean a pass!) Still more sensory overload – four names above mine in the *Variety* table of contents was the author of another article... *Jack Valenti.* I circled his name, circled mine and sent it to him with an "FYI" and best wishes. He returned it with his own inscription:

Shows you how much I know. Congrats!

The opposite won again.

It lost thirteen years later as far as my ICM agent was concerned. I was his only client with whom writer and playwright Aaron Sorkin wanted to meet about joining the staff of his brand-new ABC series, *Sports Night.* Maybe I *was* George Costanza. I did the opposite and talked Aaron out of hiring me – but towards the goal of not being hired! First step: Relaying my true worry that I wasn't a big enough sports fan to connect with all the sports banter and minutiae. (You'd think I was an authority after listening to Audible Studios' audiobook, *Tales from the Oklahoma Sooner Sideline: A Collection of the Greatest Sooner Stories Ever Told,* an arduous 2012 voiceover gig where I pretended to know something about football: **http://bit.ly/CowanOnFootball**. It was a bigger "kick" voicing Admiral Ackbar in the audiobooks for *Star Wars: Dark Empire.*) Sorkin countered that he didn't know much about the presidency when he wrote *The American President* – and he later went on to write *The West Wing*! Speaking of sports, in George's case, doing the opposite won him a job with the Yankees. In mine, it won appreciation for my candor, but ten percent of that won little appreciation from my rep. As Sorkin's show would go on to win acclaim if not big ratings, and his name continued to grow over the next decade, I couldn't quite believe I'd passed on an opportunity to work with him, but it felt right at the time. In today's market, I might have done the opposite of the opposite.

"Opposites" from the stars in this book...

The private **David Niven** and **Vincent Price** claimed to be the opposite of their debonair well-dressed public personas. Working with Humphrey Bogart and Spencer Tracy taught actor **Lee Marvin** that less was the opposite, namely more. **Truman Capote** deduced that time spent in Los Angeles was the opposite of time well spent. Theater luminary **Helen Hayes'** late success on TV had the opposite effect on her desire to continue performing on the stage. Actor **Richard Harris** was the opposite of sought after for the *Camelot* role he made famous. Actor **John Houseman**, known for his intimidating professorial on-screen demeanor, was constantly intimidated in real life. Dancing virtuoso **Gene Kelly** noted that grace can represent the opposite of femininity. Eccentric performer, **Andy Kaufman**, continued pursuing the opposite of showbiz in his part-time job as a busboy. Growing up, comic actor **Dick Shawn** was quiet on the outside but ready to explode on the inside. **Jack Klugman** bemoaned that his later roles offered the opposite of the depth his roles on *The Twilight Zone* had. Actor **Ted Knight** advised that you should smile at everybody – your friends *and* your enemies. **Dudley Moore** had a love/hate relationship when it came to women's influence over him. **Anthony Quinn** found it easier to work with women he didn't get along with. Actress **Lynn Redgrave** said the British desired American trappings but conveyed the opposite by putting such goals down. **Charles Nelson Reilly** recalled how many young, awful actors in acting class went on to become well-known greats many years later. **Mel Tormé** received standing ovations after singing poorly and apathetic reactions after singing well. As for opposites supposedly attracting, actress **Shelley Winters** felt the opposite when it came to dating an oil man. Daredevil **Evel Knievel** had vowed to quit after his most recent jump. He wound up doing the opposite. **Orson Welles** admitted that as a young man, he'd thought growing old would be great. At seventy (and on one of the last days of his life) he told me that was a dumb mistake.

It isn't a leap to say brothers Dick and Jerry Van Dyke were polar opposites growing up. Jerry told me he skipped school, received bad grades and was always in trouble, while his sibling was never in trouble "from the time he was born." Dick cited Jerry's tendency to be overweight if he didn't watch it, while Dick ran the risk of disappearing altogether if he didn't eat. "I was always trying to gain, and I just couldn't. I'm still too thin. The ladies resent it – they're all dieting!" He also professed that Jerry dated a lot more, because Dick was a one-woman-guy and afraid of girls, and Jerry wasn't. Identifying as the "lady chaser" of the two, Jerry summed it up: "Ladies liked Dick better, and I liked *them* better."

Don Rickles, as you could probably guess, was the opposite of his cutting on-stage persona, and warmly disclosed how much he appreciated being on the Griffin show. In fact, he was such a sweetheart that I remember feeling a twinge of guilt prior to his entrance, when Merv reached this part of Don's intro I'd written:

He has a Showtime special airing next month. It would have been a series, but they decided a special would last longer.

When Rickles arrived on stage and launched into combat mode, you could tell the joke wasn't lost on him. Put it this way: *C.P.O Sharkey* on NBC was his longest-running series – two years.

Bob Hope was my ten-time interviewee although I always pre-interviewed his loyal longtime publicist, Ward Grant, usually about whatever NBC special they were on to promote. I wonder if he realized here that he'd repurposed one of Hope's catchphrases:

But seriously... talk shows were still more about talk than plugging projects back then, and most guests were largely on to chat.

Hope's specials usually featured a strange convergence of veteran stars with current flavors of the month: Milton Berle. Brooke Shields. Shirley Jones. Emanuel Lewis. He would show up late and already made up, just prior to his curtain call. When his *Thanks for the Memory* theme kicked in and he made his way towards the stage, I watched him turn from a guy who looked pretty good for his age, to ageless. His daily regimen in his 80s: He ate only two meals, walked a mile or two at a brisk pace, aimed for at least nine holes of golf even on the road, hung from rings for ninety seconds at a time to stretch, and could catnap at the drop of a hat. For a theme show saluting **Phyllis Diller** (in this book) who called him her "guru," I learned that she had been working in a sleazy dive in D.C. when she and Bob first met. After badly bombing, she tried to sneak out the back before he finally caught up with her.

I dealt with George Burns, another comedy giant who'd live to 100, via his manager, Irving Fein, who'd also managed Jack Benny. Fein died in 2012 at 101. The book Burns was on to promote, *How to Live to 100 – Or More*, must have rubbed off on them. It preached nothing against cigars, the smell of which wafted from their dressing room, conjuring up memories of old uncles. Fellow cigar aficionado, Uncle Miltie (Milton Berle) sang to me the praises of two contemporary comedians whose lives were unfortunately cut short: John Belushi, a good friend, who used to "put him away," and Robin Williams, whom he called a genius. Eddie Murphy, he claimed, wasn't a comic: "I don't like him as well as I do as a comedy actor."

Murphy did a spot-on Bill Cosby impression in the '80s, someone he'd told *Rolling Stone* he wanted to emulate. Looking over Cosby's notes now, a three-time pre-interviewee, I'm reminded of how beloved he was on his number one show on television prior to his fall from grace decades later. In one set of notes about his running in track and field again in his mid-forties, he welcomed Merv's asking him anything about age, or whether he was trying to reclaim his youth: "He can be as abrasive and funny as he wants, and we'll have fun with it." It's impossible to imagine an open-ended directive like that now, nor this no longer innocent question...

How much of the Huxtable family life is the Cosby family life?

Three years prior to his series, on a Vegas show, Merv asked him if he was a hot dater before he met his wife, Camille, leading to the memory of a great date with a "good-looking girl" in Hawaii who was a terrible drinker. The audience laughed after his observation...

BC: A drunken girlfriend is a lot of fun. A drunken wife – nasty person.

Comedian Robert Klein, the first to star in an HBO stand-up special, was a major influence among his peers, especially those who shared his east coast essence. I pre-interviewed him multiple times in New York, when we visited David Letterman's future home base, the Ed Sullivan Theater (where Klein had performed on Sullivan's widely watched variety show six times). He wanted to talk about kissing on the panel among other talk show dynamics, with this opposite spin...

RK: One time I kissed (bookish psychologist) Dr. Joyce Brothers on your show, and I shook hands with (fashion model) Lauren Hutton.

In the event some of our own questions didn't fuel fruitful conversations, again as with *Jeopardy*, the talent coordinators would wind up fashioning questions after guests had given us the "answers." Re: Klein's talk show dynamics, Merv's set-up and question became:

You're one of the most seasoned talk show guests I know. Is there an art to guesting?

A rare talk show guest that landed my way was one of the most renowned actors of the 20th century – Laurence Olivier. Since I hadn't directly pre-interviewed him, he isn't represented among the star samplings in the next chapter. But I not only got to meet him, I was sent in a limousine to pick him up. Riding in a limo can be a humbling enough experience when you're not about to pick up the guy other actors worshipped as the actors' actor. He asked me to call him "Larry," which I may have snuck in once for kicks, but it was no easier than calling him "Sir Laurence" or "Lord Olivier."

Before arriving at the show, we stopped at a nearby apartment building to see if a family member was in. I remember a tiny "Olivier" nameplate on the building, which struck me as amusing.

Less amusing was when we were backstage prior to his segment, and I handed him the galleys of *Confessions of an Actor*, his soon to be published autobiography he'd agreed to sign for me. Happily soaking up the oxygen in Larry's dressing room was *Hill Street Blues* actor Charles Haid (Merv's cousin!), who grabbed the book and asked him to sign it to Merv. As Olivier's Hamlet could have recited, it looked like my personalized copy was "not to be," but I learned it was the opposite backstage following his interview. In the role of a mischievous kid, he opened the galleys and enthused, "I'm a good cheater!" before re-inking the "Merv" that led up to "With grateful good wishes, Larry" into a seamless "Andrew."

A little over a year after he'd left the White House, Jimmy Carter was on the show to promote his memoirs, *Keeping Faith*. Short of landing a pre-interview, I divided likely questions and notes into A) his life today and the family, B) world issues including the Iranian hostage crisis that sealed his fate, and C) Reagan and politics. Off his publicized comment that Reagan showed a lack of interest when

Carter briefed him during the transition, I threw in a loaded question I imagined Merv, a friend of Reagan's, might not mind seeing:

Which is a better way to govern... with your attention to details, or his attention to broad areas of concern while letting subordinates handle the details?

Merv didn't get to that one but did steer Carter to the coolly relayed detail that his current relationship with Reagan was non-existent – whereas Carter, as the notes referenced, had reached out to predecessors Ford and Nixon when he was in office.

Before the show, I handed my notes to one of the Secret Service members guarding Carter's dressing room who invited me in to meet him, something I hadn't expected.

JC: You say your name is Andy?

Faithful to what Barbara Walters reported about him, something Merv extracted from the notes on-air, he really did make you feel like you were the only one in the room. (In this case, I *was* the only other one in the room.) Getting a signed book proved to be no problem. Several years later, at the end of Carter's spot promoting another in a series of tomes that he would continue to pen for decades to come, Merv opened the book as they were breaking for a commercial, and there was the former president's inscription to another talent coordinator who'd prepped that interview. It hadn't occurred to us that Merv might want Carter to sign it to the host of the show! Short of that, we figured Merv already had a signed copy. His irritation was on rare display at the next meeting, so much so that the talent coordinator at the receiving end of his wrath quit. Unlike his witnessing signature on the Camp David Accords, Carter's signature on the book had brought the opposite of peace, and the rest of us learned to be more cautious about signed books from that day forward. If Merv had ever found out about Olivier's signature, my name could have been Merv/Andrew/mud!

. . . . .

I reached out to Carter via fax over a quarter century later during the 2012 Republican presidential primary season. In shooting a sardonic test feature report for Fox 11's Los Angeles newscast and KTTV news director, Kingsley Smith, I poked fun at one of the candidates, former Godfather's Pizza CEO, Herman Cain. My favorite exchange was when I asked a local pizza customer the obvious question...

Do you think people who feed you pizza should have experience making pizza?

Customer: Of course.

Arriving at my point...

Should people leading the free world have experience making policy?

Customer: (a beat) Quite possibly.

After asking the Santa Monica pizza store owner and viewers whether competing with Domino's properly prepared one for competing with China, I faxed Carter...

My dream would be to end by asking the home viewer whether the reverse (yes, the opposite!) holds true: Does a former president have what it takes to lead a pizza company? Would you be at all open to as little as a fifteen second phone comment simply about your views on pizza? We'd obviously work around your schedule, and it would really be the topping on the pie, so to speak.

I expected the pizza to remain topping-free, but was pleased to at least receive an email back...

November 1, 2011

Dear Mr. Cowan,

President Carter has received your invitation to participate in your two minute test piece for Fox News in Los Angeles. He is grateful to you for offering him this opportunity; yet due to his full schedule with the work of The Carter Center and personal obligations, he is unable to accept your offer. President Carter has asked me to express his gratitude to you for thinking of him and sends his best wishes.

Sincerely, Nancy Konigsmark

Maybe I should have asked for his views on peanuts.

•   •   •   •   •

Presidential progeny pre-interviews included the daughter of Carter's successor, Patti Davis, on the Griffin show a month after Reagan was shot in '81. She was angry at the way criminals in America become media celebrities, and wanted no mention of the name, "John Hinckley." In a later appearance, she only wanted to talk about her acting pursuits, rendering her ties to her father the apolitical elephant in the room. Steven Ford, also pursuing an acting career, was glad it was out of the White House spotlight versus Patti's pressures, and claimed his former First Family connections made achieving success twice as hard, because the public expected presidential-level accomplishments. As for an acting challenge that Harry Truman wasn't quite able to pull off, Margaret Truman relayed her dad's attempt to find a man with a stovetop hat to scare her friends into thinking Lincoln was still roaming the White House.

In 1982, I pre-interviewed Henry Kissinger after his triple bypass.

HK: If Merv asks a nasty question, I'll clutch my chest and start perspiring heavily.

I did suggest that Merv ask him about a notion he'd first conveyed in a book some thirty years earlier – that it was possible to design a limited nuclear war. Kissinger had since become doubtful such a pursuit could be contained. **Paul Newman** (in this book) held his own strong doubts.

I helped shape the questions Merv asked Nancy Reagan when she visited the show as First Lady to promote her book on foster grandparents, *To Love a Child.* (She'd met her eventual astrologer on his show back in the '70s.⁵) Merv and Mrs. Reagan were good friends and shared the same birthday – why one of my appearances on the show was especially nerve-wracking. The voice and phrasing of Frank Sinatra, another friend of Nancy's, was so embedded in me growing up that I was able to channel them when I put my mind to it.

1966 - Fourteen-year-old's signed Sinatra drawing

At clubs that included The Comedy Store (where I once preceded a young guy by the name of David Letterman) I'd close with Sinatra starting out "today," warbling the likes of *Macho Man, Physical, Whip It* and *If You Think I'm Sexy.* The positive reaction over the years gave me the confidence to perform a medley of these ditties on the show, which I arranged with the much-appreciated help of Merv's longtime bandleader, Judy Garland's and Barbra Streisand's former musical director, Mort Lindsey. Bandmate biggies included Plas Johnson on sax and Jack Sheldon on trumpet. It was this third Merv appearance (with other Philly transplants, Jack Klugman and *Annie* star Andrea McArdle among the guests) on which I was first billed in the show opening as "comedian, Andy Cowan." It was also when Merv first strayed from his intro cue card and called me "bizarre." Did he really think I was bizarre? Was it bizarre of me to wonder if he thought I was bizarre?

Merv: I want to introduce a young man who works on my show. He is one of our interviewers. And he izzzzzzz... a bizarre young man. No, that's not fair to say; he is very funny. He came on the show before and did Andy Rooney and it was a big hit. And today he's gonna do for us Frank Sinatra. Now what's interesting about him is – he looks so far from anybody that he impersonates that it's just amazing to watch. But if you listen, he is right on target. Now he's going to musically answer the burning question, what if Frank Sinatra were starting out today? What songs would he sing? Here from my staff, Andy Cowan... Andy?

I wrapped up with a current hit that lent new meaning to an old one...

Andy: I wish that I had Jessie's girl! I wish that I had Jessie's dame! ... That's 'cause the lady... That is 'cause the lady... That's 'cause the lady is a tramp!

Following the medley, I grabbed a stool and beat into the ground one of Sinatra's (and years later, Billy Crystal's, in his *SNL* send-ups of frequent Merv guest Fernando Lamas) favorite adjectives: "You're a *mahvelous* audience. That's a *mahvelous* band. *Mahvelous*... is a *mahvelous* word. Here's a *mahvelous* old standard." Per my request, a glass of water had been placed on the stool next to me, but I couldn't figure out a cool way to reach over and grab a quick sip, so I remained parched. (Had Marco Rubio been watching as a boy, he might have learned not to grab an uncool sip over thirty years later during his televised response to the State of the Union!) I closed with a revamp of one of Frank's majestic ballads, *Nancy (With the Laughing Face)* that parodied the First Lady. My first draft hadn't been cleared by one of the song's writers, so I toned down the edge...

When I just see her beaming at Ronnie
When I hear him call her "Mommy"
Believe me, I've got a case
On Nancy with the laughing face

It was that appearance that set me on the eventual path to clubs and special events throughout Los Angeles as lead vocalist with gifted jazz musicians, a nearly three-decade ongoing musical mission.

http://bit.ly/AndyatViper
http://bit.ly/CowanIllWind   http://bit.ly/NinaBeckTrioDylan
http://bit.ly/CowanAprilinParis

A refreshingly retro venue where we tend to favor the Sinatra songbook is one of L.A.'s most popular swing dance clubs, Rusty's Rhythm Club in Playa del Rey, spearheaded by international dancer and choreographer, Rusty Frank. In a 2015 feature story for *The Argonaut*, she quoted me to illustrate her prohibition of cell phones to promote interaction among dancers of all ages and backgrounds...

Andy Cowan, who was a writer for Seinfeld, also loves to sing the standards so he came and performed for my club. He wrote me the next day: "I loved being in your alternate universe, where handheld devices are other people's hands."[6]

In one early engagement with my quartet at a Hollywood venue owned by former *M*A*S*H* star, Wayne Rogers (before my slavishness to Sinatra transitioned to jazzier sensibilities), I scoped out the audience and noticed HBO sportscaster Jim Lampley making out with his then wife, newscaster Bree Walker. Bree was well known for a congenital disorder that produced missing digits on her hands and feet, something she claimed wasn't the big deal some made it out to be. The Cy Coleman tune of Frank's I had just begun crooning, with lyrics by Carolyn Leigh, was *Witchcraft...*

Those fingers in my hair
That sly come-hither stare
Strips my conscience bare
It's witchcraft

The Lampleys would have probably found my self-induced fear of insensitivity amusing, not that their attention was on anyone but each other at the time! "Take my arms, I'll never use them," from *All of Me*, didn't flow out of me any easier. I was glad I hadn't noticed another couple at a more recent private event until after I'd finished my set – otherwise I wouldn't have felt as loose on stage. Hearing "You really know how to sing" from Sinatra's drummer, Gregg Field, and his wife, vocalist Monica Mancini, daughter of Henry Mancini, was unreal. Gregg also liked my jazzy parody of the Ervin Drake Sinatra tune, *It Was a Very Good Year*, on the differences between Frank's love life and mine...

When I was seventeen, it was a very good year
It was a very good year for reading Playboys under the covers
I'd dream they were my lovers
It felt peachy keen
When I was seventeen

The year before my contemporary interpretation of her father on the Griffin show, guest Tina Sinatra relayed that they'd had their disagreements over modern music or movies he found more upsetting than entertaining. She also described herself to me as "his child, the one closest in temperament, the part that fights for what they believe in and speaks out even when they should probably shut up."

During my later stint as a writer and occasional performer on a CBS late night talk show hosted by Merv's discovery, Pat Sajak, we decided to end Pat's monologue poking fun at Sinatra's having just come out with a new cookbook. Pat shared an "audiobook sample" over a picture of a popular main course...

Put it in the oven, babe, a pound of ground round
Maybe an onion if it's lyin' around
Bake it for an hour until golden brown
That's meatloaf, my little meatloaf

The next day, I was taken aback when a production assistant forwarded a call from an earnest Sinatra fan who'd wondered where he could get his hands on his "record" we'd played last night – yours truly warbling with the Tom Scott band.

Sinatra's favorite singer, Tony Bennett, was a three-time Griffin show interviewee of mine. His philosophy on performing that he exudes to this day was one he'd learned from studying the great big band leader, Count Basie...

TB: It was a big band explosion of happiness, something Merv would understand, so I've adopted that philosophy. Some people put down Louis Armstrong for being extra happy, but I think that's the right philosophy to have.

The fact that Merv let me repeatedly do the show and perform a song that poked gentle fun at his prominent friend spoke to his underlying supportiveness. He also understood branding – why he doubled down on the "bizarre" handle for my fifth appearance and first panel shot, when ad-libbing off the introduction that I (bizarrely enough) had written for myself...

Merv: This'll be nice, what you're about to see. (On cue card:) My next guest is a clever young comedian and comedy writer who has performed on our show before, but he's never sat here before. He is a member of my staff on this show. (Ad-libbing:) And in meetings, I've always found him to be... odd. (Off audience laughter:) Not odd. But (back to cue card:) he's a very candid individual, and I thought it might be refreshing to talk to him today about his life out here as a single guy in Southern California. Please welcome... Andy Cowan.

I greeted him at the desk, figuring he'd stick to the prepared questions that led to my comedy hunks. But he opened with how odd it was shaking hands, considering he'd just seen me upstairs a few minutes earlier and now we were doing a "whole show business thing." I needed to respond: "I'm learning to be fake already. I love this."

Merv: You're from Philadelphia if I recall. (Off audience applause, bowing to a top TV market:) And I know you'll be wonderful about Philadelphia, because you know how important they are to my show; a much-loved city of mine. (On his blue card:) How have you adapted to the lifestyle out here?

Hitting a few jokes that hinted at my being a down guy (a theme I'd milk sixteen years later on *Up & Down Guys*) I then asked the audience if anyone lived in the (San Fernando) Valley. A few clapped.

Andy: I shouldn't be living there. It's like living in the background of a Roadrunner cartoon.

Merv teed me up with, "Really?" A simple response that makes me chuckle to hear now.

Andy: The scenery never changes: Taco Bell, palm tree, Taco Bell, palm tree.

Scored.

Merv: (On his blue card:) Things are going well for you (straying from card:) Andy. I mean you're really a remarkable addition to the show here. (Back to blue card:) I don't see why you should be depressed.

After navigating to a horoscope joke that explained why, I followed his question about whether I'd made many friends in L.A. with a joke on how friends can make you even more depressed, eliciting from Merv another succinct set-up:

"Really?" Had I not practiced it in clubs, I wouldn't have been quite as confident pausing in between the phrases as I eyed the audience, trying to draw them in...

Andy: Ever been with a friend... and you're really down... and you mention how sometimes... maybe you should just... <u>kill</u> yourself?

Nervous audience laughter. I was "odd," indeed.

Andy: And the other person doesn't say, "Don't talk like that"?

Adequate laughs. Merv quipped, "How depressing." Onward to a joke that landed about why I have a hard time buying people birthday cards: Nobody I know is as nice as Hallmark says they are. I'd "spent about an hour in the card shop" and wasn't thrilled with what I wound up buying. Merv's ad-lib, "I'm dying to see," generated chuckles as I whipped out the card to read the phony text, mentally preparing myself to recite straight lines I knew wouldn't evoke anything yet...

Andy: "There's one thing that I know is true." (Opening card) "There's no sweeter sister than Y-O-U."

Merv: (Ad-libbing) Aww.

Andy: I had to add... (reading) "Except when you have cramps."

Tossing the card, I awaited the end of extended laughter that caught me completely off guard, acknowledging it under my breath to Merv as he acknowledged it back.

When my name had first joined other guests on the upcoming shows corkboard a year after I was hired, it was scary/thrilling. I was scheduled to do a send-up that scored in comedy clubs, Andy Rooney, just starting to impact popular culture with his *60 Minutes* commentaries, in the first of two "A Few Minutes with Andy Cowan" segments. Pacing backstage and hearing the show in progress, you can't believe you're the caboose on this smoothly gliding train. As for the conviction that went into selling the intros we'd write for him, Merv was like no other talk show host...

Merv: One of the _most_ popular journalists around has got to be Andy Rooney. _Millions_ of fans watch him every week on 60 Minutes... (off script:) ... _wait_ for him on that show. And, of course, you know (on script:) his new book is at the top of the bestseller list. That's because he pays attention... (sharing with other guests on couch:) to the _little_ things... (turning back to camera:) in life... Not to be outdone, so do we... Here now is our _own_ commentator on the little things in life. A few minutes with (turning sardonic) Andy Cowan... (Off script:) Andy?

The audience applauds as they cut to a ticking clock and "A Few Minutes with Andy Cowan" modest logo, then to me, already positioned at a crummy desk center stage...

Andy: I don't know if you've noticed or not... (impression lands the first laugh) ... but there are too many kinds of toilet paper.

There I was live on tape, my first time on national television aside from a game show, trying my best to act calm and collected. When I reached this exhilarating moment about a half minute in, I discovered I had the audience in the sweaty palms of my hands...

I don't care about toilet paper until I use it, and once that happens, I care about it even less.

Considering that Orson Welles (routinely assigned to me) regularly visited the show and that *literal* heavyweight, actress Nell Carter, was on the panel watching, I can't believe I had the cojones to display the cardboard tube inside a paper towel roll as if it were a toilet paper roll and ask...

Do you suppose Orson Welles has this tailor-made too?

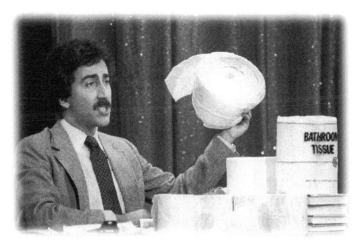

1982 – *Instead of 4 rolls to a package, why don't they give you one huge roll?*

Merv once regaled us in his office with the sight gag of slipping on a part of Welles' massive wardrobe that had been kept in storage. Orson was larger than life in more ways than one!

There are few bigger highs than reaching the end of your first national TV spot and sensing the audience is truly with you. It gave me the courage to take my time in between the final choice words...

Andy: Don't get me wrong. I like toilet paper. I just don't think it's any big deal. After all, can toilet paper do anything <u>really</u> remarkable, like renew your faith in God? . . . Nooooo . . . But... finding one last roll in a men's room after thinking they ran out... brought me pretty damn close.

You're in a fog, blinded by the moment and the lights, with a darkened studio audience your only line of sight. Clinging to your character center stage, you hope the nerves don't show. You think you did well as you hear applause. They cut back to the ticking clock logo. The applause continues. They cut to Merv, whose beaming smile that appears genuine I won't see until it airs, announcing my name again and continuing to applaud. He checks the monitor, notices he's still on camera, and continues applauding as the audience starts to cheer. They cut back (unbeknownst to me) to yours truly now out of character, visibly heaving a sigh of relief, then return to Nell Carter briskly applauding next to actor Albert Hague (the music teacher on the film and TV series, *Fame*) before going to commercial. Hague called the following day to congratulate me.

Post-Debut Toast – Hollywood Brown Derby

At work that next morning, others echoed I'd done well but it all seemed like a dream. I had returned to mild-mannered talent coordinator, "Clark Kent" Cowan, careful not to look as if my secret X-ray vision was overly focused on returning to the spotlight that shined first and foremost on the boss. I couldn't get a big head over it, because I already had one. The jumbo noggin that broke the bully's hand back in junior high had earned me then the creatively-challenged nickname, "Head," whose size my mother assured me I'd eventually grow into. Merv always claimed that audiences were drawn to physically big heads on TV, part of why he was drawn to hiring Pat Sajak and Vanna White for *Wheel of Fortune*. So, getting an even bigger head over my segment wouldn't have hurt!

Watching the airing, I cursed my TV: Seconds after I popped onto the screen, the reception faltered as the picture fluttered and color kicked into black and white, before finally correcting itself. I later discovered the interference was city-wide. Apologies to my TV.

Dick Carson (Johnny's brother) directed the Griffin show, something in which I know Merv took satisfaction. It was a kick that Dick liked my Rooney spot enough to mention it a few weeks later to **Ed McMahon** when he visited the show, among the stars in this book. (Johnny eventually started doing his own homage to Rooney.) Dick's cool professionalism lent itself well to directing, which included planning for the inevitable magic trick that Orson Welles would insist upon demonstrating at the top of most of his appearances. When he arrived for his last time on the show, it looked as if he'd managed a true feat of magic – making loads of weight disappear. But he wasn't well and died the very next day.

Johnny Carson would frequently mine laughs from the latest alleged Merv Griffin theme show he happened to catch, exaggerating Merv's periodic shoehorning of guests into a one-size-fits-all topic, common on many daytime talk shows these days. The night of the final Griffin show airing in 1986, Johnny welcomed Merv as a first-time guest, following a monologue that included what would now be a politically incorrect joke indirectly referencing the diminutive co-star of ABC's *Fantasy Island*...

Johnny: Toward the end, Merv was <u>stretching</u> for theme shows. I saw one last month – Famous midgets and their moms. You haven't lived till you've seen Bertha Villechaize.

"Newsmakers" was the theme of a legitimate show on which I was the comedy relief (I hoped) sandwiched between two deadly serious pre-interviewees

– steely U.N. Ambassador Jeane J. Kirkpatrick, and Father Andrew Greeley. (I was often assigned Greeley, not exactly my area of expertise as a non-religious cultural Jew.) I walked out center stage, positioning myself as the audience heard Merv tell the ambassador we'd all be watching her carefully in that office of hers she'd begun under Reagan's watchful eye. As Mort Lindsey's tinkling piano lightly accompanied her exit off the stage, you could hear a pin drop and my pulse. Transitioning to upcoming levity, Merv faced the camera and began reading my intro, grinning as he said "offbeat" to help grease the wheels...

Merv: Well, since today's show involves newsmakers, we thought we'd take a bit of an offbeat look at the news. With the popularity of TV news magazines... 60 Minutes, NBC Magazine, and of course, 20/20. Right now, we're going to unveil our own slightly <u>fuzzy</u> version of the important stories of the day. Stay tuned for Andy Cowan, and 20/30.

Here was another chance, as in my Andy Rooney bits, to earnestly assign more magnitude to minutiae than they deserved, a tactic I'd continue in a way on *Seinfeld* years later. As an *out of focus* 20/30 title card came into view, my chintzy pre-recorded Casio handheld keyboard kicked in, repeating an urgently silly knockoff of the 20/20 theme music throughout. With accompanying images I'd collected punching in on a monitor screen-left of me, in my most undeservedly newsworthy voice, I was off...

Tonight: People do it when they're tired. People do it when they're bored. But – could it mean much more? Tonight: a special report... Yawning!

Cheesy lettering (extra cheesy by today's standards) of "Yawning!" labels a picture of a yawning woman. Laughs trickle in from the audience. It was early yet.

Patricia Campbell Hearst. She made the headlines seven years ago, and seven years later, they're still writing her story. What is there left to say about somebody so bland, they had to rob a bank to get themselves into People Magazine?

Nice laugh.

Tonight: a special report... Patty Hearst – Boy Am I Sick of Her!

More laughs. The repeated "special report" gimmick is starting to register now.

North Dakota: One of the fifty states. Or is it?

Laughs ramp up a notch as a chintzy hand-drawn question mark pops up over the state of North Dakota.

Does anybody really live there, and why don't we ever hear about it? Tonight: a special report... A State of Boredom!

Back to previous picture of woman yawning. (Visual callback) A clap or two as laughs taper off a bit.

Electronic games. They're in arcades, shopping centers and grocery stores. But who put them there? Tonight, Tom Jerrold ('80s ABC reporter) searches for answers in a special report... Pac-Man Fever: The Communist Plot!

Hand-cut hammer and sickle plastered over video game pic. Moderate laughs maintain. (The Soviet Union crumbled eight years later, decades before Putin-Man gobbled up the Ukraine.)

Navels. Belly buttons. Innies and outies. Common expressions for the indentations in our stomachs. But what are they doing there?

Pictures of svelte and not so svelte bellies help. Picture of guy munching celery, then sticking it in his salt-filled navel really helps, as laughs build.

Tonight: A special report on a growing question, as America pushes... The Belly Panic Button!

Headed for the finish.

Brooke Shields: She's every male's fantasy, and every woman's frustration. We've seen her when she looks her best. But what about after she's eaten too much chocolate?

Nice laugh.

Tonight – Geraldo Rivera discovers the truth behind the glossy image, in a <u>special</u> report!

Cut from pic of Brooke to same pic with goofy hand-drawn spots all over her face.

Brooke Breaks Out!

The alliteration, visual and gag drove it home!

In 1982, TV news sensationalism was still in its infancy. Was I prescient, or is that just 20/~~20~~30 hindsight? If I'd been truly prescient, I would have left out the "special" report on whatever happened to the pet rock. The audience laughed when they saw the reveal, pet boulders. But less would have been more.

In a 2015 *SNL* cold open, Larry David spent the right amount of time getting big laughs as Bernie Sanders in the first Democratic presidential debate. After Larry/Bernie wondered why the banks chained all their pens to the desks, I remembered my second Andy Rooney bit on the Griffin Show back in '82...

Andy: We trust banks with our money. How come they can't trust us with their pens? (Dangling pen attached to a flimsy chain gets laughs.) Next time I make a deposit, I think I'll do it like this...

Dick Carson cut to a close-up of me dangling a dollar attached to a flimsy chain, landing laughs and an audible one from Merv off-camera.

Mining still more minutiae, at *The Pat Sajak Show* I and Griffin show photographer, Mark Edward Harris, produced *6 Minutes*, a comedy send-up of *60 Minutes*. The cast of three also included yours truly as Morley (Safer) Cowan, Harry (Reasoner) Cowan, Ed (Bradley) Cowan, Andy (Rooney) Cowan, and in the feature report, Mike (Wallace) Cowan...

Few signs in recent memory have garnered less respect than the ones we all come upon at supermarket checkout counters, with the familiar phrase, "Ten items or less." For over a decade now, this so-called restriction has been more and more loosely enforced, and oftentimes entirely ignored. And who's willing to claim responsibility for this legal and moral dilemma? Well if you think it's the supermarket cashier, think again.

The length of a stand-up spot, I thought the show would welcome this pre-produced piece (about another CBS show no less) something on which Mark and I had already spent our own hard-earned chump change...

http://bit.ly/cableace6min

They passed. The default response to most creative swings in Hollywood, this one was especially disappointing. It turned out to be the opposite, a blessing in disguise, after I cold-called Showtime, The Movie Channel (on which longtime TCM host, Robert Osborne, would reference our minimal budget before introducing it) and PBS – all of whom ran it as interstitial programming – and we were nominated for a '91 ACE (later renamed CableACE) Award for best short-form programming special! I needed a tux for the awards ceremony! I needed a date for the awards ceremony! If it were a clichéd invite to catch a movie, all bets were off. But how could the woman I'd just met turn down an opportunity like this?

Mark brought a clunky early '90s video camera to our table in the highly unlikely event our names would be called. Ted Turner and *Women of World War II* were among our competitors, and my junior high battle with the bully on the bus didn't exactly measure up. My last-minute date screamed. We won! The music soared, I received a showbiz kiss from co-host Kevin Pollak's wife, co-hostess Lucy Webb, along with the dust collector still on my mantle, and followed my thanks to Mark and other supporters with the heartfelt...

To know that cable not only opens its doors to an independent comedy project shot on less than a shoestring, but also bestows upon it an honor like this, gives us faith and we hope it gives others faith. Thank you very much.

Lucy told the audience, "I hope you guys are paying attention, because these people are moving to network."

Photo by Silvia Mautner

1991 – 6 Minutes of fame

After Mark and I, euphoric, were ushered backstage for a quick video snippet to air on multiple cable channels telecasting the major ACE Award contenders that Sunday, I told the camera: "I'd like to thank my wife. But I don't have a wife. Maybe this will help reel her in." Watching the ceremony now, on which *It's Garry Shandling's Show* also picked up an ACE for Showtime, I'm struck by the tinge of excitement among the participants – thrilled that all sorts of cable programs were being recognized. And it was teeming with stars, including a salute to Jerry Lewis and Muhammad Ali! Showtime had previously forgotten to add us to their on-air promo heralding their ACE nominees until I jogged their memory. They didn't need prodding to include us among their shorter list of winners.

With shiny ACE in hand, my date drove me to a popular Hollywood watering hole (and a favorite of Sinatra's) to celebrate, Nicky Blair's, where she gravitated to some other guy. I remember thinking I probably needed an Oscar or Emmy to keep her the entire night. Anybody can win one of those baubles, but nobody will ever be able to capture a CableACE Award again. It was axed eight years later, after the Emmys started welcoming at least the bigger cable players to the party. The real reward was when *60 Minutes'* late legendary creator, Don Hewitt, sent me this note:

CBS NEWS
A Division of CBS Inc
524 West 57 Street
New York, New York 10019
(212) 975-4321

Dear Andy:

Everybody loved your "Six Minutes."

I would have written sooner but I got behind this fat lady with a cart full of groceries on the express check-out line and you know how that can fuck up your whole day.

Best,

Don Hewitt
Executive Producer
60 MINUTES

http://bit.ly/Merv6Minutes

1989 – CBS Sajak Show ad on comedy – Cavett, Cosby, Cowan, et al.

CBS

1989 – Searching for love on CBS

Returning to the challenge of holding onto ladies, one night Pat Sajak acted as my "wingman" on his show.

PS: You have a bit of a problem meeting, getting to know, and hangin' on to members of the opposite sex.

Andy: (a beat) Not as big a problem as I'll have after they see this.

I was driven to Tom Bergen's, the Irish bar down the street from CBS Television City, where Pat would check in on my progress throughout the show and, as my Cyrano de Bergerac, secretly feed me pickup lines through my earplug, most of which I'd written for him. The patrons obviously knew something was up thanks to the lights and camera. I confessed to Pat and the viewers that I'd tried to convince women my earplug was actually a hearing aid. That way I could get to the joke: Now they're *shouting* that they don't want to go out with me.

David Letterman's influence off NBC's *Late Night* was still at its peak when Pat was tapped for the talk show, the last such CBS late night vehicle until Dave's over a decade later. Sajak's style along with the writing attempted to bask in some of fellow former weatherman Letterman's glow. Among other bits, I played a tedious scientist at the panel, as Pat took a sip of his water and drenched me with a spit take after my boring joke... And the loyal audience member wearing sunglasses who'd been there for all one hundred shows up to that point, before Pat patted me on the back, I slumped forward, and the camera cut to a fake-looking large knife in my back... And the anchor guy with a "special report" that included a reference to Donald Trump even then, which Pat conveniently caught on TV before walking out to do a monologue for which he now had material... And the guy in the audience trying to seduce the female page, as I fantasized she was on my lap feeding me grapes (a fun pre-shoot inserted into my thought bubble) as she imagined slapping my face (a less fun pre-shoot inserted into her thought bubble).

Andy Cowan

Dan Piraro / Andy Cowan

Dan Piraro / Andy Cowan

•   •   •   •   •

Spinning my wheels on the stage of real life, I'd sooner freeze in my tracks before approaching an attractive woman in a supermarket versus flirting as a character on TV. But one night in the late 2000s, I did something else that I imagined the vast majority of fellow nobodies would shy away from. I hit on Meg Ryan. The Saturday night buzz I was feeling gave me a running start. Outside Mastro's in Beverly Hills, I noticed her – with the hands of time and/or surgeons rendering her different but still adorable – awaiting a refreshingly ordinary cab with her friend, Laura Dern. Before my friend struck up a conversation with Laura, I approached Meg, attempting to communicate how much of a walking cliché I felt like, ogling a celebrity:

Andy: It's just as hard for people out of the spotlight, because _we_ know that _you_ know that _we_ know that _you_ know...

She must have understood my point, even if I barely did, and smiled.

MR: It's good you came over.

I have a fuzzy memory of asking her, "Now what?" before handing her my business card and fantasizing that she might email me. *When Andy Met Sally* meets *You've Got Mail.* My own mother predicted: "Like that'll happen." The double feature/relationship lottery ticket indeed proved a bust, but the 48-hour daydream was fun. My track record of needlessly killing a tree that goes into the business card I hand to a female stranger (famous or otherwise) I never hear from again remains unblemished.

• • • • •

It was rare being referenced by a celebrity during his or her spot on the Griffin show. The one time it happened, I wished otherwise, not that anyone noticed but me. In my pre-interview with talk show host Dick Cavett, someone I was often assigned and always admired, I reminded him of when he appeared during his early days as one of the blindfolded panelists on the old game show, *What's My Line?* and pondered to the mystery guest, "I have a feeling you're trying to guess who *I* am." Cavett prefaced the anecdote on air with, "I got one of the biggest laughs I ever got. A guy on your staff, Andy, reminded me of this." After said anecdote, you could hear crickets. In a way, the big buildup dared the audience not to laugh, and they took him up on it.

One guest who repeatedly referenced me scored with "audiences" of one for decades, and beyond the grave no less. Ernie Anderson was one of Hollywood's foremost voiceover artists, the long-time golden throat of ABC ("on *The Love Boat*") and countless other series, movies and commercials.

"If I write the copy for my answering machine message, would you read it?" I asked him.

EA: Sure, but I gotta warn you – you'll get a shitload of hang-ups.

I crafted a message and had him record it for zilch, a gazillion dollars less than his usual rate, then added syrupy music:

Missing your call is something a man like Andy Cowan would never tolerate. That's how much he cares. So please... leave a message. Because... a beep is a terrible thing to waste.

Ernie answered my phone through the remainder of the '80s, '90s, '00s and early teens (with occasional syrupy music substitutions) to callers who not only didn't hang up, but sometimes dialed a second time for an encore. Alas, even Ernie wasn't immune to replacement by computers, when I finally decided the voicemail chip that protects my identity should take over, putting the kibosh on Ernie's longest steady gig.

I also asked one of the most revered voices in the business, Warner Brothers giant Mel Blanc, to record Bugs Bunny answering my phone. As for what Mel thought of contemporary cartoon voices...

MB: A lot of them are good, but most of them are copies of other people's voices, like Jimmy Durante (veteran comedian, actor and singer, "the Schnoz," voice of Frosty the Snowman) and I don't believe in that. To me, it's like stealing from somebody. So all of mine have been created from scratch.

My least comfortable experience with a guest involved an original with a voice all her own, the late Broadway musical star, Ethel Merman. No one had filled me in on precisely why she was doing the show. In asking her what's been happening, I may have even dropped the "g" in "happening," thinking it might somehow connect with her Queens, New York roots.

EM: What? You don't know about my concert at Carnegie Hall? Oh my God!

Andy: Oh, that's wonderful, Ms. Merman. Please. Fill me in.

EM: They screamed. They applauded and howled for five minutes. Clive Barnes wrote me a love letter in the New York Post.

As I continued worming my way back into an amicable line of questioning...

What do you remember about your first show with Ginger Rogers in "Girl Crazy"? ...

Looking back over your career, is there anything you didn't get to do but wished you had? ...

You've never missed a performance. Did that require having to perform when you were ill ... depressed? ...

You released a disco album a few years ago; what do you think of where music has gone since then? Could the old standards ever be put to New Wave?...

Have audiences changed as much as music has over the years? ...

Who are your favorite singers today?

She offered up truncated responses before returning to the task of rubbing my nose in it.

EM: I don't go to the theater.

As Merman herself warbled, "There's no business like show business!"

Showbiz and my two-time guest, Jerry Lewis, were of course long intertwined. Though I only pre-interviewed his manager, I remember a steely reserve in Jerry's eyes as he passed me in the hall, not dissimilar to the character of the stalked star he'd played at the time in Martin Scorsese's classic film, *The King of Comedy*, a dramatic role Jerry claimed was a piece of cake compared to doing comedy. He resented that Hollywood had little respect for the latter genre, and felt marginalized in the same way Hollywood had treated Charlie Chaplin. Backstage he greeted another guest on the show, three-foot nine-inch character actor, Billy Barty, who'd appeared in Lewis's *Hardly Working*. Later I heard Jerry remark, "I can't believe I'm on the same show with a hood ornament." Decades later in 2011, I drove to Las Vegas with comedian, Jeff Wayne, for a sit-down with Lewis at his office, and *Cops* EP, Morgan Langley, whom I brought in as showrunner. Jerry had responded – to his own surprise – to our pitch for a reality show, L*ewis* O*ut* L*oud,* about his young daughter and family, and takes on popular culture.

JL: If I'd read a project about a reality show six months ago, I would have vomited. But when I read this, it was like I had 600 milligrams of Demerol racing through me. I'm ready to go.

When he brought up another reality show about obese contestants losing weight, he asked, "What's next – watching a bowel movement?" He longed for a show about a man his age, out to conquer yet another milestone – outliving George Burns by a year and making it to 101. One way was through the life force of his twenty-year-old adopted daughter, Danielle, the "air in my lungs," whose potential suitors he might introduce to his gun collection, just in case they planned on pulling some of the antics he pulled at their age. He referenced his missed opportunity as a young man for a fling with Marlene Dietrich, with whom he "stupidly" talked about movies all night – and fulfilled fling with Marilyn Monroe. He lamented that the marquees in Vegas advertised steak in a restaurant, when you had to work years to earn your place on a marquee in his day. Well into his 80s and only slightly mellowed, he still relished being an active part of the biz, which I found worthy of respect. He'd also address contemporary society on the show, including Lady Gaga, someone he respected. As he unexpectedly snapped our pictures, I was reminded of how this habit he'd unleashed on talk shows over the years spoke to a continued creative fixation of sorts with capturing images through his viewfinder. Another moment that came out of the blue – when he popped on his clown nose! As for the circus elephant in the room, his age, one show idea of mine shone a bit of a light on it...

Jerry tries to minimize future crotchety-ness by asking smiling and grumpy-looking people which side of the bed they got up on that morning... right or left... to gather once and for all (as a running tally shows the results) which side is the *wrong* side of the bed.

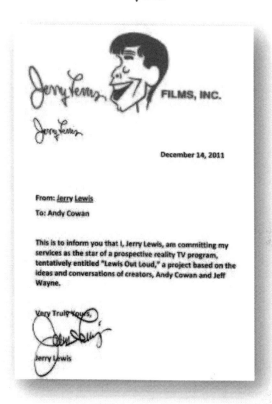

FILMS, INC.

Jerry Lewis

December 14, 2011

From: Jerry Lewis

To: Andy Cowan

This is to inform you that I, Jerry Lewis, am committing my services as the star of a prospective reality TV program, tentatively entitled "Lewis Out Loud," a project based on the ideas and conversations of creators, Andy Cowan and Jeff Wayne.

Very Truly Yours,

Jerry Lewis

According to my twin, Ellen, Jerry Lewis was the first "nice Jewish boy" she had a crush on as a little girl, something I made sure to tell him in a later phone call.

JL: Y'know what? Give me her number. And let me call her and tell her there are rumors around town that she likes me.

After reaching her in a store on her cell, he called me back...

JL: She almost fell apart. I said, "This is Ellen, isn't it?" She said, "Yes, who's this?" I said, "This is an old flame. Someone you loved <u>years</u> ago." And she says... Jerry Lewis? She knew right away! So, the surprise I had for her *backfired and it was a surprise to me! We talked for three or four minutes; it was lovely. I said, "If you get lonesome, call me." She was really very sweet.*

He sent me a cassette of the call, which included this aside to her:

JL: I want you also to know that one of the nicest people I've ever known in our industry is Andy.

It felt cool to be on the receiving end of some showbiz schmaltz. Jerry Lewis may have had his steely side, but he could also be thoughtful and a softy. Aware of the benefits that could accrue from treating people nicely, he had written about how gestures of goodwill had won the devotion of his film crews over the years.

On the phone with someone seeped in the music of my childhood, I felt obliged to mention how important that creative outlet was for me too. Springing a "quick little vanity exercise" on him, I shared a snippet from a recording of an early singing gig when I was more glued to Sinatra (adding I'd since worked towards becoming unglued and finding my own voice) ...

Andy: I'm gonna play just a few seconds, and you tell me if this reminds you at all of the person who joined you with your former partner (on Jerry's telethon in '76) ...

JL: All right.

After cradling the phone near the computer speaker for *some* of me singing *All of Me...*

JL: Very nice! Very, <u>very</u> nice! Why are you hiding it?

He sounded sincere. But I felt like it was time to shine the spotlight back on him.

Andy: I still gig around town, write songs here and there. When I watched your documentary and how important music has always been to you, on a small level I could connect.

JL: I can't get up in the morning unless there's music. I've been that way all my life.

On a festive holiday 2011 night, I attended his documentary premiere at the studio where he'd been top dog, Paramount. I met a blind date there, something I wrote about in one of various pieces for the *Los Angeles Times...*

Here I was inviting a JDater I'd not yet met to a red-carpet screening at Paramount Studios. Stars with bucks versus Starbucks — how could I not get a few brownie points for that? [7]

I later secured an old college roommate's help in reaching out to Eva Price, the producer of Carrie Fisher's *Wishful Drinking* Broadway show. Eva wondered if Jerry might be interested in a potentially lucrative (if it sold out) two-week Broadway one man show, like the kind she recently produced for Kathy Griffin. I discovered Jerry's "mouth had been watering" about returning to Broadway ever since he'd closed in *Damn Yankees* on Broadway many years earlier.

JL: It doesn't have to be two weeks. I'll do it as long as it works. I was so excited reading your letter; I was gonna wake you up this morning. And I looked at the fucking clock and said, Andy won't be thrilled it's ten minutes to eight. I've got what I think can shake up a Broadway theater audience. Not only comically, but in the stories, in the film.

So it would basically be him holding court, I asked?

JL: That's it. That's it. I don't need any musical help. I don't need anything. Give me the audience and I will turn that into fucking pay dirt. What we're talking about now can really be the fucking utopia.

I also suggested it wouldn't be bad buzz for the reality show. "I think it would be great. I think the whole idea is fabulous," he enthused. He wanted to do it "tomorrow." I couldn't wait to relay his excitement to Eva, a step he wanted me to take before he talked with her. She was still fuzzy on what the show would be, and whether an extended run was something he or the market could bear, but she thought a "genius and legend" deserved a conversation.

If I were in effect helping to secure a gig, would I be out of line asking him for some kind of commission (I'd split with Jeff and my college roomie) should things move forward? When I danced around the notion in my next call to him, he chuckled, "Anything you want, kid." A part of my role as genuflecting celebrity worshipper had transformed into Mr. Mercenary. Eva and he met, she presented him with numbers... and never heard back from him.

As for the TV show, an agent reported TV Land could be interested but Jerry might have to be willing to do it more like *Curb Your Enthusiasm*. Producer Joe Revello noted that "somewhat scripted" takes a long time to shoot and wasn't easy to get right. My hunch was that something more creative and artistic might intrigue Lewis even more than a reality show. But the big questions I had, besides his age: Could we deconstruct the Jerry Lewis image and play that for laughs? Would he be willing to poke fun at other aspects of his reputation? Would he be comfortable sharing the spotlight and creatively collaborating? We'd also need a sizzle reel to show he was up to the challenges. Before we could broach him about it, TV Land passed. The age issue made them nervous. Meanwhile their Betty White, Jerry's senior, was still *Hot in Cleveland*.

Whether you're a legend, or a newbie clamoring to get in, the entertainment world is such a hit and miss proposition that the "buzz" can often wind up coming from the proverbial fly in the ointment. Like most projects in Hollywood, the reality show didn't ultimately find buyers. *That's* reality.

Lucille Ball was another showbiz legend I didn't happen to pre-interview for the Griffin show. We met briefly backstage when I picked up a vintage *I Love Lucy* photo she'd pre-autographed "For Andy" with "Love" from Lucy. Her "Who are you?" sounded condescending to my ears, but maybe she was having a bad day. I'm sure it must get tiring for people in the limelight to always be on their best behavior when encountering the public. Nevertheless, the impact of a tiny nice gesture, or the opposite, can last beyond their lifetime. When I greeted Carl Reiner, on to promote his underrated Steve Martin comedy, *Dead Men Don't Wear Plaid*, I mentioned that I still had makeup on from my earlier appearance on the show, feeling a little embarrassed. He advised me to never feel embarrassed about that – a tiny nice gesture remembered all these years later. Among the other nice gesture practitioners from this book ... Steve Allen ... Phyllis Diller ... Jack Lemmon ... Jay Leno ... David Niven ... Vincent Price ... John Ritter ... Robert Stack ... Dick Van Dyke ... Orson Welles ... Robert Young ... to name but a few.

.　.　.　.　.

After more than 5000 guests and twenty-three years, Merv's last words on his final show in '86 were the last ones I wrote for him:

> *I (he said "we" on air) will not be back after this message. Th-th-th-th-that's all folks.*

In 2007, the first line as written became his epitaph.

What the Stars Told Me

Originator of what evolved into The Tonight Show, this comedian, writer, composer and musician helped launch a lot of careers. David Letterman acknowledges the influence Allen had on him. He may not have seemed as "hip" as he was early in his career, but I had the sense his brain was as sharp as ever.

STEVE ALLEN

On how the old standards compare to contemporary music...

I'm just as appreciative of quality music that was produced last Tuesday as I am of what was produced thirty-five years ago. No matter what the time period, you'll come up with plenty of garbage. Most music today is garbage, and that's probably as true today as it was thirty-five years ago. Yet thirty-five years ago, we benefited from some of the greatest composers the world has ever known. Irving Berlin wrote over a thousand songs but only had fifty big hits. Although the average guy would kill for one big hit, there was obviously a lot of garbage in there somewhere.

On his need for 10-12 hours of sleep...

It's a pity, because it means I'm unconscious for about forty percent of my life. I wonder how many more songs, novels and plays I might have written had I needed only the traditional eight hours.

Allen wasn't shy about mentioning that he, himself, had penned well over a thousand songs. *This Could be the Start of Something (Big)* was the one people remembered.

He's most linked with Thurston Howell, III, on *Gilligan's Island* and the voice of *Mr. Magoo*, but he had numerous credits, including working with James Dean in *Rebel Without a Cause*.

JIM BACKUS

On first meeting Marilyn Monroe...

The first time I ever saw Marilyn, she was stark naked. She was late coming to work and asked me if I would mind if she changed right then and there. Also, what many don't know – she copied her walk after Robert Mitchum and John Wayne.

On Gilligan's Island...

That show is much maligned and an easy target, but it was very pleasant to do, and it's been played nearly as often as *I Love Lucy*. Of course, I don't get any money from it anymore. So I sit in my chair and watch myself on television, and go crazy. I get no residuals for *Mr. Magoo* either!

This author, playwright, raconteur and famed party-thrower never minced words, which is why talk shows loved to book him. I remember he showed up in the green room with his good friend, Joanne Carson, Johnny's second wife. He died at her home when he was only 59.

TRUMAN CAPOTE

On Southern California...

Los Angeles is the biggest dump. Your IQ drops three points for every year you spend there. They have the social life all analyzed – Group A, Group B. The thing is – the people in group A in L.A. wouldn't be in Group Z in New York. Los Angeles society people look down on everybody in the film industry, except for the heads of studios and a few broken down old actors like Gregory Peck and Kirk Douglas, who spend their whole life kissing their asses. The industry is the lowest thing there is in Los Angeles society.

TONY CURTIS

On Marilyn Monroe...

I had the same problem of low self-esteem as Marilyn. The reason I survived, and she didn't, was that she was never able to look outside herself and see who she was. I don't mean to demean her, but I thought she was just an ordinary woman with an extraordinary body. What destroyed her was a combination of what she was willing to do for success, and the resentment she felt against all the movie moguls who took advantage of that.

On his own demons...

The ones I'd invited through years of drug abuse are almost gone now. I used cocaine and all the prescription drugs I could get, to enhance my own self-esteem and to reduce tension. It's an easy trap to fall into, because it makes you feel good and you think you have control over it, but you never do.

On the young actors in the '80s unwilling to promote their movies...

They're not going to last. They're not enigmas, they're just nothing. I think they're afraid that if they give something, they'll get caught. People will know there's not much there.

On the Oscars bypassing well-known actors like him, Paul Newman and Cary Grant...

(Tongue somewhat in cheek) We never get 'em, because we're too good looking.

The last time I met actor Tony Curtis was long after the Griffin show, on my third lucky trip to "Paris." In March of 2001, I spoke about comedy and Jewish culture at the Paris Hotel in Las Vegas, and the featured guest on the dais was Mr. Bernie Schwartz, aka Tony Curtis. Well into his 70s, he was still a cool character, married to his sixth and final wife, some four decades his junior. Curtis starred with Jack Lemmon (among the stars in this chapter) and Marilyn Monroe in what the American Film Institute called the greatest comedy film of them all, director Billy Wilder's *Some Like It Hot.*

As for my other lucky trips, I'd savored my initial free excursion to the actual Paris in '79, after winning a grand tour of France on the short-lived game show, *All Star Secrets*, hosted by Bob Eubanks. Years later at the Griffin show, I told beauty industry magnate Vidal Sassoon that he'd changed my life after I'd guessed he was the only celebrity – among Zsa Zsa Gabor (in this chapter) and other '70s kitschy "stars" Eubanks pointed to – who thought people should be fined if they don't vote, moving me from last place to grand prize winner. I landed once again in the real Paris and the very same hotel in '81, to pre-interview such Griffin show guests as former JFK press secretary Pierre Salinger along the Seine River.

Merv used to throw annual Oscar parties at his home, where the staff would come to watch the ceremony on what passed for big screen TVs in the '80s. Shortly before my trip to speak with Tony Curtis, I was looking forward to zoning in on the Oscars on my own TV, minus any distractions, eagerly anticipating Steve Martin's first hosting gig. The pizza arrived, I was all set, and moments before it began... the electricity went out, and it looked like the entire street was without power. Having no time to scope out a bar with a functioning TV on which inebriated sports fans wouldn't mind not watching sports, and after calling friends, none of whom were home, I dialed my parents three thousand miles away in suburban Philadelphia. As I sat there in my darkening apartment wolfing down cold pizza, I heard Martin hosting the Oscars over my speakerphone, courtesy of my folks holding their phone up to their TV. On the dais in Vegas, it was this story I contrasted for comic effect with the glamor of Tony Curtis's past Oscar show experiences – not that he ever won, something he was disappointed about – as I pretended that instead of Steve Martin's commentary, I heard my mother's commentary about the commentary. "I didn't think that was funny." "Ma! He's introducing the In-Memoriam segment."

In 2004, I was pleased to hear L.A.'s longtime entertainment reporter for KNX News Radio, Tom Hatten, quoting my letter in *Variety* about how to improve the telecast[1]... "Here's another way to fix the Oscars: The second a winner is announced, punch up a news crawl at the bottom of the screen that would be pre-programmed with the names of people he wanted to thank in the event he won, freeing (and requiring) him to spend his time making a victory statement that reflects on life, not ego-massaging." In 2016, producers unveiled a plan to move the ceremony along – a scrolling text of names to thank under each winner, submitted ahead of time by each nominee.[2]

Phyllis Diller had a life-affirming energy about her. Though she relied on cue cards in the same way her mentor, Bob Hope, did, her mind remained astute and plugged in. She signed her book, *The Joys of Aging & How to Avoid Them*, "to my trusted friend & writer...Andy Cowan... Love, Phyllis Diller." Sweet.

PHYLLIS DILLER

On cosmetic surgery...

You're a whole different person after plastic surgery. You like yourself, so you treat people better. The main thing about getting along in the world is liking yourself. That's why cosmetic surgery is a good thing. My mother went to a doctor for actual surgery because she hadn't had her period for three months. And the doctor decided she had a tumor. So they took her to the hospital to remove the "tumor" and it was *me*.

Most famous for being famous, she pre-dated reality shows but personified one. Never at a loss for words about love and marriage, by 2016 and the end of her life at 99, she had walked the aisle nine times. She was more cautious about revealing her age.

ZSA ZSA GABOR

On showing her birth certificate...

I want to bring my Hungarian birth certificate; I never had it on the show before. You can see the date: February 26, 1928. (She was born in Budapest on February 6, 1917.) I'll use it to illustrate why this gigolo I married cut his own throat. He said at night I look like 67 without makeup. First, I never take off my makeup in the evening, but I never put much on. Secondly, I'm very beautiful in the evening – nude or dressed. People think I'm forty. Plus, how could he tell because he admits I never let him close to me anyway. And he says he met a woman who claims she went to school with me, and she's 67. Well everybody I meet claims they went to school with me – old, young, black, Chinese.

We married in Puerto Vallarta. It wasn't an official marriage, because I wasn't yet divorced. I thought if you marry in Mexico, it didn't count in America and at least I wouldn't be living in sin, which I never have. Nothing attractive about the jerk. All day he sits in the sun, meditates and eats. He gives me this bullshit: "I love you." I said, "Look, Phillip, if you tell me that one more time, I'll throw up. I know you don't love me. You want my name and my money." He even stole my car.

On whether she'll marry again...

I can't live without a man. If I meet a man I love, I will marry him. Other women sleep with more men in one month than I have in my whole life. I just kept making it legal, because I was raised in convents and my very stupid brain tells me you have to get married before you go to bed with someone. My mother keeps on saying you don't have to.

I never met a man yet who didn't ask me to marry him the next day – including Winston Churchill's son, William Paley, William Randolph Hearst Jr., JFK, Mr. Nixon – who's my best friend for fifteen years. He called me yesterday. He's in love with me for over twenty years, but we needn't mention that on the show.

On quitting older men and trying a younger guy for a change...

No, I can't do that. I have such a strong father complex. I've been so in love with my father that I must have a man like that. I like the chauvinist pigs! That's attractive. The moment a man says to me, "Shut up and listen," I fall in love.

Long before his fame as Dumbledore in the *Harry Potter* films, Richard Harris visited Merv's show. When he first made it big, he had been equally known for his rowdy antics and imbibing with fellow actors Richard Burton and Peter O'Toole, a lifelong friend. And boomers won't forget when he sang about that cake recipe he'll never have again in the big hit, *MacArthur Park*.

RICHARD HARRIS

On begging to play King Arthur in "Camelot"...

Jack Warner wanted nothing to do with me for the movie. I sent him a telegram every day: "Harris is Arthur." And it led nowhere. I burst into the suite of the director one day and begged him to test me. He said no way. I heard he was going to a party that night. I went into the kitchen and borrowed the waiter's white coat, entered the room with a tray of drinks. I still had to insist he test me and he finally agreed. Got the part.

This philanthropist and "first lady of the American Theater" worked for nearly eighty years and appeared to me to be the embodiment of the ideal grandmother: sweet, dear, wise and classy. She reinvented herself with an Oscar best supporting win for *Airport*, and in later TV roles in the Miss Marple mysteries, which didn't sit well with her.

HELEN HAYES

On romance...

My husband once told me when we were first married, "Don't try to win, Helen. Let's just keep it neutral." And it stuck. We always listened to the other's point of view. Today they're doing something wrong. And romance isn't a word much in vogue these days, but it should be remembered more. Flirtin's fun. The best part of being at a social gathering used to be what was called innocent flirtation, which pre-dates loveless sex and drug-induced highs. And it's all right to tell someone how sexy she looks, even if you're both in your later years.

I think this is a very difficult time for women, because so many options are made available to them, and they've been made aware of so many "bad deals." I wasn't aware of getting so many bad deals, that there was so much trouble for my sex. Young women today are awfully sensitive to anyone trying to downgrade them, and it might be one of the things making marriage so difficult.

On being watched on TV...

I was in a silly little murder mystery on TV last month that thirty million people watched. And I stopped and realized I hadn't been seen by that many people in my whole stage career. That's what put the cap on my ambition to keep performing. I got angry and thought this isn't fair.

Photo by Alan Light

As Professor Kingsfield, his Oscar-winning role in *The Paper Chase*, he reminded me of an off-putting grad school professor I'd had at the time. Years later, he milked that persona in a series of Smith Barney commercials. Early on he worked with another intimidating presence, (in this chapter) Orson Welles.

JOHN HOUSEMAN

On the role of intimidation...

I'm constantly and perpetually intimidated. But back in school, like everyone else, I had one or two teachers who scared the shit out of me, and they were the ones who taught me something. As far as learning, fear is an important element with me but not with everybody.

On contemporary theater...

Theater today is lamentable and desperate. It's so revolting that nothing good gets done in New York anymore. Nobody takes a chance. All the good shows originate in England or regional theater. Unless you have a "smash hit," you die. And what constitutes a smash hit? A low common denominator... On the night following the opening of a show, you don't sleep all night. Not because you pay much attention to the aesthetic views of the reviewer, but because you live or die by them. It's a fair system, but it's lamentable that in New York, we're down to two papers. When I started in theater, you had nine dailies. You shouldn't have the kind of power they have now.

I saw Meryl Streep when she was at Yale. There's no question that when you see a Meryl Streep, you're looking at serious theater.

From the moment I first watched this performance artist on *SNL*, I couldn't stop watching. Never afraid to confound the audience, he could simply stand there and lip-sync *Here I Come to Save the Day* from the theme to *Mighty Mouse*. As Latka on *Taxi*, and his obnoxious alter ego, Tony Clifton, he didn't just play another character – he became the character. I remember his delight in suggesting what Merv could press him about, and how he'd go on to refute it.

ANDY KAUFMAN

On always being out of town when his obnoxious alias, "Tony Clifton," shows up...

I was in Europe at the same time Tony was on your show in Vegas. And when he was hired for *Taxi*, I wasn't in town that week, but I heard about it. I'm not on every show. It's not my fault they happened to write a show for Tony Clifton that I wasn't on. And as far as us two never being on stage at the same time, I'd rather not comment, all right? ... I can say that to Merv, and I can start trembling. He can really grill me if he wants. And if he wants to ask me about that fight on *Fridays* (the early '80s ABC late night live comedy show that featured Larry David) and whether it was staged, I can deny it.

On channeling different characters...

One of my favorite hobbies in New York is becoming a different character on every block and talking to people where I sometimes don't have any control over it. It started happening on *Taxi* in the middle of the show. At first the cast complained; the producers wanted to fire me. But then they said, "Wait a minute! Let's make use of this!" So, my character became schizophrenic. Last year I got stuck in my favorite character, "world champion," to the point where I'd be dreaming in this character and talking like him with my friends and family.

On his ongoing part-time job as a busboy in the San Fernando Valley's Jerry's Deli...

I like it, because working in a deli was the first job I had. It brings me back to my roots and makes me feel part of working America. This is a service job, show business isn't. I punch a clock and get an hourly wage. What I sometimes do just for fun is say, "Would you like coffee?" They say yes. I say, "Would you like regular, or Jerry's famous special brew?" They say what's that? I say, "With a special ingredient!" They say, "Oh, I'd love to try that!" And I'll bring over two pots with the same coffee.

On meeting women...

You meet a lot of snobby women in Hollywood. I can't even bother to talk to them and I'm extremely shy. It's very rare that I go up to a woman. I'm lucky to be in this business, because the way I usually meet women is by them coming up to me. Sometimes I'll bring home a girl and wrestle. I have mats in my house. It's a nice alternative to tennis.

On getting hate mail for wrestling women on TV...

I like to answer hate mail by phone and explain myself: "Do you really hate me? Why? Let's talk about it." When I'm wrestling, I'm competing and don't want to lose my money. Or my hair. Sometimes I've offered to shave my head. I don't wrestle men, because I'm an intergender champion as recognized by the intergender wrestling commission. I just defended my title against the *Playboy* September playmate. She hates me!

On involving his audiences...

I sang *100 Bottles of Beer on the Wall* in its entirety last spring. The audience loved it. I'll bunny hop an audience around the block. I once drove an audience on a bus to get milk and cookies. My next plan is to take them around the world on an ocean liner.

This Old Hollywood star went back to those 1930s Busby Berkeley musicals, where the over-the-head camera captured a kaleidoscope of glamorous human pyramids that helped take audiences' minds off the Great Depression. Barely recognizable compared to her heyday, she seemed to evoke ancient history when I met her on the show. I guess millennials think the same thing today about actors from the '60s!

RUBY KEELER

On working with Busby Berkley in the 1932 movie musical, 42nd Street...

You never said no to Buzz. He was like a machine. He had everything worked out in his head. He'd tell you to do something with one of his contraptions that came out of the floor. And you'd do it without having any idea of what it would look like on-screen. Kids were always getting their toes caught in the rocks, running to jump into the pool. The songs were the most difficult thing for me. I'd have to react to everything (singer, actor, producer) Dick Powell sang, and of course, the song would have nineteen choruses! After enough of that silly smile, my mouth would get crooked. I cry a little when I see the stage show of *42nd Street* today, because I'm not up there with that wonderful cast. It's like watching a time capsule. We worked long hours, but we enjoyed it. When I read today about somebody who has a good job in a TV series and they quit because they need a vacation, it makes me chuckle. They really don't know what work is.

Ms. Keeler was a spring chicken compared to the oldest actress I'd covered for the show, hundred-year-old (in 1983) Estelle Winwood. Her publicist forewarned me that she was hard of hearing and that Merv would have to basically shout the questions. I also learned that she'd broken her hip, punched a nurse in the mouth, threw away her wheelchair, and continued to smoke three packs a day. The next year marked her final wrap.

The first back-to-back ('36, '37) Oscar-winning actress, Luise Rainer, died at nearly 105 at the end of 2014. I pre-interviewed her in 1982, long after she'd turned her back on Hollywood, a lifestyle she claimed she was too "normal" to enjoy. She also echoed a lot of other vintage stars' feelings that contemporary culture exposed too many celebrity details, leaving glamor and mystery in the dust. And this was decades before Instagram!

The powerful and athletic yin to Fred Astaire's graceful and elegant yang, dancing great Gene Kelly struck me as a guy who didn't suffer fools gladly.

GENE KELLY

On grace...

I don't think you should confuse grace with femininity. Grace can be strong and virile. Any male who looks like a sissy dancing is a lousy dancer.

On withstanding the test of time...

Many of my old movies are dated, even the one that's probably my best known, *An American in Paris.* The one that holds up the best is *Singin' In the Rain,* because it's a period piece parodying the changeover from silent to talking pictures. American westerns also hold up because they're period pieces. A musical has less of a chance, because the attitude of the times is reflected in the singing and dancing.

On MTV...

It doesn't thrill me. I like some of it but as a whole, it doesn't do anything for me to see the music visually produced.

Jack Klugman was another actor who told it like it was. He'd long since traded Oscar Madison for NBC's *Quincy*, but he still fondly recalled his work on *The Twilight Zone* on a theme show honoring its late creator, Rod Serling. Jack's remarks seem to foreshadow what many would call today's second golden age of TV.

JACK KLUGMAN

On whether TV's golden era was as good as they say...

The people who say the good ol' days weren't that good are full of shit. They were the magnificent days. People still tell me they saw me on *The Twilight Zone*. I did three half hours and one 1-hour episode. People loved those shows because they were well-written, three-dimensional fuckin' characters, which you don't get today. Today you just get the plot, and maybe find out the character likes his coffee black. But Rod Serling delved into desires, loves, hates.

Most performers occasionally worry about having to top themselves. This daredevil's modus operandi was *constantly* topping himself in stunts that offered up greater and greater "wow" factors. Meanwhile, his son had to worry about topping his dad.

EVEL KNIEVEL

After my last jump, I said I'd never jump again. Here I am five or six years later, and the old feeling's coming back to me. Once you retire and have nothing to do, you *are* nothing. I've never done anything in my life as exciting as jumping. I've always held on to the handlebars. I'm crazy, not stupid. But my son is 23, so he can do what he wants and jumps with no hands. Nobody can say he made it on my coattails. He's much better than I am.

This actor was part of the glue to *The Mary Tyler Show*'s continued hold on classic sitcom lovers – especially once he layered Ted Baxter's humanity into the pomposity and ineptitude. He was only 62 when cancer took him.

TED KNIGHT

On how success has changed him...

I've mellowed out. I don't feel as aggressive anymore with my career. My enemies have turned into friendly acquaintances. People that I envied and despised because of their successes I now tolerate and even smile at. The envy's gone, because it's a wasted emotion. Smile at everybody – your friends and your enemies. You'd be surprised at how many people come up to you and say, "What the hell are you laughing at?"

On staying child-like...

I never did grow up and I don't intend to. I'm just a kid with an old face. In show business, we're all kids looking for love and affection, and we never grow up emotionally. We're all emotional wrecks. I know I am. The difference now is that I know this. I didn't know it till I hit fifty. My credo is "vanity, nepotism and fear." Fear will keep you young, because obviously you don't want to die, and you'll do things to avoid that. Vanity is an important part of it. And so is nepotism – being alive long enough to make enough money to pass along to my kids.

In 2013, I had the kick of rehearsing and performing several of my sketches with Ed Asner for a multi-generational pilot that musician and producer Mitchel Delevie hired me to write. Asner's first words to me: "Don't change your face." Mine to him were about how much *The Mary Tyler Moore Show* meant to me.

In one sketch, he played a man on a blind date with a much younger woman...

Danielle: Whose picture was that on Match.com?

Man: Me.

Danielle: You? When?!

Man: (thinking) The one in Hawaii was... oh... when did they become a state?

Danielle: A hundred years ago?

Man: Don't be silly. (remembering) 1959.

Danielle: That was you in 1959? You couldn't find a less old picture?

Man: I wouldn't call it... old. I'd call it... mature.

Danielle: That would explain the poodle skirts. How could you misrepresent yourself like that? You said you were "30ish!" That's one healthy... "ish!"

Man: Part of me is. I got a hip replacement in '82.

I didn't want to ignore his dramatic chops, so I threw in some tension in a sketch in which he robbed a bank teller – me...

Neil: (sotto) I want you to act perfectly natural or this will be the last day on earth you draw breath. Am I making myself clear?

Teller: Yes.

Neil: When we're done with this exchange, I will approach the exit and shoot each of your security cameras. If you make so much as one false move before I leave the premises, I will use an additional bullet on you. I'm an excellent shot. At this proximity I don't have to be. Do you understand?

Teller: Yes.

Neil: (handing over) I want you to take this check. Look at it. Stamp it. Open the cash drawer, calmly count all of it out as if it covers the entire amount.

Teller: Okay.

Neil: Stop looking so scared. Laugh at something I just said.

Teller weakly laughs.

Neil: You call that a laugh?

Teller forces a stronger laugh.

Neil: I'm not Tina Fey!

Apropos of the '70s, another sketch of mine for the Delevie pilot depicted a retro *Hollywood Squares*. The host's questions (Peter Marshall, tentatively booked) and pre-infamous celebrities' answers (Robert Blake as Baretta, Afro era OJ Simpson, Phil Spector, etc.) all wove in murderous connotations...

Peter: OJ, to make a football, do you have to kill a pig?

OJ: Hmm. I've never killed a pig before. Of course, I don't generally associate with pigs. (audience laughter) Yes, you do have to kill a pig.

Peter: No, footballs are no longer made of pigskin, they're made of cowhide. Circle gets the square!

Speaking of my least favorite subject (except for when the Philadelphia Eagles finally won the Super Bowl) – in 2011, I pitched Dan Piraro a *Bizarro* cartoon panel gag that described a big clown shoe kicking a football over the caption, "Clown College Football." Dan rightly suspected the joke needed another layer. I wrote back: What if a close-up of the big shoe ready to kick the football is on a big flat screen, and a beer-guzzling clown husband is watching, ignoring his clown wife who's with him, a sad clown, per image (I sent Dan)? And caption is: "Clown College Football Widow." With football season about to end, I waited ten months to laugh out loud at his rendering.

Photo by Alan Light

His love for being an actor was still obvious, part of why audiences continued to embrace him.

JACK LEMMON

On the movie business...

It's awful difficult to maintain the quality level of pictures like *China Syndrome, Tribute* and *Missing*. So, I'm just gonna bloody well wait till the next one, no matter how long it takes. It's nostalgic watching my son pursue the same path. It keeps me young – going back to the days when I'd flip if I got a job, finding fifteen thousand ways to do a part. I still flip over the right part.

On acceptance as you grow older...

I tend to be a little more patient with other people's faults and I hope mine too. But as an actor, you're very absorbed with why people behave as they do. Too many people walk around with so much guilt about what they think they are, rather than accepting a lot of it and realizing that's not so damn terrible, as long as they're aware and can control what faults they may have. There isn't anybody who doesn't have faults according to others' opinions. When it becomes your own opinion, then you can do something about it.

On the environment...

I've been very, very ecologically concerned for over two decades. All you need to do to get really depressed is to listen to Cousteau for an hour. You'll blow your brains out. But the slow, creeping cancer types of problems people don't pay as much attention to as a plane wreck.

This guest struck me as more circumspect about his devotion to acting. As he once told Roger Ebert, "You spend the first forty years of your life trying to get in this business, and the next forty years trying to get out."

LEE MARVIN

On the men behind the actors...

I'm not sure the audience cares about the real Lee Marvin. They want to believe the screen image. Other actors all surprise you because you think you know them through their film work. And then you work with them and find out for some reason, they're nice guys! You never even consider that. You figure anybody who's "big" is gonna be a prick. Guys like Bogart were very real men. I learned that when you do a scene with them, don't fool around. With Tracy, I did *Bad Day at Black Rock*. With Bogart, I did *Caine Mutiny*. They did so little. No unnecessary theatrics. And if you got fancy with them, they could absolutely eat you. They could do it with just a look. They used that look and the audience laughed at you.

On being a grandfather...

Actually, I hate grandfathering. After about twenty minutes, I have to go out for a walk. Dealing with kids is a job for the parents. If I had a choice, I'd rather spend time with my elders.

Long after appearing as a kid with lifelong friend, Elizabeth Taylor, in *Lassie Come Home*, this actor remained a Hollywood fixture, one of the few child performers to transition into a successful adult acting career. He was known for opening his home to golden era stars as well as contemporaries like Johnny Depp.

RODDY McDOWALL

On being a child star...

Stardom is not the healthiest of conditions in which to spend one's childhood. But one survives it the same way one survives other traumas. Don't forget, a lot of child stars stopped their careers, because they didn't want to go on. And others have had very successful careers in other areas. Shirley Temple has had four careers. It would be marvelous if I had the concentration I had as a child actor. As a child, you're not acting. You *believe*. At 17, Fox loaned me to MGM where the drama coach told me, "You'll never work again until you're 27." It didn't make sense to me.

On working with animals...

The original Lassie was a lot smarter than a lot of people I know. He remembered me four years later. The horses were different. There were six "Flickas" and nine "Thunderheads" for the *Son of Flicka* sequels. After that many horses, one loses rapport. I loved Lassie, but I hated the main Flicka horse. She was mean and kept stepping on my feet!

I had the feeling it was therapeutic for him to spread his wings away from Johnny from time to time, still never forgetting who put him on the map.

ED McMAHON

On milestones...

I love birthdays. They don't bother me at all. I celebrate the octave of my birthday. I celebrate for eight days. Next year is big – 60. My wife is handling the whole thing, and I don't know what she's planning, but it'll be a biggie. For our sixth wedding anniversary, I surprised her by putting her on a private plane, flying up to San Francisco and going back to our original honeymoon suite. We returned to the restaurant where we had our wedding supper, and the city where we had our after-wedding party. Then I surprised her by taking her on a train from San Francisco to Chicago. She knew nothing about it in advance. I just told her what to wear each day. In that way, I'm an old fashioned romantic.

On knowing ahead of time when Carson will make him laugh...

When we have something like the famous Carnac joke – "Sis-boom-bah" (written by Kevin Mulholland) ... Describe the sound made when a sheep explodes ... Johnny always sets me up beforehand at the office. He'll say, "I've got one for you in Carnac tonight that's gonna put you away." Now I'm primed. Then when he looks at me, I know this is the one. So, when people see me fall off the chair laughing, it's because I've been set up. He gets me out on the diving board, and then the line pushes me over.

Photo by Alan Light

This actor's sadly too short career was in high gear when he visited the show. Nobody else is quite like him today. He was sophisticated yet silly, and an accomplished pianist. There was also an underlying melancholy to him.

DUDLEY MOORE

On women's influence...

One discovery I made, which may or may not be the result of therapy, is that I sometimes hate women for having such an effect on me. It's a love/hate thing, because the emotions that are brought out by even pleasant people give rise to anxiety over *losing* these emotions or people. Which is why I once sarcastically said, "I wish everybody would drop dead. Then we wouldn't have to worry about each other anymore."

On intellectuality...

My intellectual friends think I'm stupid. My poorly educated friends think I'm a brain surgeon. Overt intellectuality, to the point where it gets patronizing, aggravates me. I'm not intimidated by overtly intellectual women so much as by their lack of communication and emotion. You can have a woman who's intellectual *and* emotional – like Barbara Walters.

He's most remembered for his role in *Happy Days*. And, of course, *The Karate Kid* movies.

PAT MORITA

On whether he ever had to defend himself like The Karate Kid...

I got into one fight with my cousin over some dumb softball game. I slugged him and ran. And I ran till I was fifty. I'd been running from him in my dreams. Finally, we became friends again. We're at that age – Mama's gone, Papa's gone. So, it was time to let bygones be bygones. I reminded him of how I'd been running scared ever since. And he said, "Dummy, I was just trying to catch up with you and ask, What the fuck did you hit me for?"

On his stand-up days and the fallout from World War II...

I used to tell people that on December 8, 1941, I became colored. It got laughs everywhere – The Apollo, The Shrine. In fact, I was a kamikaze comedian, because I used to open with this line and it was all downhill from there. World War II was one of the most trying times that we as a family had to endure. Being uprooted and thrown behind barbed wire is a totally foreign environment for human beings, period; especially to Japanese, because we are so home-rooted. We felt we earned a spot on earth by being willing to do manual labor. We were good workers. In the early thirties, we were starting to feel like we really belonged in this country. And then in the late thirties came the yellow journalism.

This superstar seldom appeared on talk shows. A longtime political activist, he had serious issues he wanted to discuss.

PAUL NEWMAN

On the threat of nuclear proliferation...

I hope we get loud and noisy about this. I can't stand the people in Defense who discuss this thing so calmly. What really gets me are those yo-yos who say everything will be all right if we have enough shovels – that what we need to do is dig a hole three or four feet deep, get a couple of doors and cover them with dirt. Tell that to a farmer in Montana in the middle of January. Washington and Moscow are still dealing with a concept of first and second strike, and that simply doesn't work anymore. If you're sitting in a basement full of explosive gas, and you have eight matches and I have ten, who cares who's first? If you're talking about spears or revolvers, the concept works. But if the Russians have a million nuclear warheads, and the U.S. has 980,000, what difference does it make?

Einstein said the atomic age has changed everything but the way we think. The time has come to call a halt and freeze it while we still can. Eisenhower warned us to be careful that we weren't held hostage by the technological elite. They hide behind "national security." But the truth is that they don't know anything either. Technology is mindless in any case, and we can't control it. That may be the biggest sickness of all. The fact is that a lot of people in the scientific and military worlds are defecting from the position that hardware can create national security. The more weapons we have, the less secure we are.

On actors speaking out about national security issues...

I'm not going to abdicate my rights as a citizen just because I have high visibility. The Pentagon and the Defense Department have such high visibility and access to the media that the people are brainwashed. They think they're getting the truth, but they're not. Television and newspapers hardly covered the special sessions on disarmament. They'll cover the issue after the war, because then it'll be an event. It's not an event yet.

Photo by Allan Warren

This old school movie star demonstrated a humility and gentility that I, a young guy not long on the job, remember appreciating. He didn't look or sound in the best of health, and later in that year of 1981, he was diagnosed with Lou Gehrig's Disease.

DAVID NIVEN

On his upbringing...

I was a nasty little boy, a total shit. It was nothing awful, but I was expelled from one school. It was tough for me to get on the right track. I had no father, and my mother didn't understand the situation. I was sent off to boarding school at the age of six, which was frightening. Bullying and all that. But there was this one schoolmaster who treated me like a human being and not a horrible child. More like a grownup. He had a profound effect on me growing up.

On Hollywood's Golden Age...

What made the great Bogarts, Coopers, and Dietrichs so immortal was the fact there were more writers behind them. Take Gable. When he was king of Metro, the biggest, he had six well-known, highly competent writers. They had nothing to do except perfect and polish the ideal vehicle for Gable's personality. That meant that every Gable picture was pretty damn good. Errol Flynn (with whom Niven shared a house) liked to discomfort his friends. He got a great kick out of putting his chums in a bad spot. If I were to say, "Errol, Betty's coming over to have a drink this evening, and for Christ' sake, don't say that Nancy was here last night," he'd be at the door with that news.

On finding work...

Years ago, it was much tougher to get started. You had to do what I did – become an extra and hope for the best. And it was grossly overpopulated. Now it's much easier to get started, because of television. But it's much harder to keep going, because actors have to scratch around to find the ideal thing for themselves. I've never been very ambitious. I don't think I've ever seriously, consciously gone after any part. I always felt that if they want you, they'll let you know. Movie acting is so much luck. When I was an extra, there were 22,000 of us scratching around for eighty jobs. Think of the talent that got trampled and never had a chance.

On competing with his screen persona...

It's terrible having to live up to the suave, debonair image. I think it came from being very well dressed in *Around the World in 80 Days*. I had thirty-two changes of costume. Otherwise, I'm a slob.

On owning two homes...

We have a little cuckoo clock of a home in Switzerland where we go during the winter. And then we have an old, broken down place we go to in the south of France. It sounds very rich, but it's not. Any actor who has two houses to look after is mad. He should have two psychiatrists, one in each.

If ever an actor was identified with one defining role, it was Carroll O'Connor. His persona was so different from Archie's in *All in the Family*, it seemed like he was hiding part of himself when you met him. He knew how daunting the odds were to reach the level of success he had. And he didn't flaunt that success.

CARROLL O'CONNOR

On what he'd tell young people who want to come to Los Angeles to break into show business...

Go down to the beach, take a swim and go right back home again. I wouldn't encourage anybody. The sheer numbers would be discouraging, a very overcrowded industry. But you wouldn't want to actually tell someone not to come here. So, with a falling heart, you say nothing. But I think the theater is growing in other parts of the country, and so is regional filmmaking, which is healthy for the industry.

On the California lifestyle and trappings of success...

We have a beach house, but I don't do anything. I hardly move. I don't care for outside stuff. But I love watching outside stuff on the tube. My favorites are tennis matches and baseball. The money from *All in the Family* went straight to my head, but I never bought the yacht, never bought the plane. The beach house was the big deal. I didn't care for all those other things, and my wife's taste is kind of quiet. I really don't think actors go hog-wild with expenses or drugs, for that matter, to the extent the public believes.

His son, Hugh (an actor in Carroll's later series, *In the Heat of the Night*), had a long history of drug addiction, which his father acknowledged after Hugh took his own life in 1995.

I still get plenty of fan mail for Archie and loads of requests for pictures. I've got a big bill for that, but it is a business expense. Forty cents postage, not counting the cost of the picture. People all over the world tell me they still watch the show.

Another classic dancer from Hollywood's Golden Age, he was most remembered for his *Make 'em Laugh* number in the classic musical, *Singin' in the Rain*. He seemed more reserved and serious than a laugher, per se.

DONALD O'CONNOR

On whether he ever feels like not performing...

You're damn right. That's like every five minutes with me. When you get tired, you get a lot of crazy thoughts. But once the music starts and the people are there, it's a different story.

On whether his kids are following in his footsteps...

I would have liked them to continue along the same path. They can all sing and dance, but they don't have the burning desire to be in the business. It would be nice to have another generation coming up in the family. But it's hard to follow in your parents' footsteps. As for my mother, just before she died recently at 91, I asked her if it was true that I'd danced for the first time at thirteen months old. She set things straight. I was *four* months old! I did a dancing routine with mothballs.

Before Fallon, Leno and Carson, there was Jack Paar. He appeared with Merv when we visited New York, where he'd hosted his signature version of *The Tonight Show* in the late '50s and early '60s. It highlighted urbane talk and his nervous idiosyncrasies, the latter of which I sensed he still had.

JACK PAAR

On New York...

I'm very happy living in Connecticut, fifty miles from Manhattan. I've always had ambivalent feelings about New York City, and I think the distance is just right. Miriam (his wife) and I still enjoy going there once or twice a month – mainly to see a foreign film, eat at the Russian Tea Room or my old hangout, The 21 Club. We see ten or fifteen shows a year. I have my own way of rating shows. I call *Dream Girls* a "thousand-dollar show." You'd have to pay me a thousand dollars to see it again! I have a theory that the theater can exist only in a large, vertical society. If people live in stone caves on top of each other, they'll go out to watch anything – even cockfights. If they could walk in the woods or a beach, theater would be unnecessary.

On working in the hospital...

I wrote my latest book in the hospital for a prostate condition. I used to make the nurses run out and look up the spelling of words. One day, I said to a nurse, "Bedpan." And she asked, "You want one, or you want me to spell it for you?"

As a kid, I first remembered him from his co-starring role with Audrey Hepburn in *Breakfast at Tiffany's*, the film adaptation of the novella by Griffin show guest Truman Capote. By the time I pre-interviewed him, he was reborn to a new generation of fans in his co-starring role with Mr. T on *The A-Team*. He died at the still relatively young age of 65.

GEORGE PEPPARD

On stopping drinking...

I love to talk about it. I think about it every day. The last guy to know they're drinking too much is the guy who's drinking too much.

And multiple divorces...

Facing the fact you've made a major life error makes anybody feel like a failure. It's a humbling experience. You start doubting other people and yourself.

I'd been under the mistaken idea that after you get married, the love started, and marriage would change your life. I don't think it changes anybody's life.

After Ashton Kutcher and Demi Moore separated in 2011, I pitched Dan Piraro a *Bizarro* cartoon panel gag that described a tail-waving dog carrying a picture of Ashton in his mouth. Caption: "Demi's dog still hasn't learned not to retrieve *everything* tossed into the yard." Dan wrote back, "I love this gag and would have used it six months ago, but now that I'm going through the divorce thing again I can't bring myself to. :O["

Here was the original jack-of-all-trades. Writer, editor, actor, journalist doesn't quite do justice to his participation in everything from boxing to stand-up comedy – towards the end goal of writing about what it was like to experience it.

GEORGE PLIMPTON

On figuring out what he'd be good at as a kid...

I took an occupational exam at age eleven that told me I had every aptitude to be a Hollywood producer. I guess I had the same mental makeup as Cecil DeMille. I took it with a friend, who was disturbed to find out everything on his test suggested he should be a hairdresser.

On the ideal occupation...

I don't know if there is any. I've always walked away from sports feeling glad I wasn't in it. You can't have very much fun having to watch your body all the time. And your whole career stops while everyone else's goes on. I'm not even sure I'd like to be a musician. I've tried that. I don't even like writing very much. It's too hard. I would like to be extremely rich, young and living in the south of France. I take that back. There's nothing more tiring than not doing anything.

This actor always seemed to have fun with his ghoulishly campy image that harked back to his horror heyday in the '50s, only one chapter in his long career. Around the time I met him in the early '80s, he would add his unmistakable voice to Michael Jackson's *Thriller* title track. In recurring *SNL* bits long after his death, Bill Hader was one of many whose sincerest form of flattery imitated him.

VINCENT PRICE

On his reputation as a snappy dresser...

I'm kind of a slob. I once won a prize for being one of the best-dressed men in Hollywood, and I picked up the award with one brown sock and one blue.

On horror films...

Now there's nothing left to your imagination at all. The old days were like fairy tales compared to today's brutality. I find audiences reacting against too much blood and obvious horror.

One of the most enjoyable dastardly acts I ever performed in a motion picture was in *Theater of Blood,* where I killed off all the critics. A part dear to an actor's heart.

Photo by Alan Light

Lust for Life, one of two films that earned him an Academy Award, was an apt description for this actor and painter's philosophy and aura. I remember thinking his way with the ladies in his 70s (and beyond) even trumped young guys in their prime. Okay, me.

ANTHONY QUINN

On acting with leading ladies he doesn't care for...

I've found it much easier to work with women I don't get along with. The minute I work with a woman I'm likely to fall in love with, I am horrendous. I throw all the scenes her way. Things work better when there's a little resentment involved. Ingrid Bergman and I didn't work quite as well together as we should have, because I was in such awe of her beauty – almost more than her talent.

On his own continued sex appeal...

I think sex appeal is very much like lady luck. If you try to be lucky, luck will not come your way. Lady luck only comes by when you tell her to go screw herself. So as far as the ladies are concerned, if you tell yourself, "Look, I'm not really looking," they come looking for you.

On the strain touring has on family life...

Touring in *Zorba* has become a bit much for my wife. She wants me to settle down in New York, so the family can be together. But if I do agree to play Broadway, it will be strictly up to me and not my wife. She has always cared for the house, while I take care of my career. I'm Latin in that respect.

On growing into the role of Zorba...

I'm twenty-two years richer in the life experiences that define the differences between playing an old man and *being* that old man. The play has become a very personal thing. I'm using my own pain. There are many differences between Zorba and me, but many traits are alike. We're both against war. And I'm in complete agreement about his love for women.

A member of the Redgrave acting dynasty, she was predisposed to enter the theatrical world, much like her sister, Vanessa. She died of breast cancer at 67.

LYNN REDGRAVE

On her visit back to her mother country...

I really don't miss a thing about England. I know that sounds so uncharitable. English people get so upset when I say that. They knock California, saying it's so awful, so large, the roads are frightful. We recently passed by an English tea shop in Santa Monica and I got the urge for some "proper" English tea. I ordered a salad and they brought me what the English would call a salad, which is quite frighteningly bad. I looked at my husband and said, "This is the reason we immigrated to California and haven't been back." I would love to be on a health kick like everyone else in California, but I just don't have the time.

When I go home and see my nieces and nephews who were brought up in English boarding schools with structured home lives, they are absolutely charming. I do sometimes wonder whether the wildness of our youth in America is a good thing.

I am amazed by how sentimental the Americans are about the Royal Family. I arrived in London the day after Princess Diana gave birth. It was wild excitement there as well. The flags were out at all the houses and shop windows posted their congratulations.

On Britain's misconceptions about America...

They have a reverse snobbery about Americans. They greatly desire what Americans have but think there's something low about wanting it, so they'll put it down. And they're also surprised by the fact America is so cultured.

On American versus British actors...

They're too intimidated by British actors because of their accents. American actors are generally more prepared and more professional in every way.

This director and comedy personality was a natural for the show, because he loved to mix it up. It was also why he was a fixture on game shows throughout the '70s and '80s.

CHARLES NELSON REILLY

On his chilly relationship with his mother...

My mother never had a good word for me. When I did *Charlie's Aunt*, my first major part, I bowed to tremendous applause and thought: at last, my mother would have something nice to say. She came backstage and said, "Before your father gets here, I just wanted to tell you – he was very upset about the dress."

I will say I've never been sick, thanks to my mother's philosophy: We never had any money to be sick! I don't have any bandages, medicine. I never vomited. Never had acne. Another thing that keeps me healthy is never getting up in the morning. I never set an alarm or leave a wakeup call. I never do anything in the morning anymore.

On actors' phobias...

The five fears of an actor are falling, dizziness, grabbing onto actors, furniture, and the fear of going blank. Twice I've blacked out and didn't know where I was. I'd read about these fears in a handbook and thought, "these things don't happen to me." And that night, all five happened to me at once.

On actors' humble beginnings...

Plenty of young, awful actors in acting class went on to be great years later, like Geraldine Page, who was always so sweet. The worst scene in my class in twenty-four years of teaching involved Lily Tomlin. And every time Hal Holbrook and Steve McQueen would get up to do a scene, the whole class would go, "Oh no, not them again."

On hating his neighbors...

I moved my big boat into a better real estate area, the 35-60-foot level. And the neighbors don't like me because I'm a silly, giddy person on TV, and they think I'm gonna ram their boats. But they don't know I make the Coast Guard films and piloted the Staten Island Ferry.

Another actor who died at a young age (54), he was someone you could sense had a mutual connection with the audience.

JOHN RITTER

On being religious...

I am. I used to preach on the hood of my father's station wagon as a preschooler and talk about saving souls. I feel there's an afterlife and we're here to help each other.

On being a new father...

I love every child alive now and I just want to hug every pregnant mother. It's a whole attitudinal change to live for something bigger than yourself. I want to clean up my act, not stay out too late, not work too hard and just be available. It's good to have something bigger than the neurotic concerns that go with acting.

On taking his two-year-old to the theater...

The youngest kid in the audience, he was transfixed by *Peter Pan*. When Sandy Duncan came in, I could feel his little heart start pounding. I started to cry. I remember making out on the couch with my girlfriend when I watched the show. And here I was, way over the puppy love stage, with my little boy, and thinking about growing up and how timeless that is. When Sandy said, "I am freedom, I am youth, I am joy," I was just holding it all in my lap. During the intermissions, I flew my boy around, so he became Peter Pan. He'd been such a good boy, but in the middle of the second act, he started gawking at the people behind us. Then during the last sweet moment of Peter and Wendy grown up, when you could have heard a pin drop, my son went, "Peter Pan!" And all these heads whipped around.

Personally chosen by JFK to portray him in the film, PT 109, he was later blacklisted by some in Hollywood, after pointing the finger at Columbia Pictures head David Begelman for forging his signature on a check Robertson never received. The infamous embezzlement scandal was something Robertson said helped Hollywood to clean up its act.

CLIFF ROBERTSON

On being clean-cut...

I've heard talk that the grubby, unshaven, poor look is on its way out, and the hero is coming back. Certainly, Tom Selleck would indicate that. Maybe it's no longer going to be a disadvantage for some of these handsome younger men. They won't have to look like they've just come out of the gutter which, in itself, can be an affectation.

On confronting corruption in Hollywood...

Looking back, I wouldn't have done anything differently. The town was behind me and said it was good for the industry. And the result is that you see less creative bookkeeping today. People who supported me asked me not to mention their names, and you couldn't blame them. It was just several powerful individuals who felt their honeymoon was over and tried to discourage the industry from confronting corruption by setting me up as an example.

Here's an actor who worked from the '30s till the '90s, but his standout role, for boomers that is, was as the Joker in TV's *Batman*.

CESAR ROMERO

On never getting married...

I got close a couple of times. It wasn't too hard to find Miss Right. It's that Miss Right never wanted me. I wouldn't get married today on a bet. I don't mind being alone one bit. You get married, have children, the children grow up and leave you anyway. So that's nonsense. There are nursing homes all over the country full of old people whose children don't want anything to do with them. I go around with young girls, but I doubt very much that I'd marry one. Marrying a young girl can be very dangerous.

On how Hollywood has changed...

People used to go to the movie theater to get away from the humdrum of reality. Today you get all the rotten, dirty things that go with life. And there was a great and very elegant social life in Hollywood years ago. A definite motion picture colony, and within that colony was a very definite society. Everybody knew each other; it was like a big family. That's all gone. I go to quite a few Hollywood premieres, but they're all the same now – benefits. Not like the parties Marion Davies, Mary Pickford and Carole Lombard used to throw that were great social functions.

You always had the sense this former number one box office star still loved being connected to the Hollywood community. It was his longest marriage!

MICKEY ROONEY

On his many marriages and recipe for a happy marriage...

Cary Grant, a man I adore, has been married five times. There's never been anything terrible made about that. But with me, it's another story. But that's all right. I used to think it was maybe my fault – that I was emotionally unstable. But most of the lovely ladies I married didn't stay married after our marriage either. The secret of a happy marriage is – you marry someone you like, your best friend. And you've gotta care about yourself. So many don't care. They say "I'm gonna get fat. I'm gonna belch." They grow comfortable in their unattractiveness. They become professional slobs.

On the ease of divorce...

People don't get married any longer for love. They get married for the divorce, so they can run, as did Joanna Carson. This has got to make people around the country regurgitate. Divorce is so easy today. And very seldom do you find the male leaving the nest. They may go out to play and think some naughty thoughts, but they always want to go home to mama. But if a woman gives you the cold shoulder and turns her back, that's the end of it. There's no reasoning, no listening.

As the son of a successful early Hollywood producer, this celebrated screenwriter of *On the Waterfront* and author of *What Makes Sammy Run?* was uniquely suited to relaying the town's quirks. Counter to contemporary scandals, he labeled early Hollywood starlets the sexual predators.

BUDD SCHULBERG

On his father's (B. P. Schulberg) early influence on Hollywood...

He discovered many big stars as head of Paramount on the West Coast during the twenties and thirties. Clara Bow, the "it girl," symbol of the jazz age. My father called her "Crisis a Day Clara." Every day something dire happened to her. Her success was so enormous, and she was so unprepared for it that she was a patsy for everyone who came along, ending up mired in scandal. He discovered Gary Cooper... Cary Grant, who recently called me and reflected on where he might not have been without my father's help.

On hiding symbols of his family's wealth...

We had a crazy car, a French eighteenth century carriage built on a Lincoln chassis, with a uniformed chauffeur sitting inside. I hated that car. Hated the look, hated what it stood for. I'd lie on the floor of the car, so nobody looking in could see me. At the same time, like any other healthy American boy, I was selling magazines. Sometimes I'd be dropped off a block away from my route, crawl out of the car on my belly, dress down to sell on Western Avenue, and then later be picked up by James.

On stars' insecurity...

I can think of hardly anyone who wasn't. My father gave a welcome party for Maurice Chevalier, and all the top stars came to the house. I was sitting on top of the stairs watching. They asked Chevalier to sing, and as he started to, Charlie Chaplin went to another piano and, like a child, started to pound on it. It was like he was saying, "Look at me! I want attention." He couldn't stand Chevalier stealing the spotlight.

Although I was surrounded by starlets, I went off to college, believe it or not, as a virgin, because I had no faith in these girls. All of them were predators, because everybody had something to offer for stardom. All were trying to get that seven-year contract. Since the moguls did have the power to offer that, the atmosphere was very sexual. I'm not sure it's changed all that much today. But the power was so much greater then.

Many stars overdosed. Mabel Normand, Barbara La Marr – people now forgotten but very big in their day. It wasn't heroin so much, but many were into cocaine. And Clara Bow basically died of alcoholism, as did Jack Gilbert. It was because many became famous so fast and the fear of falling was so great.

On Louis B. Mayer...

He and my father started a studio together. They were great partners and friends then. Later when he became the "M" in MGM and the dictator of Hollywood, they had a falling out, and like everything in Hollywood, it was on a large scale. They both owned trade papers just to attack each other. L.B. was made for his time. He could play on people like a harp, make people laugh or cry better than many an actor. If he wanted to cut secretaries' salaries, even though he was making a million, he'd have them in tears, begging him to cut theirs. You could either love him or hate him for it.

On what yesterday's moguls would think of '80s Hollywood...

They'd be disgusted and contemptuous of the lack of control, the fact it's such a grab bag, the fact somebody comes up and goes down so fast that there's no continuity. Even the meanest of the moguls, like Harry Cohn, you still had to admire for organization. They'd also think today's stories don't have enough structure. As for today's sex, L.B. would have them all arrested. There's a lot I despised about the moguls, but you can't entirely put them down.

There aren't as many outstanding actors as there were in the past, because they don't make as many films and don't have as many opportunities to develop. There were many more great character actors in the days of Bogie, Robinson, Garfield and Muni. You can mention George C. Scott and De Niro now, but you run out faster than you did then.

Remembered for his roles in *The Producers* and *It's a Mad, Mad, Mad, Mad World*, this comic actor died the way many performers wish to – on the stage although at the too young age of 63. It seemed fitting that this avant-garde performer left the audience thinking it was part of his act, until the medics showed up.

DICK SHAWN

On his sheltered childhood...

I lived in one room with my parents and brother, behind my father's clothing store in Lackawanna, New York. I was so sheltered, I didn't even know I was a Jew until I got in the army, and when I started dating Gentile girls. Gentiles were tall. Jewish girls were small and round. When I dated Gentiles, my mother would always come knocking on the door.

I was quiet on the outside, and ready to explode on the inside. If I hadn't learned to do comedy or find a way to express myself, my hair would have blown off.

On reincarnation...

Ideally, I'd want to start all over again knowing what I know now. I'd have to start again with the same brain, but it doesn't happen that way, and that's why I don't believe in reincarnation. What good is coming back if you start out as stupid as you were when you began the last time?

This Hollywood veteran who made Elliot Ness his own decades earlier still seemed hip, young for his age, and displayed a good sense of humor. He hadn't even begun his fifteen-year gig hosting *Unsolved Mysteries.*

ROBERT STACK

On JFK...

When I was just starting in the business at about nineteen, I shared an apartment with JFK, Ambassador Kennedy's son. I met him through a friend who brought him onto the set one day. This friend and I shared an apartment in Hollywood, and Jack had one of the keys. He got lots of use out of that apartment. In fact, I once told him, "I think you're wasting your time in politics. You oughta go in pictures. You're an action man, you'd be a smash!" We were a bunch of young guys sowing our oats. We had what we called "the flag room." It had a large couch in it and flags of various nations hanging from the ceiling. If a girl couldn't memorize the nationalities of the flags, she had to pay the forfeit.

On Reagan...

As for President Reagan, yes, he's a friend, but I have no ambitions to intrude on him. I approach America like a naturalized citizen, because I spoke French and Italian until I was six, and I know what the rest of the world is like compared to America, which is why I treasure this country. So, I want none of the perks or invites that come with knowing the president. When he was SAG president, I recognized presidential timber in him and urged him to get into politics.

On whether the public ever challenged his toughness when he played Elliot Ness...

It was the diametric opposite! People would always test Bogie, or Mitchum – who had that look in his eyes of wanting to get into trouble. But for some reason, there was kind of a half-assed respect that went with Elliot Ness's character. I even had real gangsters say, "Y'know, you're all right." No one ever wanted to come up to me and pick a fight. I don't think they'd come up to Eastwood either.

On whether he understood his profession any more now versus when he was starting out...

There is no sense. We're all hired help. We're all peasants who wait for the phone to ring. It's the old story – you, the blonde third from the right, show us your legs. Whether you're a male or female, you never cease to be pigeonholed unless you stop becoming an actor and you produce. I wish there was more continuity, that it wasn't as haphazard. But by and large, it's been good to me, what the hell. My wife said something interesting to me: "I would like you, for once in your life, to find the fulfillment that comes from the interaction between an audience and a performer." That helped me decide to do La Cage Aux Folles on Broadway. How the hell many times does something like that happen? I know people who've done stage all their life and never really had one thing that grabbed the audience. There aren't many shows that work.

This veteran sitcom star and producer (and father of Marlo) remained devoted to his St. Jude Children's Research Hospital he founded. Semi-retired by the time he was on Merv's show, he refused to totally quit the business.

DANNY THOMAS

On retirement...

What little I'm doing show business-wise are the big banquets around the country for St Jude. The ego is massaged, and you get a standing ovation for showing up. I did an airport management convention for AT&T the other night. It was the first time I've worked in Los Angeles like that since I can remember. Like Bob Hope and George Burns, I don't want to quit. You quit, you die.

Photo by Alan Light

Since this famous jazz vocalist was now including *Steely Dan* tunes in his repertoire, I remember asking the "Velvet Fog" whether he agreed at all with my offbeat but (I thought) accurate assessment that Donald Fagan had a hint of Rosemary Clooney in his voice timbre. Mel scoffed. For you younger readers, she too was a notable classic songbook and jazz vocalist who frequented the show – and George Clooney's aunt, with whom George lived as he awaited his big break, several years before he appeared on the show. She once told me that if she had it do over again, she might have passed on stardom in lieu of a working career as a singer.

MEL TORMÉ

On his first performance in New York...

It was at the Copa in '47, the home of established stars like Durante, Sophie Tucker, Joe E. Louis. The mob ruled it. One guy used to bang the table with a big pinky ring when he got mad. It was a very traumatic experience. No one as young as I was had played there before. The reviews were awful. People were throwing ice cubes at me. Sophie Tucker was at ringside and turned her back on me during the show.

On audience reaction these days...

When I receive a standing ovation now, it doesn't impress me because I can sing badly and get one. When that happens, I can walk off a stage in deep depression that may last several days. Other times I get apathetic reactions when I know I've been great.

On never singing anything the same way twice...

This led to my being crossed off Richard Rogers' list, and I idolize his music. He heard me sing *Blue Moon* in a rehearsal and I phrased it a bit differently. And he said, "No, that's not the way to sing my song. You do it this way." I told him I was simply trying to make the lyrics sound more conversational.

On bringing the emotions he's feeling to his work...

Singing upbeat songs when you're feeling down is harder than singing sad songs when you're happy. But you always have to remember the audience is there to have a good time and to escape. Performing is very tricky. It's a good idea to allow some small piece of unhappiness from your life to be a part of your work every night. It gives your singing depth.

Why age hasn't deteriorated his voice...

In fact, it seems to be improving. I don't smoke, don't drink and I sleep enough. This, more than anything, strengthens the voice. Vic Damone and I compared notes on this the other night and found we're exactly alike. Seven or eight hours sleep is good for me. Vic sleeps as much as ten.

On paying attention to the critics...

I don't read reviews. I've long since decided that my reviews come from the audience. Music lovers are usually far more qualified to give an instant review. Whereas a lot of newspapers are hiring very young guys who are rock-oriented and have no business reviewing classical or jazz. So, artists like me get unfair comments, because it's not their kind of music.

Photo by Allan Warren

Actor, writer, director, humorist, wit – he was the kind of well-rounded guest that talk shows favored years ago. I remembered him from his Oscar-winning supporting role in *Spartacus*.

SIR PETER USTINOV

On living in Los Angeles...

I think it's rather riling in a free society to always be told to have a good day when you're leaving. I was told about an Englishman who came over here and was told for the fifteenth time to have a nice day. And he turned around and said, "I have made other plans."

On his many interests...

It intrigues me when I'm asked why I do so much in so many different areas. I'm not putting myself on a pedestal. In fact, I'm prostrating myself. I think if you'd ask the same question to Leonardo da Vinci, it would have been regarded as an impertinence. They would have said, "If you can do the Mona Lisa, why do doodles?" But I think some of his doodles are more valuable than the Mona Lisa. They have all sorts of extraordinary insights into civic planning and traffic control. In any case, I can't stand the Mona Lisa, because she looks like a relative of mine.

One phenomenally successful advice columnist in the family is rare enough. But two – that was bizarre. She wanted to make a point that contrary to continued rumors, she and her twin sister, known as Ann Landers, were no longer on the outs. Their birth names were Pauline Esther Friedman and Esther Pauline Friedman. Too close for comfort?

ABIGAIL VAN BUREN / DEAR ABBY

On evolving over premarital sex...

I've become more understanding, flexible and less rigid. If seventeen to eighteen-year-olds are mature enough to handle sex at that age, who am I to lay a guilt trip on them? Others are still immature at 21 or 22. When it comes to sex, I believe anything goes that's agreeable between the two people. As for pornography, I think adults should be able to see whatever they want to see. I'm very much opposed to censorship.

On pot...

I've changed my opinion on this many times. At first, I thought if they legalized it, it would take the profit from the dealers and the drugs from the back-alley types who'll sell kids anything. It would have to meet specific standards. But many more people could have it if it were legalized. It's a tough question. Yet I know people who've been using pot for a long time, and they're not freaked out.

On whether her kids rebelled growing up...

Yes, they thought I was square and old-fashioned. Like most kids, they wanted privileges before their parents were ready to grant them. It's the same hassle: "I'm the only one in my crowd who can't!" I gave the same answer other parents do: "*They're* not my kids. You are." Kids still need discipline. They don't always want what they ask for. Sometimes they hope you'll say no.

On jealousy...

I got a letter from a woman who's married to a very jealous man. She wanted to know where she could have a chastity belt made, the only thing she could think of to satisfy him. I heard from many in the metal works industry who said they could do it. Somebody asked, "What if she loses the key?" I said don't you worry, there's always a Yale man around when you need him.

On her estrangement from her sister, Ann Landers...

I walked around with a hole in my heart for seven years during our tiff. People were pouring fuel on the fire. I begged her for years to forget our differences, but she was very cool. Suddenly in '64, she called me, and I choked up. She asked if I had any plans for my wedding anniversary. It was hers too, since we were married together. Thus began our reunion. There's nothing that can come between me and my sister. We're the best of friends, and all the garbage that's been printed won't stop it. I want to say this on the show.

Another classic talk show guest who wittily called it as he saw it, this celebrated writer and intellectual ran for public office several times. He was about to enter the U.S. Senate race against California Governor Jerry Brown in the Democratic primary but wasn't ready to officially announce it on the show.

GORE VIDAL

On the Reagans and his own political ambitions...

Ron and Nancy have met everybody in Washington now. They are essentially social climbers. I actually think he might quit the White House and go back to Santa Barbara. The pressure gets too great. He's old. He's getting in a lot of trouble.

If I decide to get into the California Senate race, I won't announce until March. I have no committee and I've raised no money, and therefore they can't say, "Oh, you're really running," which I am, between us. But I will not say that on television. Otherwise it gets very messy with rules and regulations.

On his childhood...

I was kind of a mean kid, sort of a bully, though I must say I only bullied more powerful people – schoolteachers. I was particularly hard on them. There was always a war over what was right and what was wrong. I wanted to know why people did things, why they justified what they did.

I remember meeting the acclaimed author of *Slaughterhouse-Five* and *Breakfast of Champions* in a hotel along with his wife. I also remember breathing in secondhand smoke.

KURT VONNEGUT

On his image...

I think I represent a reputable strain of American liberalism, which is really the backbone of the country. It's never aligned itself with the Communists. It's born out of idealism during the Great Depression.

On a North Carolina school's burning of his book, Slaughterhouse-Five...

I feel so sorry that children aren't taught what's wonderful about the American experiment. It's wonderful that we don't have an established religion.

Wonderful that you can say anything you want to without being told to shut up. What kids are learning is that some ideas are hateful and should be thrown into a furnace. These school administrators are certainly entitled to worry about what the schools are learning, but this rage of hating ideas is wrong. My books have been attacked over the years, but never me personally. So I'll write letters like the one in the *Times* and tell them, "Hey, I'm a living human being. I've got some dignity." They think all writers are dead.

On magazine gossip...

It's cheap. You don't have to travel too far. I don't think there are enough well-known people in this country for *People Magazine*'s quota of fifty-two each year. I think they get about forty-seven, which leaves them five short. They have to repeat Liz Taylor a lot.

Two of my favorite Jack Warden roles were in *Shampoo* and *Heaven Can Wait*, both earning him Oscar nominations. Fans weren't always sure who he was.

JACK WARDEN

On being mistaken for others...

There was an article in the paper the other day that confused some of my life history with Jack Weston's. Sometimes I'm confused for James Whitmore, Eli Wallach. It doesn't bother me. Being a character actor, I'll work till I drop.

On giving up drinking...

I don't go to a lot of parties anymore. I used to try to get loaded in the first five or ten minutes just to tolerate them. I feel much happier now. When you no longer drink, there are three or four hours in the day that seem to accumulate, because you're not off drinking somewhere. I used to love to sneak out early in the afternoon and go to a bar.

I pre-interviewed this legendary star and director of *Citizen Kane* eight times. His final appearance was the day before he died in October of '85, and some of his remarks were picked up by the wire services in reporting about his death. His unwritten rule on all of his previous appearances had been that he didn't want to travel down memory lane and relive his past. But with the author of his new biography on for what turned out to be his final appearance, he traveled away – deemed one of "The 60 Greatest Talk Show Moments" by *TV Guide* in 2013.[3] Although imposing, I remember he was one of the relatively few guests who would answer my question before directing it back to me with: "What do you think?" I think I'm trying not to sound intimidated talking to Orson Welles, that's what I think!

ORSON WELLES

On turning seventy...

Nobody celebrates being seventy years old. If they do, they're out of their minds. Years ago, I thought seventy was younger than it is. I was always looking forward to being old. I thought it would be great. What a dumb mistake. Do you know what Charles de Gaulle said about old age? "Old age is a shipwreck." (Merv made sure to ask about that on the air.) I think Americans behave very badly about old age. They all get dressed up as though they were going to a fancy dressed ball. The men wear funny little checked shorts, the women dye their hair blue, and they all call themselves boys and girls. And then they're angry because nobody treats them with respect.

On the young, and the old...

When I grew up as a young man, it was much easier to be young than it is now, much more fun. When you're told that you're liberated, it's no fun to be free. Nobody told us that we were liberated, and we were perfectly free, so it was naturally a lot more fun.

On travel...

I was a travel junkie as a child and young man, but now I don't like to travel because every place is the same. It all has a Hilton or Sheraton and the same airport. Tourism has destroyed traveling.

Being a tourist and a traveler are two different things. One travels in a package, and the other decides to go off and see the world and has no idea where he's going. That's pretty hard to do nowadays without advanced booking. You must never travel with anybody – particularly if you're in love. Alone you'll have adventures. Nobody will ever bother to involve you in anything if they see you with a lady.

On assimilation...

It's a bad idea for minorities not to assimilate and learn English. It's ridiculous for people to come to live in a country and expect to maintain their language, except in home and their community. Otherwise we're going to find ourselves with Latin American states, like Quebec is a French state.

On learning about technology...

The computer hasn't touched me at all. I was born too early to understand it. People who have no hot and cold running water have color TV, so in the next five years, we'll probably see computers in shanty towns.

On directors playing tricks on actors to elicit a certain performance...

I don't believe in it. The director is the servant of the actor and shouldn't play any tricks at all. I think the actors play the tricks on the director. A lot of their tricks come from the actors' new power, which is too great these days. The studio system has been destroyed and the slaves have broken loose from the galleys.

There have only been two directors in history that people have gone to see – Hitchcock and DeMille – the two who imposed their personalities onto the public. The directors today keep putting their names up there in big, big letters, but nobody reads it. I don't think they really know who Spielberg is. They confuse him with Lucas, or whoever. Maybe the kids know him.

On never having been scared by a film...

At an age when I was frightened by entertainment, what scared me was a thriller on the stage. If the lights went out and there was a rumble of thunder, and a hand came out of the library, I yelled my head off. But never in a movie. I never believed movies much.

On whether there's never been a great motion picture performance in color...

What I really said was that the greatest performances have been given in black and white. But I'd just as soon answer the question the spicier way you expressed it.

On seeing his own work...

I don't ever see myself on the screen, except by accident – if I'm flipping from station to station and I happen to be on. I've never seen any of my movies all the way through in a theater, except for *The Trial.* It was revived in France, and I was stuck at the time having to go to an opening. I just don't like to see my work. I always think I could have done it better. If you're a writer, you can correct new editions of your work, but you can't do that with a movie.

The reason this two-time Oscar winner was one of my favorite actresses and guests: She seemed all too human. Merv was especially playful during her interviews. When she promoted her first kiss-and-tell memoir, he tossed out a comparison to the "big bang theory." Her spots could dovetail into what felt like therapy sessions, and her comment about women running for higher office was ahead of its time.

SHELLEY WINTERS

On her early films versus these days...

I don't like to watch my own movies, but the other night was like Shelley Winters night on TV. I was on *The Tonight Show* and two movies the same night. It's terrible to watch yourself get old and fat! I sure was cute in the '50s. I've turned down several pictures this year – one with a girl's head being crushed, where I was the murderer. And another that's pornographic. When I was 22 with a great body, I didn't do it, so I'm not gonna do it now. I'm appalled at the steady diet of horror films. When they used to make them, they had great imagination.

On her on-screen mishaps...

I'm always playing the victim! I've been strangled by Ronald Coleman. Run over by a car by James Mason. Executed. Drowned by Robert Mitchum. James Garfield shot me. Gene Hackman made me have a heart attack. Only in pictures in Italy do I live. There I kill other people.

On her favorite co-star...

Montgomery Clift was the greatest actor I ever worked with. He surprised you. When the camera was on, he never did it like he rehearsed, and it was wonderful. Some leading men were artistic fascists. They not only memorized their lines at home, they memorized how the scene was going to go. And if they had clout, they'd insist that you make it go that way too. I'm not an easy person to make do that. What happens on camera happens between people, it's in the air. You can't plan it.

On the advantages of dating when you're older...

You're beyond playing games. This is me. If you like what you see, fine. If not, forget it. If the guy doesn't call, you take off your girdle, watch TV and say tomorrow's another day. I've reached the point where I'm not interested in the physical part anymore. The humor is more important, especially as you get older. I'd never want to be sixteen again. I like young men, but not kids. I have a seventeen-year-old godchild I was with recently. And somebody took me aside and said, "Shelley, I know you like younger men, but this is ridiculous." I don't know who to go to parties with. All my friends are too old! They got older than me. Or they look older than me! If I was a man and went out with somebody thirty, nobody would think twice about it, so why can't I go out with a thirty-year-old guy? It would end up in the *National Enquirer*.

On the freedom young women have...

I'm really jealous. With them, marriage is an alternative, not a requirement. I see them showing up at functions by themselves. I'm still very reluctant to go to a public function without an escort. To the movies or restaurant, I can go with another girl. But not public functions.

I'd like to meet somebody connected with the industry. Otherwise I have nothing to talk about. I've gone out with businessmen. I went out with a guy who owned a big oil company, he wanted me to marry him, was very rich and intelligent. But we don't realize how involved we are in this business. It's ninety percent of our conversation and I couldn't be relaxed with him.

I often go Dutch on a date or treat when the man isn't doing well.

On a woman running for higher office...

I think women are more interested in promoting life. With all the birth control devices that have been invented, women still manage to somehow unconsciously forget to take their pill. Gynecologists have told me that the need to produce children is so strong that they'll never find the perfect birth control device. So, keeping all this in mind, I think there would be less of a chance of war with women.

Merv's show was indeed ahead of its time – the time it ultimately aired, sometimes months after taping. Another case in point Leno recalled for me in 2015...

Jay: The guy who played Captain Binghamton in the old sitcom, McHale's Navy, Joe Flynn – he drowns in his Beverly Hills swimming pool. I'm watching the show two months later. Out walks Captain Binghamton – "Merv, I just put a pool in my house. It's the best thing I ever did!" He'd already passed away!

This veteran actress (and first wife of Ronald Reagan's) enjoyed a big career resurgence playing a baddie on *Falcon Crest*. We saluted the cast up in California's Wine Country.

JANE WYMAN

On why she decided to come back to television...

I'd turned down so many things, and when *Falcon Crest* came along, I wasn't going to read the script. But my associate said I should, so I told him I'd get around to it. I finally read it, put it down and thought – I better read this one again. I saw so many ways to go with it. They were waiting for a yes or no, and I said yes! I surprised myself, because I made the decision so fast. Two days later, I was on an airplane. And the fourth day, I was shooting. I'm really having a ball! And I think it shows. I haven't played a character like Angie before. I've played stern characters in films, but not devious like Angie. She charms them, giggles and smiles, plays girlie on them, and suddenly – whammo! This girl is tough. She wants to get her own way, and she's gonna get it no matter what. I've never known any people like the characters in *Falcon Crest*. Sometimes when I get into heavy drama, I'll find a model in my mind. But with this character, we created her from scratch. Now I get mail, are you ready, from eleven-year-old kids! They're fascinated with this old broad. They don't know from the birds about anything else I've done.

Having grown up on *Father Knows Best* and *Marcus Welby, M.D.*, I got a kick out of pre-interviewing this relatively rare talk show guest. Here was another actor who knew Reagan from the early days.

ROBERT YOUNG

On work... and matrimony...

It interests people as to why a man of my age, 77, would feel the need to work. It's not an economic requirement, why do it? The only way I can answer that is because I have a helluva good time... I don't have a hobby. My wife and I love to read, we talk a lot, go to the market, take care of the homes. We've been married fifty-one years. There's no way to advise someone how to build such a marriage. You do it one day at a time. There's sharing, compromising. It isn't always fifty-fifty. It can be ninety-ten. And it takes fifty-one years of living to find out how to make such a marriage work. It's like a pair of thoroughbred horses pulling a carriage. When they're first put in the harness, they're so unaccustomed to it that they fight it and develop sores. They eventually find out how to get it into step.

On learning his craft...

I had the best training you could possibly have. They'd start young players and put them in *everything*, usually the B pictures. Some of them were unbelievably dreadful. But I thought, if I can make something out of *this* piece of junk, I deserve an Oscar! It was always a challenge to bring it off, and I was the one who grew.

Before Reagan was SAG president, Young told him why he didn't think he (Young) would be successful at politics, because he couldn't bring himself to carry out the "promising game" during the campaigning. But he suggested Reagan could accept it as the way to get into office and do the good he'd like to do...

We had a good understanding at the end of this, put our arms around each other, and that was that. I felt that Ronnie had great promise, because he had the essential ingredients – including the actor's gift of making self-deprecating remarks in front of a group.

Like an Alien

"The Opposite" continued to pay dividends. In the summer of '95 I would move to yet another "bunk" on the same studio lot where *Seinfeld*, *Double Rush* and *Take Five* had filmed, as executive story consultant on the brand new 3rd *Rock from the Sun*, scheduled for midseason on NBC. Showrunners Bonnie and Terry Turner, former *SNL* writers, thought my first draft had a "whimsy" separating it from the other *Seinfeld* scripts they'd read, a tone they thought could marry well with the show they were figuring out. Nearly twenty years after I'd stormed into *SNL*, I would now be writing for Jane Curtin (with whom I didn't have much contact) and the talented John Lithgow (always a gentleman) French Stewart (ditto, a guest star in "The Opposite") Kristen Johnston and Joseph-Gordon-Levitt, whose professionalism belied his youthful fourteen years and voice yet to change.

John Lithgow

I was drawn to shining a light on life through the fresh eyes of newly arrived extraterrestrials posing as humans. Everything would be brand new to the "Solomons." Pitches included...

A story about perfection and the impossibility of obtaining it on earth: There's always a flaw somewhere, unlike other planets where the creatures are born airbrushed. Maybe a subplot about Harry (or Tommy) watching a law firm commercial and realizing that suing could be a way to take advantage of things not being perfect enough? Or the Solomons could start feeling insecure about their looks after hearing that humans "lift their faces" and "land work for their noses." (Get nose jobs.) In order to fit in more, Dick decrees that they all need to visit plastic surgeons.

The noisiness of earth... car alarms... boom boxes... starts getting to Dick, so he sets aside one day of absolute quiet in the classroom and at home, an impossible task. Maybe he sees an ad singing the praises of "Toledo Hills," a place where you can "rest in peace," and winds up learning about a whole other side to earth, making him long again for noise. Or Sally suggests who better than a guy they call justice of the peace to help make Dick's world more peaceful? Unexpectedly becoming man and wife doesn't help.

Harry is traumatized to discover the world is growing blurry. After buying glasses, people start treating him with more respect, which Harry likes at first. The Solomons surmise that humans think the inability to see means you're smart. If all humans wore glasses, perhaps they'd be smart enough to elect a bat president or someone as blind as one. Harry ultimately switches to contacts after not being able to handle the stress of acting as smart as he imagines the world now thinks he is.

Having been on earth long enough to have formed memories of earlier events, Dick discovers his brain is becoming overloaded and he's starting to forget things, like where he put the keys or that putrid smelling milk. Unfortunately, he's remembering goofy things like the theme to *Gilligan's Island*. He needs to figure out what he's learned so far he should forget in order to have more space for the important things he'll be learning in the near future. One upshot: He chooses to forget not to talk about something he was told was confidential.

Sally learns it's possible to offend after eating raw onions and thereafter thinks nearly everything will offend.

Tommy picks up a new language at school, cursing, and sees its powerful effects on people. Dick encourages everyone to use this language as often as possible.

Harry learns that you can have anything you want for thirty days, free of charge, with a little thing called a "credit card."

Tommy experiences the shame of being in close proximity to your relatives after Dick chaperones him on a date.

They wait around to discover who's writing the mysterious graffiti they see everywhere... maybe it's a kind of interplanetary language they understand?

Sally starts feeling strange maternal instincts and tries to meet a guy for the sole purpose of procreating. No guy is willing to bite with such an unsubtle approach, so she decides to apply for adoption. Falling far short of the "ideal mother," she tries visiting a sperm bank for a loan. As Tommy enters a gawky adolescent stage, her maternal instincts subside, and she thanks him for being so disgusting.

The Solomons wonder why their clothes aren't fitting like they used to. One day when Dick hears one of his overweight students before lunch say, "Boy, am I starving," Dick deduces he, himself, isn't eating *enough*, consumes even more, puts on even more weight and discovers on earth there's a thing called "exercise." They buy a rowing machine or stationary bicycle (highly illogical in that it doesn't get you anywhere) and Dick must contend with which is less unenjoyable – using it or not eating. (He does learn the rowing machine makes a delightful contraption on which to hang his coat.) One day a hungry Harry spots a homeless guy carrying a "will work for food" sign, gets him to perform work and asks, "Okay, where's the food?" thinking the "food" is for himself, not the homeless guy.

After a holiday weekend (the first time he's not worked for three consecutive days) Dick is dreading returning to the university more than ever. The less he works, the less he feels like working. He calls in sick and gets immersed in afternoon TV. He winds up seeing the futility in everything. Why shave, you just have to shave again the next day. Why shower, you just have to shower again the next day. Why go to the bathroom... No, that doesn't quite work. He discovers the perfect way to make money without working – lottery tickets. Too lazy to pick them up, he has Harry do it, who sees "tonight's winning lottery numbers" on TV, asks the convenience store cashier for the identical winning numbers and thinks he's won eight million dollars. Other get-rich-quick schemes: looking under the cushions of enough sofas for enough change to retire on... and street performing. Too lazy to perform, Dick just stands there holding a guitar. Sally and Tommy try snapping him out of his laziness and keep food away from him until he's hungry enough to go back to work. But the less he chews, the less he feels like mustering up the energy to chew. He doesn't like how the laziness is making him feel but he's too lazy to care. Since sloth is obviously a natural human instinct, he wonders why the entire world isn't lazy, how anyone on the planet has the energy to get up in the morning and do anything. Until one day, in bed under the covers, he accidentally teaches Harry something, very loosely involving Dick's specialty of physics, and remembers again the exhilaration and self-respect that comes from contributing something to society.

My script, "Dick's First Birthday," was the third episode of that first season and tackled birthdays and aging on earth. Lauren Graham, later of *The Gilmore Girls* (and Larry David's girlfriend in season nine of *Curb*), guest-starred as Dick's young object of his desires. I did a quick uncredited voiceover as the host of the Miss Universe pageant, which I made Harry think was fixed since it only included contestants from earth. When the now age-conscious Dick shows up at work in skintight leather pants and a bad dye job, Jane Curtin's character, hiding her shock, asks him to pick up a pencil from across the room to revel in his ridiculous getup as sound effect squeaks accompany his every step. They both kept losing it along with the audience and truly made the scene come alive. A joke of mine I'd always liked made it to the table draft final scene when Lithgow's and Curtin's characters were reflecting on life in Dick's car. After she notes gray hair makes him look distinguished, he tells her *she'd* look distinguished with gray hair...

Dr. Albright: I don't think so. When men get gray, they look distinguished. Women just look old.

Dick: When women get breasts, they look sexy. When men get breasts, they look old.[1]

For the filming, the "when men get" setup changed to "Men look distinguished with gray hair. Women just look old." Though that connection to "when *women* get" sounded a little less flowing to my ears, it seemed to have worked just as well.

•　　•　　•　　•　　•

A joke of mine I've yet to use anywhere: Hair is a lot like real estate. It's all about location, location, location. Head – good neighborhood. Back – bad neighborhood.

. . . . .

In the end, although the 3rd *Rock* cast was first-rate, I didn't feel as connected to the showrunners' sensibilities or methods of writing as I had with *Seinfeld*, notwithstanding my frustrations there. On 3rd *Rock*, our first drafts would be rewritten the way most are on sitcoms – by committee in a room. And if you weren't artistically or emotionally joined at the others' hips, it was easy to feel like the odd man out, especially when you did your best and more efficient work in your office near a white noise machine drowning out distractions. One writer who seemed to thrive in the fraternity-like environment would literally do stand-up, standing up on the table to tower over us as he seemingly dared us not to be captivated by his antics. The show appeared to be moving in a broader direction than I'd anticipated, and subtler jokes were often challenging to pitch. I thought one tapping into Dick's wide-eyed innocence would work for a scene about why he didn't want to chuck his old car, and offered it up multiple times for executive producer (and future *Malcom in the Middle* creator) Linwood Boomer's episode, "Angry Dick," until they finally agreed to use it...

Dick: It has a compartment. Just for gloves.[2]

"Dick" jokes continued popping up (sorry) in the episode titles to come, another tiny sign that my slightly less wacky leanings may have been between a 3rd Rock and a hard place. This show was like a girlfriend who made me pine for the previous girlfriend I connected with more who'd broken up with me, *Seinfeld*, still frustratingly nearby where I could envy her latest "suitors." (She could be wacky too. But New York wacky.)

Up & Down

I wasn't through with the opposite. In this case, it was cultivating opposite personas while tapping into therapy, the career path I flirted with in my undergrad days as a psych major at American University. Examining neurotic behavior was why *Seinfeld* and *The Bob Newhart Show* resonated with me. I would interweave therapy into my other creative projects but undertook it only briefly in real life. The projects themselves proved more therapeutic.

Up & Down Guys, a comedy/therapy/talk show, originated in live streaming video on the web in 2000. In all matters of life, whether they were embellished "problems" in an upfront mini-therapy session, or other news and popular culture topics we'd later address as co-hosts with real and imaginary guests, my "therapist" (psychologist, Scott Kopoian, and on the later radio show, therapist Matt Casper) saw the glass half full. I, as the down guy, saw it half empty. Avoiding anger or the oppressively dark or negative, I wanted the audience to pick up on the humor in my bummer-vision. This was four years before Rachel Dratch's reliably funny "Debbie Downer" debuted on *SNL*.

A typical *Up & Down Guys* would open with Dr. K mooning over whatever was positive that day. On Election Eve it was about the wonderful crispness in the air, the thrill of the electoral process, the freedom to vote. Finally, he would say hello to his patient and ask how I was. I'd bash democracy, leading to the reason: I'd been called in for jury duty. And if I made up an excuse to get out of it, I'd be subject to perjury...

Down Guy: Some democracy. Let them arrest me. I'll hire a lawyer. He'll tell a jury of my peers: "This man tried to get out of jury duty." What are they gonna say? "He was smarter than we were."

Taking solace in the fact I was "up" enough to predict my acquittal, Dr. K would help me reach a mini-epiphany towards the goal of seeing the half bottle half full next time, instead of half empty.

The opening therapy was largely improvised off bullet points, and in this case, a made-up premise about overly concentrating on the concentrate ...

DG: I'm obsessing as I usually do on the red flags as to why this date I had didn't work out. She comes over to my place to watch a video.

Up Guy: Was this the first date?

DG: Yeah.

UG: Wow!

DG: I had no idea she'd be coming back. I apologized for not cleaning up. She says, "No problem," meaning she must be a slob too. Anyway, I asked her if she wanted a beverage. Right away she says, "Nothing alcoholic." So out of the gate, that's a sign she doesn't want to let her guard down. That's about as non-sexy a drink order as you can get: "I'll have the platonic juice."

UG: She didn't want to dull her senses around you.

DG: Why, because I'm already dull?

UG: No! She wanted to take in everything about you, without clouding her judgment.

DG: Have you been drinking? Because I'm not sure about your judgment right now. Anyway, I tried to be the gentleman, opened the refrigerator, offered some juice. I'm almost embarrassed to admit this to the world... There was a carton of... concentrate orange juice. And a carton of non-concentrate. And I grabbed the concentrate. I grabbed the cheap stuff. So I poured her a glass of OJ. I kind of made a mental note: "Is she special enough to have the non-concentrate?" I think she noticed that gleaming "Not from Concentrate" carton there.

UG: Couple of comments I'd like to make to the audience. Remember Andy initially said she didn't let her guard down, because she wouldn't drink anything alcoholic? That was an incredible statement. I mean, what does he want? She's in his apartment! Isn't that letting the guard down to a tremendous degree? Andy, are you familiar with the term, "Don't sweat the small stuff?"

DG: How come your terms always have more than one term to them? (Not that terms can't be a phrase, but I liked where this was going.)

UG: (starting to laugh) Okay...

DG: I'm familiar with the term, "don't." I'm familiar with the term, "sweat"...

UG: I guess that was an inaccurate use of the word, "term."

DG: I guess so. Are you familiar with the term, "term?"

As for presidential candidates seeking another term, here was a show where I could talk about how I wished they impacted me more personally. Sure, health insurance was important, but what about failed date insurance? It was time the credit card companies wiped off the restaurant charge that arrives a month after the woman you took there never speaks to you again. In that case, the restaurant *didn't work.*

. . . . .

Cologne doesn't work either, but cologne manufacturers are smart! They know women hate the smell of too much and that we guys forget this on first dates when trying to impress. So we dab on enough to gross the woman out, and before the relationship can advance to the stage where we no longer care enough to woo her with cologne (and the cologne companies would lose money) the woman breaks it off – forcing us to find a brand-new woman we try to impress by wearing too much cologne. Cologne manufacturers are smart.

2007 – *Comedy Central Stage, taking advantage of another guy's cologne*
http://bit.ly/AndyonComedyCentralStage

. . . . .

Among later up and down departments post-therapy, we'd review real personals ads (when online dating websites were fewer and farther between) ...

UG: I always love it when Andy tries to connect...

DG: Get this one... "Mid-fifties. Looks forty. Feels twenty!"

UG: Ooooh!

DG: That's quite a spread there.

UG: Did you notice that tactile there? "Feels?" So she's obviously a sensuous individual...

DG: She could "feel" nauseous. Does that mean I'll be attracted to that? ... "Avid traveler" ... Uh-oh, that means she's gonna want to go places all the time... "I love to love and be loved. I love hugs and cuddling..." There's such a thing as too much of a good thing... "One-ness is all that there is..." So why get together? If one-ness is all that there is, what does she need two-ness for?

UG: I think she's referring to two merging into one. I think you might have found your soulmate, Andy!

DG: "Been called famous actress look-alike..."

UG: Oooh!

DG: That could be anybody. Bea Arthur. Lassie. You want to be a little more specific?

•　　•　　•　　•　　•

A joke I added years later to this actual news item: Researchers have just discovered a sound wave equivalent to 57 octaves lower than a middle C, the deepest note ever detected from an object in the universe. Except for Bea Arthur waking up.

•　　•　　•　　•　　•

Well before dissing infiltrated the web, we'd review the reviews, asking why movie blurbs should have the last word...

DG: *"Mission Impossible 2 is a blast pure and simple with Tom Cruise as you've never seen him."*

UG: *Sounds exciting.*

DG: *There's something inherently wrong with that review. It's a sequel! We've seen Tom Cruise like this before!*

And Kim, our married Midwest *Up & Down Girl* (who called me "Down Guy") would check in, forming our "human graphic equalizer" as her mid-range perspectives balanced out my relative lows and Dr. K's relative highs.

Up & Down Girl: The down side of marriage is you'll never have that cloud nine feeling of falling in love again.

DG: *I'm single and I never experience it. I'd settle for cloud three. Does being under a "fog" count?*

UG: *But isn't there a comfort level that goes deeper than that, Up & Down Girl? You can be yourself around a partner. You know and accept each other for who you are. That's the kind of bond that lasts.*

DG: *You call fifty percent of the time "lasting?"*

U&DG: *Now Down Guy, there is an upside to feeling comfortable with someone. When you're dating, you have to worry about brushing your teeth or washing your face before hitting the sack...*

DG: *Wait a minute. When you were single, you didn't always brush your teeth at night? I'm surprised you snagged a guy to begin with.*

If there were fun opportunities to shine a light on real life lessons, so much the better. As when I'd tell Dr. K how I only appreciated things when they were about to end. I hated summer camp in June; by the time it was over, I was bummed about going home. What if it's that way with life? I'm the down guy now. But by the time I'm on my deathbed...

UG: You'll realize how great your life really was. Maybe if we all lived life like it's our last day on earth, Andy, we'd appreciate it more.

DG: At least people would tell me I look great. They never tell you that when you've still got life left in you.

As for "guilt-trippings," another occasional department, I could unload my guilt over minutiae like resenting a lower lifeform that has it better than I do – a dog in Bel Air. The up guy would point out how the dog probably resents how well I have it. And in visualization exercises, Scott would help me imagine peaceful, stress-free environments when I was at my relative best, as when driving through a carwash, what I likened to returning to the womb when mom had a beer. (All those suds.) Unfortunately, my down ways would return as I imagined them forcing their chintzy wax on me and scratching my car, leaving me even more stressed.

In this department and its rejoinder, I could have fun with the language...

DG: It's time for the <u>down</u> word of the week...

(Foreboding music up)

DG: "Remains." The next-of-kin identified the remains. I hate that word. Remains...

(Foreboding music down)

DG: Okay, next on the agenda...

UG: Wait! It's time for the up word of the week...

(Cheery music up)

UT: "Remains." He remains healthy. I love that word. Remains...

(Cheery music down)

DG: What if the guy who "remains" healthy is the killer of the guy whose remains the next-of-kin identified?

In another bit, I'd remind listeners how the latest awards ceremony led to a lot of up guys *and* down guys, by accessing our own celestial version of the old search engine, Ask Jeeves... (Echoey) Ask God! (Musical fanfare)

DG: Let's ask God why he rejected the Emmy losers' prayers. Tina Fey lost this time.

UG: She's so talented!

DG: Let's see why He rejected her prayers. (Typing) Why did You... that's capital "Y" ... reject Tina Fey's prayers? ... (Pitched down with echo) "Thou shalt not kill bison." Wow. Even God can't tell the difference between Tina and Sarah Palin.

Steve Smallwood / Andy Cowan

21ˢᵗ century men: shaved heads and earrings

In another occasional segment, we'd travel up and down the space-time continuum (work with me here) in "sick but true future prediction from the past," going back in history and predicting something that sounded sick in context but would eventually become true...

DG: Today we're going back over fifty years... Ready, Scott? First, let me get the software ready...

UG: Andy is configuring the special, cutting-edge software. We'll be going back into the past to make a prediction. And it'll be sick. But true.

DG: Okay, let's go back into the past...

(Foreboding music with cheesy visual effects)

We're going... We're going...

(Period music)

DG: It's 1954, Scott! Anxious young children are forming lines to get shot with toxins to help erase the scourge of polio from the face of mankind... And now, the sick but true future prediction from the past!

(Timpani drum)

DG: In fifty years... those same children, forming lines around their mouths, will happily get shot with toxins to help erase wrinkles from the <u>faces</u> of mankind!

Now let's go back into the present!

(Foreboding music with cheesy visual effects)

DG: No wonder L.A. women keep giving me blank looks; I've been taking their Botox injections personally.

UG: See? You're not toxic to them, the Botox is!

And even further back...

(Classical music)

DG: It's 1907... We're at a gathering of families in a museum in New York. And it's readily apparent that everyone abides by the credo, "Children in public should be seen but not heard." And now... the sick but true future prediction from the past!

(Timpani drum)

DG: A hundred years from now, not only will it be all right for children to be heard in public... It'll be all right for women's body parts to be heard in public... in The Vagina Monologues!

• • • • •

A true future prediction of the past happened in 2000 when I called (Griffin show interviewee) Larry King on *Larry King Live* and unexpectedly made it through[1]...

LK: Santa Monica, California. Hello!

A measure of how long ago eighteen years is in politics? This topic hadn't even been publicly broached yet...

Andy: To what extent, if any, does anyone on the panel think Hillary is using her senate run as a steppingstone to the presidency?

New York Mayor Ed Koch next rolled his eyes on my TV, saying he didn't believe that was in her planning. Republican Congressman Rick Lazio, who'd fail in his senate bid against her, thought it was "absolutely her plan." Conservative political commentator, Robert Novak, declared there was no doubt and that Democrats and Republicans in New York he'd spoken with off the record "all think she not only wants to be the first woman president but feels she'd be a better one than her husband."

RN: And Ed Koch, it might not be that far off. It could be 2004 when she runs!

Or Kerry, the Secretary of State that follows her, will! When the future has passed, future predictions are a lot easier. In the event Hillary and Bill wound up dancing at another inaugural ball, I posed this question in March 2016 on *The Michael Smerconish Program*: "Who leads?" So much for that future prediction of the past.

Another sick but true future prediction from the past aired in Los Angeles on live TV in 2013. Fox 11's news director suggested I appear on "Big Deal, No Big Deal," a new feature segment on their live morning show, *Good Day L.A.* Longtime host Steve Edwards and Maria Sansone would weigh in on three current topics from the world of news, politics, sports (uh-oh) and entertainment, asking two other panelists whether they were big deals or not. In a trial run on-set, days before the telecast, they floated the oddity that Facebook once again was allowing beheadings on the site to foster discussion about terrorism. Calling it a big deal, I won a laugh with "It's not Faceless book!" and was booked. They were to email me three stories in advance, one of which came from my suggestion – the 50th anniversary of JFK's assassination. Arrival time for this non-morning person was 7:15 A.M. for the 7:40 A.M. live airing. Pacing backstage in my badly needed new blazer, I ran a line by producer Josh Kaplan...

JFK will always be a huge deal. It's the big what if. To this day, I watch the motorcade and yell, "Use the bubbletop! Skip the trip to Dallas. Come back in twenty years when they shoot JR, you'll be much happier."

After a beat of silence, Josh burst out with a laugh and said, "Go ahead, use it." I certainly wanted to inject some non-levity as well about this solemn anniversary and how the assassination represented the loss of the country's innocence. But they were introducing me as a comedy writer and I figured the JR line was a reasonably clever and benign initial deflection that tied into what *Dallas*, the TV series, would cook up nearly two decades after the Dallas assassination.

After the JR part met with stony silence on-air, I knew the hosts had reflexively focused on "shoot" and not the innocence behind the remark. Maria and another panelist chattered on about a president obviously before their time before Steve wrapped up on JFK's unreported peccadillos (four years before Edwards was fired in the wake of sexual harassment allegations). But I made it a point to jump back in with a reason JFK was a big deal: "He rallied us behind the big goals... The Peace Corps... The moon... Back then it was, 'Ask what you can do for your country.' Not like today's politics (when the Tea Party was at full brew) – ask what you can do for your party's extremists." I was barely able to squeeze in the last part on what I figured was a right-leaning station.

As Steve finally introduced the third story, the nightmare of studying for the wrong exam dawned on me over live TV. When Josh had earlier asked backstage if I'd caught the email, I'd assumed he was referring to the "sorry this is so late" message and story replacement I'd received at 12:40 a.m. before finally turning off my computer for a few hours of challenging shut-eye. They'd changed the last story yet again at 5:40 a.m. partially due to the station's state of flux after the news director, my benefactor for whom I'd done the test shoot about Herman Cain a year earlier, unexpectedly resigned. Suffice it to say my response to a story I was first hearing about then and there – how posting sexually explicit photos on the web without the other person's permission was a hot issue in the Maryland Attorney General race – didn't exactly fly out of my sleep-deprived mouth. Was making "revenge porn" illegal a big deal or not? After I sputtered out a response about Anthony Weiner, Maria rightfully pointed out he'd done the damage to himself. Josh later apologized for the last-minute confusion.

• • • • •

As for an *Up & Down Guys* bit that contrived confusion, "recapping the chatting" posited that after one of our reruns, we liked to monitor and read back that show's chat room exchanges to gauge what was on the viewers' minds while we were away. The confusion came in when I'd always misinterpret a delayed response to mean the worst...

SeriousSurfer: The Down Guy's really funny.

UG: See? Look at that!

DG: Wow! I love SeriousSurfer!

Supermodel2: I'm a down girl after my hairstylist does that to the loose hairs on my neck.

DG: What's she rambling about?

Vera: I came in late. Does what, Supermodel2?

SeriousSurfer: What do you guys think of this Up & Down Guys?

Supermodel2: Blows.

DG: What?! Screw you, Supermodel2.

UG: Wait, look at the next comment. She was answering Vera.

Vera: Yeah, I hate it when my stylist does that too.

DG: Oh! "Blows" on her neck. Sorry, Supermodel 2.

Celebrity phone-in, my favorite *Up & Down Guys* bit, was fun to both write and perform, and flexed the muscles I'd developed pre-interviewing talk show guests on Merv. But this time, I could shoot the breeze with any bigshot imaginable, because the audience would only hear my end of the conversations (a twist on the old Bob Newhart one-sided phone calls, which were twists on the old Shelley Berman one-sided phone calls). A few chatters watching the web show actually believed I was interviewing Oprah Winfrey among other A-listers, as I tried hard to sell it with little rituals. One, as the guest "responded" back to me, was pushing on my headset piece to better hear them, in the way announcer Gary Owens had on *Laugh-In*. Darting my eyes upward as I absorbed what they had to say also seemed to help, along with cutting off part of my words before they'd resume "speaking." The conceit: Initially up, I nervously anticipated each call, surprised and yet again disappointed when the guest informed me they'd prefer not putting their voice on the web or air (thereby lessening their exposure on our nickel-and-dime show) ...

DG: *This is so exciting. There was one person on our wish list we were brazen enough to even* think *about talking with. And she is standing by on the phone. I can't believe we're making her stand by.* The *talk... show... queen. If just a fraction of her success and good luck rubs off on us, I'll never be a down guy again. Oprah Winfrey!*

UG: *Wow!*

DG: *# 1 on the Forbes List... Where are we on that list? Scott, you're right behind the inventor of Red Dye #2; he's not exactly rolling in dough these days... Yeah, we're ready when she is! ... God, am I nervous...*

Hi! ... Andy Cowan and Dr. K. on Up & Down Guys, *it's so great to hear your voice! ... May I call you Oprah? ... Okay, Ms. Winfrey.*

Do you mind if we put your voice on the air? ...

UG: Yeah!

DG: Okay, we won't ...

(Up guy SIGHS, uncharacteristically down, whenever we learn yet another celebrity won't be putting his or her voice on the air.)

DG: This is such an honor to talk to you . . . I understand why your audience cries for joy when they're in your presence... I cry too, not for joy but . . . No, you're right, this isn't about me...

Your empathy for other people... maybe not me... is what is so powerful. It's so clear you understand their pain . . . Pain . . . When something hurts . . . When something isn't right . . . Not important...

Here we are starting out. Just like you started out . . . No, I know you were on TV, but still . . . Ms. Winfrey... We would kill to reach one thousandth of your level of success... that would be about a million bucks, if my math is right... (to Dr. K) I should get more than you...

I would give anything for any advice you might offer us . . . Besides "quit the business"...

Scott, do you have a question for Ms. Winfrey?

UG: Yes, Ms. Winfrey, a pleasure.

DG: With you, everything's a pleasure.

UG: When you're as powerful as you are, how do you know whom to trust? Who your real friends are?

DG: That question had a hint of down-ness, Dr. K, I like that... Ohhhh ... Interesting ... The non-friends kiss up to you, the real friends ... aren't afraid to ... tell you when you're full of it! ... I disagree ... Okay... Tried to tell her she was full of it so I could be her friend, she saw right through it...

You want to help people ... No, I realize that ... Uh-huh, give them hope ... Show them the way ... Uh-huh ... Make them ... believe in you ... worship you? And ... what? ... Reach the promised land? ... (getting creeped out) Ms. Winfrey, you're just a talk show host. I mean, what are we talking about here? ... Oprahism?! ...

UG: Oprahism?

DG: Sounds like a religion ... Oprianity? ... Which is it, Oprahism or Oprianity? ... (to Dr. K) Ah, she welcomes Jews and non-Jews alike ...

UG: That's good, we can both get in then.

DG: Merry Oprahmis? Oh. It's her birthday. Merry Oprahmis to you ... And happy... Chhhhhopranahkah...

As for a sick but true future prediction (2079) from the present...

Steve Smallwood / Andy Cowan

Eternity in Style!

We'd have real guests too, as when the late comedian, Robert Schimmel, relayed an ultimate up and down moment from his life, when he was called in to read for the part of George in the pilot for what would become *Seinfeld*...

RS: This guy is sitting next to me on the couch outside the audition room. And he goes, "What did you think of the script?" And I said Jerry's a funny guy and I really like him a lot. But whoever wrote this doesn't know squat about script writing; this is garbage." Little did I know I was talking to Larry David. I go in later to read my part, and there's Jerry, Larry, and Jerry's manager, George Shapiro. And they go, "This is Larry David. He created the show." And I go, "I really don't have to bother reading, do I?" "Nope."

Or when *Seinfeld* writer, actor, comedian and honorary down guy, Fred Stoller, talked about feeling invisible minus benefits like sneaking into women's locker rooms to catch them naked. (In these sensitive times, I'm sure he'd imagine feeling invisible somewhere else.)

Kevin Fagan tallied more ups than downs when it came to his career churning out the droll *Drabble* comic strip for Universal Press Syndicate.

Kevin Fagan

Drawing upon my own big head theory, I showed Kevin and the streaming video audience some of my own comics from the '80s I'd both written and drawn, *Howie*, whose handle partially reflected *how* he was always trying to connect with his world.

A few hinted at the opposite. (I was a social smoker in bars then:)

I later worked with several other freelancers to present a variety of *Howie* art styles to the comic strip syndicates, including this artist, in another nod to therapy...

Dan Povenmire / Andy Cowan

But when it comes to *Janet's* catering to him, a la Groucho Marx and Woody Allen's character in *Annie Hall,* Howie is wary of being a member of a club that would have him as a member.

(This pre-dates email:)

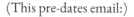

Dan Povenmire / Andy Cowan

I also drew on my substitute teacher days from the late '70s. (At the Buckley School, an upscale private school in Sherman Oaks, California, I remember watching students arrive in limos and thinking, "They should be teaching *me*!" Among those I substitute "taught" was one attractive senior who would eventually become a *Desperate Housewife*, Nicollette Savalas, Telly's stepdaughter, AKA Nicollette Sheridan.)

Over a decade before "The Opposite," my character posed in a thought bubble to himself: "Why should kids listen to me? I wound up a sub." And in the next panel, this reflection: "Whatever I tell them, they should do the opposite." After the spelling bee continues in the next with my word, "foreign," a student's reply proved he was already ahead of me: "D-O-M-E-S-T-I-C."

Howie Connects with Jason
& Seinfeld Director

Another sick but true future prediction from the past...

Howie will be whittled down to five comic strip contenders out of three thousand submissions at Creators Syndicate. There will be an association with future success at Disney. The Disney Channel's first animated hit. A future merchandising bonanza leads to riches!

The animated hit was *Phineas and Ferb*, co-created by my aforementioned freelance artist on *Howie*, Dan Povenmire (*The Simpsons*, *Family Guy*, *SpongeBob SquarePants*) after sixteen years of pitching it to the other networks that ultimately passed on a good thing.

The winning contender at Creators turned out to be *Crankshaft*, Tom Batiuk's comic strip about a grouchy old bus driver, currently in over 300 newspapers.

But wait, the sick but true future prediction from the past continues...

In 1991, you'll write a *Howie* half-hour animated pilot script. Republic Pictures will option it and commission a sample animation reel, animated by Pantomime Pictures' veteran Oscar-winning director/animator/designer, Fred Crippen (*Sesame Street*, *Teenage Mutant Ninja Turtles*). You'll voice Howie, write and sing the *Howie* theme song...

Fred Crippen

Cassandra   *Brent*   *Janet*

Get set for Howie
Get set for mopin', copin', gropin,' hopin'
To get up to speed and try to succeed

How he'll make it he hasn't a hint
But Howie aims to find the blueprint
For how he can break through
So Howie can go... "Whew!"

It won't break through. Keep hopin'!...

In 1995, you'll write a *Howie* half-hour *live action* multicam pilot script about a substitute teacher who lives in his parents' guesthouse with his one dependent, Sid (a depiction of my eternal housemate, a potted plant). Howie's parents are occasionally heard over the intercom but never seen, as they "monitor" his life without his always knowing it. He saves on the really cheap rent, until he can figure out the career he was put on this earth for – which might help land him the woman he was put on this earth for. With so many choices out there, one of them is the right choice, which means millions of them... are wrong. Not even Uncle Al, his mother's brother and gratis shrink (thanks again, psych degree!) knows the answers. But Howie's friend, Brent, does: "The hell with the destination. Enjoy the ride!" An attorney who attracts the "Cassandras" of the world (and lets his litigious side wander outside the courtroom) Brent's in the driver's seat of life. Howie's stuck in traffic.

Meanwhile Howie's other friend, Janet, an *actual* teacher, could be the substitute for what's missing in his life, the one woman who accepts him for who he is, not who he could someday be – one reason he doesn't exactly respect her taste. In the opening, I set up their platonic relationship...

Howie and Janet are wandering through The Gap. Janet is focused on the clothes. Howie looks bored.

Janet: So, she goes, he never listens. And I go, I've seen him listen. And she goes, how can you see somebody listening? So I go, that's ridiculous. You can see somebody listening. And she goes, what are you, taking his side? And I go, it has nothing to do with sides. And then she dredges up all the times she's listened to me. And I go, so, I've listened to you plenty of times too. And she goes, my listening to her has nothing to do with her listening to me...

Howie: (glassy-eyed) Uh-huh.

Two attractive young women are eying him.

Howie: (noticing them) Figures.

Janet: What?

Howie: Oh... Those two over there. The only time women give you the eye is when you're already with one. They only want you when they think they can't have you.

Janet: (noticing) So... go over there.

Howie: Go over there? And do what?

Janet: They noticed you. You noticed them noticing you. Go ahead.

Howie: That's okay, Janet.

Janet: Don't be silly. Tell them. I don't know. I'm your sister. (off his hesitancy) Go ahead.

After a beat, Howie tentatively moves their way.

Howie: Excuse me... Are you sisters?

Woman: No.

Howie: Oh. 'Cause I'm with my sister.

Woman: Who cares?

Howie makes a U-turn towards whence he came.

Janet: How'd it go?

Howie: It didn't. They know I'm available.

Avoiding the proverbial "will they or won't they syndrome," I have them sleep together in the pilot (careful to make it more Janet's idea than Howie's) before he fears crossing the platonic border was a mistake, she minimizes its significance and says whatever happens or not is fine, and we back away and reexamine the friendship. Howie may be neurotic, but I couldn't make him a loser. Playing off the "there's got to be something better out there" theme, he's optimistic enough to believe that he should strive for a life that's A Plus, not (as Uncle Al advises him) C Plus. If and when he comes to believe, deep down, that he deserves a high grade for himself, maybe then... he'll believe he deserves somebody like Janet.

Ahead of his first freelance writing gig profiling Ms. Philly Cheesesteak, at least the visual personification of "the one" he'd described to Uncle Al, Howie buzzes Janet's apartment intercom late at night, days after he'd last seen her in bed. Stressing how he's a journalist now and needs to be objective, he's not sure if what's coming up is supposed to be an interview... or... *A date*, asks Janet? Is it... okay if it's *both*, asks Howie? Journalistically, that is? Janet tells him he'll figure it out. A few days later at Howie's guesthouse, with Brent, after learning Ms. Cheesecake's personality was nothing to write home or the newspaper about, there's a knock on the door...

Howie: Yeah?

Janet enters.

Janet: Hi.

Howie: Hi.

Brent: Janet, haven't seen you in a while. What's new?

Janet: Howie and I slept together.

Brent: Wwoh.

Howie: (covering intercom) Wwoh.

Janet: (to Howie, re: Brent) Didn't tell him?

Howie: Guess not.

Brent: (shakes Howie's hand) Congratulations. (shakes Janet's hand) Congratulations.

Howie: Sorry I haven't called to get together or anything.

Janet: Don't be ridiculous. I haven't called you either.

Howie: That's true. You haven't.

Brent: You two always had a lot in common.

Janet: So... how was your interview... slash... date?

Howie: (sarcastic) Great.

Janet: The interview? (off his nod) The date? (off his nod) Too bad.

Howie: When I said "great," you knew I meant lousy. (off her nod) You know me so well... It's good to see you.

Janet: (letting some affection seep out) It's good to see you.

Howie: (reinforcing it's platonic, to Brent) It's good to see you.

Janet: (attempting same, to Brent) It's good to see you.

Brent: Good to be seen.

Five years later in 2000, you'll send the script to Jason Alexander's production company. He'll "love" it and favorably compare it to the first Seinfeld script, which he'll recall hadn't yet found its spine. He'll cite that the networks are looking for the next Seinfeld but won't risk attaching himself as a star and inviting more comparisons to Seinfeld than warranted, saying Howie is original unto itself. His team will seek out a showrunner to appease the networks, one who will protect your vision. Dottie Dartland Zicklin, co-creator of the ABC hit, Dharma & Greg, will enthusiastically sign on, after reading some hundred scripts in the past year and finding "maybe one" that was funny. She'll say the script shouldn't change too much or you'll screw it up, and reconfirm she's there to protect your vision, and that if you don't agree with something, say so.

The pitch will be turned down by ABC and CBS and finally land at Fox. Jason will assure their senior VP of comedy, Tracy Katsky, that the network won't get a better team, and uses his eventual return to sitcoms as a bargaining chip, were he to do a show at Fox, in that he'll need a companion piece. With no show on their lineup yet that could fit the bill, could that be Howie? After incorporating their minimal notes, you will carefully lay out each beat of the pilot outline in a conference call to Jason's development team—Dottie, Jamie Widdoes (the show's chosen director) and Tracy, who'll respond, "I'm psyched. You've bettered our notes and used them for the forces of good." Fox will sign off on the pilot script you'll complete and hand in after the Christmas break.

March 6, 2001, your agent will report the network has passed on a lot of projects but you're still very much in the mix and not dead yet. A Fox executive who reports to Tracy will say it's a "really great" script. Not ready to send it to pilot, they'll probably wait for other rewrites to come in before deciding to pick you up or not.

It won't break through.

March 21, 2001, Jason will relay that many at Fox were in favor of its future development, but one or two less smart opponents ruled the day and passed. He won't stop believing in something just because it doesn't get set up right away and will want Howie back. With Fox having spent money on it, Jason will guess that nothing would make them happier than to be reimbursed and have it fail somewhere else. And with his return to a sitcom now being explored at ABC, assuming it gets the nod and does well, he will have the ear of ABC in a whole new way as far as Howie is concerned. Jason's starring role as a dysfunctional motivational speaker in Bob Patterson will premiere on ABC October 2, 2001. And end October 31, 2001. He'll fold his production company thereafter.

Keep hopin' ...

In September of 2001, you'll call the Paramount office of Andy Ackerman (well-liked director of Seinfeld and Cheers) and leave a message about a project developed for Jason Alexander's company that you think would be right up his alley. You'll meet up in October at the Bob Hope Building, where you'll pitch Howie among other projects, and leave behind the script. (Ackerman will note

Jason was great in Patterson, but that the pilot had him reacting too much, and he wanted to see more of George Costanza.)

In December you'll learn that *Howie* was the one that spoke to him, that he "loved" the relationship with Brent, and Janet – likening it to the relationship with his own wife that started out platonic. He'll agree the apartment intercom is a great device for dealing with the parents.

Howie is in the guesthouse perusing the want ads. Brent is perched in front of the TV.

Howie: (reading) "Looking for vocational growth? Looking for challenges? Then Taco Land is looking for you."

Brent: Why?

Howie: Maybe they want to become Taco World. (then) I'm leaving teaching for this?

Brent: Since when do subs teach?

Howie: I'm leaving babysitting for this? ... I've got so much to do. I've gotta change my life... I've gotta change the refrigerator baking soda with the medicine cabinet baking soda...

Brent: Big deal. Tomorrow I've gotta get a cranky judge to feel sorry for a healthy guy who parked in a handicapped spot, who became handicapped after a handicapped guy ran him over. And I haven't even prepared the case yet.

Howie: Whew. He really is handicapped. (reflecting as he combs through paper) I wasn't even a sub. They called me when they couldn't get other subs.

I was a sub sub.

Mom: (V.O. over intercom) It's fine that you didn't want to go to med school.

Brent shoots Howie a look.

Howie: Mom, I know it's your guesthouse. But it's my life. Please don't listen through the intercom.

Mom: (V.O. over intercom) I was making sure the wiring worked.

Howie: Besides, you know I stunk in science. And I can't stand the sight of blood.

Mom: (V.O. over intercom) You liked "Rocky IV."

Howie: Liked. Not loved.

Mom: (V.O. over intercom) It's fine that you didn't want to go to law school.

Howie: Like the world needs more suing? (to Brent) Sorry.

Brent: Suing is a very dignified profession.

Dad: (V.O. over intercom) So is babysitting.

Howie: Dad! This isn't a call-in show!

Andy will suggest you add a beat or two to help further clarify Howie's guilt over having slept with Janet, short of his spilling the beans, when he later hits the Ms. Philly Cheesecake competition with Brent.

A singles bar with mostly guys, including Howie and Brent. But a few women.

Brent: Ooh, ooh. Check out the one in the blue dress.

Attractive woman in blue dress is talking to unattractive guy.

Howie: What's she doing with him?

Brent: Women don't need looks.

Howie: Yeah, right.

Brent: I'm serious. Why do you think they're the opposite sex? We're attracted to the outside. They're attracted to the inside.

A beat as Howie works up the nerve to talk to lady nearby.

Howie: (to lady) Hi.

She barely stifles a yawn.

Howie: (V.O. to himself) She must not be attracted to bile.

Brent smiles at her. She smiles back.

Brent: What's with you?

Howie: Me?

Brent: You're sending out faulty pheromones.

The beat I added...

Howie: Oh, I don't know. I'm feeling a little weird on the prowl. And I have no reason to feel weird. (a beat) Can you keep a secret?

Brent: No.

Howie: Appreciate your candor.

With Ackerman on board, it'll be a whole new ballgame at the networks. He'll be able to shoot a pilot in the spring. His agents (mine when I'd written with Dave Williger) will love the new draft.

In January, Paramount executives will give it real consideration, but in the end, don't "get it." Andy will call, "bummed," reiterate how much he liked the script, and wonder how we could be so wrong. Being non-exclusive to Paramount, he'll put his thinking cap on about where else to take it. Eight months later, he'll reluctantly convey that the studio is pressuring him to develop something for his last year there. Forced to put *Howie* on the back burner, he'll suggest maybe the best thing to do for your sake is for him to unfortunately pass for the time being, and hope that the way things work in circles, maybe it will come back to him somehow. Eric Poticha, a senior VP at The Jim Henson Company, became another *Howie* fan but couldn't get any bites.

After the co-head of Ed Asner's GrantWorks Productions, Maggie Grant, met with Ed and his daughter and fellow partner, Liza, in September of 2017, Maggie emailed me that *Sub* was something they all were "very interested in pursuing."

MG: We all think that you are a terrific writer, very funny, that Sub can find a home on TV, and we want to work with you to get it there.

What is *Sub*? The *Howie* strip-turned-animated-pilot-turned-live-action multicam... now newly tweaked single cam. Maggie and I signed a basic non-disclosure agreement regarding the potential financing and/or sale of the project, followed by no further word as of this writing.

Keep hopin'.

More Up & More Down

After streaming fifty hours on the web I still felt up about *Up & Down Guys.*

Andrew Singer, a junior executive with Lorne Michaels' Broadway Video (who has since risen to their President of Television) was "really into" our videos...

AS: You have such a clear dynamic and chemistry, and the show has many layers of irony and charm. You seemed amused rather than oppressively down. There was a cynicism, but it wasn't unpleasant or uninviting. And I really enjoyed the improvisation. It's refreshing and very interesting, especially with so many digital distribution avenues for television.

He asked how I thought an interactive and experimental web show would translate to TV. In a way, it was "slightly defanged Larry David meets a more up Dr. Phil." First, an interactive therapy session among "patient," psychologist and occasional callers if feasible, who offer up their therapeutic two cents on the personal travails that connect with listeners' shared experiences. When their time is up, theme music kicks in, and patient couch transforms into a talk show couch. And therapy morphs into a multi-faceted comedy talk show loosely hinging on the up and down themes, hosted by the slightly down guy and his mostly up therapist.

The up and down attitudes would permeate the show...

AS: Whether you're interviewing people, real or imaginary, or talking with each other, or he's administering therapy, the show is about that up and down dynamic, and how that dynamic changes all the other aspects of a talk show. It's the absurdity of a therapist and patient manning a talk show. And the audience can relate with the up or down side depending on how they're feeling that particular episode. You're sort of personifying aspects of the human condition.

As far as their network projects for NBC, they were overloaded and understaffed.

AS: But this is something that has really sparked my interest. And because the cable development environment is continuous throughout the year, it's something I'd like to visit.

He needed to get his supervising development exec excited about it. The downside: Still buried a month later, he hadn't yet had the opportunity and worried he'd be unable to dedicate enough time to setting up and producing another project. The upside: He forwarded the material to several other companies and producers who might be interested. The downside: nothing came of it.

At lunch the following spring, with primetime scripted programming for NBC still their mandate, he saw it as a smaller show and was intrigued with exploring MSNBC, CNBC (where he ultimately didn't know anyone) and Bravo, divisions of NBC. As to whether he could get Lorne Michaels excited about it, he had no problem sending it to him. A month hence, he admitted getting him to look at anything was nearly impossible, even when it came to scripts for their latest project, *The Tracy Morgan Show*, with Lorne's name on them. It would be several years before we'd move on to new primetime TV projects of mine.

An executive at Merv Griffin Enterprises, veteran *Smother Brothers Comedy Hour* producer, Ernie Chambers, was "very intrigued" with the therapy part of the equation. But...

EC: Before we could get involved; Merv is a great fan of yours, and asked me, "What do you think?" I said it's a great idea and obviously Andy's a very talented guy. But there's nothing here to convince a buyer of what the show is. So, it's a very simple matter and very cheap for you to do a new demo. You could spend a weekend with a digital camera, do about ten minutes of the therapy, and maybe about ten of a collateral talk show. He's the up guy. You're the down guy who sees no hope. Right now, he's laughing too much. You're like two guys over coffee. It's not like you're the patient and he's the doctor.

Merv offered Ernie an interesting note about how my own neurotic perceptions could humorously color things. I could be talking about my mother or a girlfriend – before we later see how she's nothing like the way I'd described her. All that the therapist would know is what I'd expressed to him, which might be the opposite of reality. My new goal was to focus on portions of a therapy session where Scott came off more as my shrink. After I dreaded an upcoming blind date, Dr. K would periodically pop up in my mind later during it to call me on various tidbits I'd shared with him in-session, a surreal offshoot of Merv's note about contrasting my real life with how I'd conveyed it on the couch.

Producer/director Brian Kahn and I gathered a small crew to shoot a fourteen-minute video in 2005 that included Brian's wife, actress Stefanie Ann Kahn, playing my date. We added jazz stingers that sounded organically produced, visual still inserts from a supermarket photo shoot over which I complain to Dr. K via voiceover about being ignored by the customer in line on her cell (already a growing malady in 2005) and checkout girl with a cold who touched my fruit. We were excited about how all the elements came together. Some thirty strangers of all ages, none of whom owed us their allegiance, exhibited healthy laughter throughout a screening, along with palpable interest in what happened next to my character. Ernie asked me to send him a copy, adding that it was nice to hear that I was "UP." Our *Up & Down* DVD logline: "Half full. Two-thirds empty." He wrote me back...

EC: I think the biggest problem is that, inevitably, it invites comparison with Curb Your Enthusiasm and your resemblance to Larry David. And your shrink is scarcely what I would call "up." He doesn't give you much support. Forgive my bluntness, but I don't think I do you any favors by lying to you – unless you happen to be perched on a ledge. I should have prefaced my email with my customary disclaimer: "This is just one man's opinion." Best of luck with it.

I referenced back eight instances where Scott had expressed support about something. As for Larry, I couldn't disassociate from also being Jewish, self-deprecating and an observer of the down side. (*Bizarro* cartoon panel gag I once pitched to Dan Piraro: Young Jewish parents with newborn squeamishly notice the mohel's "Tip Jar.") But Larry's character was the bull in the china shop; mine was the down-on-his-luck guy trying to turn things around.

About Dr. K, Ernie replied...

EC: He ought to be a cheerful, enthusiastic, positive, life-affirming force – none of which your guy is capable of. He should be a guy who says, "HAVE A HAPPY DAY," and really means it.

Re: Ernie's original note about Scott's laughing too much and seeming more like a buddy than a shrink, our reining him in for the video probably made him seem too somber.

There was always radio. A talk programming executive at the largest network, Westwood One, "loved" the up and down concept, along with the web show's execution and comedic sensibility, what we pitched as more class, less "crass." The challenge, as echoed by its iconic founder who also liked the show, National Radio Hall of Fame inductee, Norman Pattiz, was where to put it on the radio amid limited shelf space. Once it was proven locally at a big enough station, they could conceivably take it out nationally. My champion at Westwood One sent it to their New York affiliate sales team working with WNEW. But the station was set to switch to all music the following year. He and a fellow exec then opened the door to WJFK, a huge D.C. station that programmed Howard Stern and was looking to fill an hour or two.

They were moving fast on opportunities for the one hour between Stern and Bill O'Reilly (Fellow B.U. broadcasting students) which I thought could be a middle ground for our sensibility. Open to our broadcasting from Los Angeles, their general manager asked if we could do it live. Our web show had been live, no problem there. He asked us to overnight a tape and later confirmed "you guys put on a good show." The next step – hearing from their young program director with whom the general manager left all programming decisions...

PD: I don't know if it's something we're gonna be able to use. I don't know, I just didn't get it. Maybe I'm just missin' the boat.

Echoing my frustration, Westwood One labeled him an idiot and lamented the extent to which the industry was full of fellow idiots. Trevor Oliver with Premiere, the nation's top radio syndicator, wasn't one of them. He liked the show "at first glance" and sent new programming ideas to their corporate wing, a slow process, with our show atop the "good pile." Still, the best bet remained generating local numbers somewhere...

TO: If I thought I could roll this out and sign up a hundred stations for it, I would. But if a local commercial station could test market it for us a bit, I'd be happy to provide technical support and anything I could do to move it along.

An upside he inferred from executives undergoing indecency training as broadcasters monitored shock jock repercussions: our show didn't fall into that category. A downside was that talk remained extremely segmented – whether conservative political talk, or hot (shock) talk. John Mainelli, the program director at New York's Free FM CBS Radio affiliate, WFNY-FM, called it "breezy, clever, hip and engaging," but was targeting "slightly less sophisticated and not quite so urbane young guys . . ."

JM: If I could get my hands on a second FM station, I'd fill it with shows like yours. There's a sizeable opening in talk between what we're doing and public radio. Especially in cities like New York, Boston, San Francisco, Seattle, Minneapolis, Chicago.

He sent our CD to all the CBS FM talk stations. Each would flip over to music.

In 2004, author Lori Gottlieb filed a *Los Angeles Times* profile on the show, when we were awaiting a tryout slot promised at KLSX, a big commercial talk station in Los Angeles.[1] Whether it ideally worked into a permanent slot or not, Westwood One felt a tape of *Up & Down Guys* on a commercial station in the second biggest market in the country was "huge" and could help generate interest elsewhere.

"The home of Howard Stern and Tom Leykis may seem an odd fit for a personality more akin to Woody Allen's," reported the *Times*. But I hoped there was an untapped audience of neurotic listeners that hadn't been properly serviced by the airwaves. I also thought radio didn't always need to provoke or titillate to be entertaining and hip. As for *Curb Your Enthusiasm*, my tongue in cheek response to whether there was any conceptual comparison: *Up & Down* was far more creatively challenging, because Larry had a life. I had no life and nothing to draw from. "*Seinfeld* was all about identifying with doubt and insecurity and unhappiness," added a friend and *Seinfeld* former staffer, Bruce Kirschbaum. "It's amusing to see other people suffering that way too – you feel better about yourself. And Andy is wound so tight that if I pulled my finger back and flicked him on the side of his head, he would ring like fine crystal for 15 minutes."

Trevor Oliver also tossed in quotes...

It's very original and engaging. The main point of Dr. Laura is the help and advice and solutions. But a smaller part of the appeal might be our own wicked sense of curiosity about other people's neuroses – and that's what fascinates me about Andy's show.

Looking for "a diamond in the rough," KLSX commissioned two other test shows as well, one co-hosted by Drew Carey and former *Simpsons* executive producer, Sam Simon, and the other featuring Casey Kasem's daughter, Kerri Kasem. After our September airdate for which we'd carefully prepped was suddenly postponed to either Thanksgiving weekend or over Christmas, I tuned in to hear the show they ran in our place. Puzzled, I checked in with the station to *carefully* broach how it had turned out to be a Leykis rerun. The program director had a meltdown while I basically cowered ...

PD: Lemmee explain something to you right now. I'm utilizing some of the time periods for the testing of shows. I really don't need Andy Cowan, Drew Carey, or any-fucking body, 'cause I've got a radio station that's on fire here. For whatever reason, yeah, I ran Leykis. I don't answer to you. I don't even give a shit. I was trying to work stuff out and it didn't work out. Sorry. Tough. Deal with it, my man. And when I'm ready, when I've got the time for Andy Cowan & Drew Carey & everybody else's grandma, I'll put you guys on. It didn't happen over Labor Day, and you know what, it just didn't happen. So work on some other projects and call me back, or never, or ever. I really don't care. Okay, my man, thanks.

Meanwhile Lori hadn't appreciated his trying to promote the rest of his lineup at the expense of the article's original focus, us. In as unentitled a way as I knew how, my goal had simply been doing the best show possible. I'd gained them at least extra publicity with the *Times* piece and this was my reward. With the article set to run in a week or two, I offered Lori a revised closing remark, what the newspaper described as a "silver lining in the disappointing news" ...

Andy: This may sound sick, but being the Down Guy just got easier.

KLSX flipped to Top 40 in 2013.

XM and Sirius satellite radio (not yet merged) liked the format, pacing and chemistry. The former likened it "in the most positive way" to a "Seinfeldian sensibility crossed with Woody Allen," but never found a spot for it. Sirius talked about starting a channel for "seriously cool shows that didn't fit anywhere else" like ours. A downside: If they created such a channel, asked Sirius, how would they get the message out to people who might like us when there were 128 other shows going on? An upside: A CBS Radio VP with the Jack FM network (for whom I wrote weekly one-liners in 2007 and 2008) wrote me that "radio needs more of this quality of humor and content." Another upside: America's highest-rated public radio station, New York's WNYC, "loved" the demo. The downside: it couldn't air the show unless it was funded elsewhere.

Up & Down didn't find another home until we landed at Southern California's oldest public radio station in 2010, KPFK-FM, an unpaid labor of love that continued into 2011.

http://bit.ly/upanddownguysKPFK

As right-wing AM talk was overtaking the airwaves and music was largely sweeping aside FM talk, commercial radio remained more elusive than ever. Apart from the down guy handle, a Westwood One Executive VP, Dennis Green, dubbed me "the most persistent guy in showbiz."

Opposite Andy

My own show that touched on therapy was about to provide me with some. The *Up & Down Guys* video that had been turned *down* was about to be picked *up* for an option as a half-hour TV hybrid by GRB Entertainment, producers and distributors of over a hundred hours of reality shows for American and international markets. It was nice to see my name attached as executive producer, writer and star. GRB's best-known show at the time ran on A&E for three seasons – *Growing up Gotti*. Victoria Gotti's father was a Mafia boss. Mine was, for a short while anyway, an FBI interpreter. There's your opposite!

A big *Seinfeld* fan, the GRB exec pitched another title for our show: *The Life About Nothing*, which I thought cozied up too much with the *Seinfeld* handle. Plus, the argument-provoking behavior in another pilot GRB had taken out featuring John O'Hurley (who'd played "Mr. Peterman") was deemed too close to *Curb Your Enthusiasm*. This project was and had to be its own animal. With "The Opposite" among the exec's favorite *Seinfeld* episodes, the title nevertheless became *Opposite Andy*, which took initial adjusting to on my part. I did notice one quirk I later highlighted. The first four letters were nearly mirror opposites...
Op pO site Andy.

GRB's domain was reality, as murky as that definition was on TV. My goal was to combine the beauty of seeming real, with enough story bullet points to keep it interesting and funny. Along with my sometimes-imaginary shrink, could we still try to portray the somewhat surreal that came from my life? Such was the case in the original video when a fly grazed my face (a raisin Brian Kahn threw at me that seemed like a fly when we added the buzzing) and I unexpectedly *liked* it. Cue romantic music. I liked the feel of another life force brushing against mine!

(I'd briefly pondered this once when a gnat grazed me in real life.) I set up that my therapist, the up guy, wouldn't think it was weird. Noting you can grow so used to being alone that the notion of someone "invading your space" can be more disturbing than loneliness, he would call it promising and a sign I was ready to have a relationship. After lovingly gazing at the fly, then whacking it with a newspaper, I told him, "Can't even commit to a bug."

Unlike *Seinfeld*, I opted for an occasional poignant moment if it felt organic – as in our video, where I complained about feeling invisible and the up guy/therapist asked if I thought I was capable of a relationship. Ernie Chambers may not have thought that was "up" enough, but I thought it was worth leading the way to a reflective response...

DG: In a way, a partner's a mirror on me. Maybe all these years, I've been avoiding the mirror.

UG: If you're avoiding the mirror, maybe you want to be invisible?

I'd introduce myself in the revised sizzle I'd build along with GRB as both an up and down kind of guy. "Up one decade." Cut to Merv in the '80s welcoming me to the couch, then the "Everybody Knows Your Name" theme accompanied by my handle on a *Cheers* credit. "Down the next." Cut to the '90 Sajak show clip where he references my problem meeting women, followed by my comeback. Go to the *Seinfeld* staff picture and how at that point I was really up, leading to W's State of the Union clip from *The Daily Show* and Stewart's likening Bush's 180 from earlier positions on climate change and balancing the budget to the clip of Costanza deciding upon "the opposite," eliciting *Daily Show* audience cheers. The amended sizzle would then showcase the subheadings: "Andy hasn't had a successful date in 10 years." (How they came up with that number I never asked.) "Andy is determined to make his life the opposite of what it is today."

Andy: I'll avoid my <u>agent's</u> calls! As soon as he starts calling.

After a plus-sized black woman sat on my lap, I declared, "I'll date women the opposite of my ethnic background!" Or instead of Mr. Nice Guy, I might try "Dangerous Jerk" on for size. As a fashion leader versus a follower, I could test if wearing a different shoe on each foot might catch on. It could earn derision at first until I notice somebody else wearing two different shoes, and it starts to spread – before the "somebody else" takes all the credit away from the true fashion pioneer, me.

Unless all of this seemed too scripted?

Maybe we could explore surfing dating sites on the web, landing on a woman's profile that interested me, and later zeroing in on her during a date (with permission), the opposite of how she'd looked and acted in the profile. A mix of real people and restrained improv actors might give us more control.

I might hook up with my writers' group cronies at the local deli, bitching and moaning about the business, as long as it wasn't too showbiz-centric, a red flag for buyers. I could be the one obsessed with eating healthy, but attempt the opposite, because I can't afford to extend my life unless I start making some real money. Maybe the others are passive-aggressively envious I have my own reality show, short of aping hostility as in *Curb Your Enthusiasm*.

We could pop in brief music gig snippets, and the misspelled marquees that go with them. (The rest of the world thinks "Cowen" or "Cohen" is right and my birth certificate is wrong.) I could heighten sounding like Sinatra for the comedy angle – that I'm down about it when yet another patron asks, "Do you know who you sound like?" Because I've heard it a million times, and I'm trying desperately to find my own style. As for trying to find a woman, maybe I'd meet Mia Farrow. I sound like her ex-husband, Frank. I look like her ex-partner, Woody.

Another angle: I finally get this big break, a comedy/reality show about my life, but the problem is... I have no life. So, I'm forced into adjusting my up-till-now reclusive ways (See *Inside Al* in **Tooning In**) and introduce myself to my neighbors who never talk to their neighbors, shining a light on the inherent isolation of modern society, and especially L.A. Maybe I return to the kind of short-term furnished apartment complex many newly-arrived Angelinos initially move into. I'd play the only guy still living month to month, who can't commit beyond a month relationship with anything, who was always waiting in vain for the big break to last long enough to afford a piece of the rock. I'm there over twenty years, and I still don't know my neighbors, who move out after a year or so, tops. I'm like the oldest kid in class who keeps being left back. Short of my moving in, we could rent out an apartment as a set piece. And the pool, barbecue, tennis courts – all foreign to my sun-shunning ways – I'd embrace as part of my opposite doctrine. We could also try connecting with the "young, hip, stylish, trendy" coveted demo in the L.A. jungles from which I and a bar buddy feel more and more estranged. Young bouncers who help us could be another window into their world.

Another way in? The geeky star of Fox's *Beauty and The Geek*, Richard Rubin, was a young old soul and new friend, who also had a deal with GRB. Maybe the occasional imaginary "shrink" is a graduate student in his twenties going for his master's in psychology. And my character pays him a tiny stipend to see me, not thrilled to be, in effect, his guinea pig? Aside from the savings, I'd kind of need him as a window into "up-ness" and the young generation, and he'd kind of need me.

With reported interest at Bravo, should we pitch the less than real elements? It didn't matter. Ultimately the "reality" version attracted interested looky-loos, but no bites. The fling with GRB had run its course.

Years later, I decided to give Andrew Singer plenty of room not to bite on what by then I'd turned into a largely scripted half-hour pilot by posing, "This isn't something you'd be interested in, is it?" He countered, "Not so fast," calling it a "very cool project." Upon later catching our video link to the sizzle reel during the Writers Guild of America strike (when writing and pitching activities were no-nos) he wrote, "Am I allowed to tell you that you did a great job on this?" Months later, seeming more hamstrung in terms of development that didn't originate in-house, he emailed me...

As you know, I am a fan of your writing. It is simply that the nature of our company is to do projects with the roster of talent here at SNL, and so my hands are often tied when it comes to taking on new projects. Please do keep me posted as to its developments, and I would be happy to discuss the notion that we could attach it with Lorne – depending on the network and if there is a model for us to do so.

Bottom line: If interest came directly from NBC, he'd be willing to talk to them.

My goal was to give buyers the best sense of its multiple layers and how the series wasn't a one-trick pony, and not reliant solely on "the opposite." I wished they could follow the opposite of their inclination to not read more than the pilot script (if even that much) before passing. So, I included a second episode outline and thirty additional stories, unlikely though it was they'd take the time to see all the directions in which this thing could go.

The pitch...

The guy off *Seinfeld* who *didn't* make a killing, Andy Cowan, reaches the point in his life where he needs to shake things up and do the opposite of his instincts, the theme to his top ten *Seinfeld* episode that's spawned frequent discussions in the art, social and economic worlds. An occasional witness to how he attempts to carry this out: his shrink... at least in Andy's imagination... a *twist* on the therapy angle.

No one else could write or play the Andy character, not to mention tap into a story that explores new permutations of "the opposite," a pre-marketed *sparingly used* hook that could help pitch the show. <u>It's just one of *many layers*</u>. (I went overboard reminding them it was about much more than the gimmick.) It's also about a still single boomer who looks and acts younger than his years trying to remain visible in youth-saturated Los Angeles.

Andy (to bar buddy, Doug): Where are the youthful women our age?

Doug: Youthful, or our age?

Andy: Mature. As in wine or cheese, not fish or yogurt.

Younger audiences can connect with reinventing themselves, along with young YouTube stars with millions of hits in the roles of Andy's niece and nephew-in-law (Ashley and Zach).

In-session with Dr. K in the pilot, Andy's reflections about his family lead to a recent dinner scene with his elderly parents, Harold and Ruth...

Harold: Business must be good, Zachary?

Zach: (eyeing handheld) Cha-ching! (shows handheld to Ashley) eBay obeys!

Ashley: (playfully punches Zach's arm) Told ya my hair clippings had CASH-ey.

Zach: (caressing Ashley's hair) My little YouTuber. Two million, four-hundred seventy-nine thousand views and <u>counting.</u>

Ashley: (re: hair, playfully) Hands off the merchandise!

They kiss, slip each other a little tongue.

Harold: (to Ashley) Your grandmother mentioned some kind of invention?

Ashley: G-Spot PS App. It's awesome. Zach came up with it.

Harold and Ruth shoot each other confused looks.

Zach: G-Spot Position System Application. (to Ruth) Gives directions to your G-Spot on your smartphone.

Ruth reacts.

Zach: Ashley's my little Siri.

Ashley: (robotic) "Make a left at the thighs. If you've reached the pubic bone, you've gone too far."

Harold: (resumes eating) I never ask for directions.

Andy reacts.

With my character also freelancing for the King Features comic panel, *Bizarro*, I included one in the treatment that spoke to the opposite and age – a trendy club bouncer carding a guy old enough to be his father, with the explanation: "We don't let in anyone over 45."

I stressed my persona would be the opposite of Larry David's on *Curb*. Less annoyed at the world, I'd be more put upon, but not as down as in the video sizzle link I was sending out, the one Andrew Singer had appreciated that still showcased some of the "down" character from *Up & Down Guys*. On *Opposite Andy*, I'd at least be a cautiously up guy! The pilot summary (including my George idea from years earlier about competing with movie actors' looks) would hopefully interest them enough to read the script:

Andy's therapist winds up suggesting he follow the credo of "The Opposite," the top ten episode he wrote for *Seinfeld*, and try shaking up his own life a little and do THE OPPOSITE. For starters – stop anticipating negative events about a potential blind date (she's obsessed with her dog, didn't sound that into Andy, etc.) before they occur and go out with this Lori with an open mind. Stay positive! ... Which proves challenging at times on the date... Andy also does THE OPPOSITE of avoiding the word "awesome," THE OPPOSITE of avoiding movies featuring good-looking actors in the lead, and THE OPPOSITE of not being inclined to heartily laugh out loud in public – carefully laughing in sync with his date and the others in the theater, until he mistakenly laughs when she chokes on some popcorn (what he thought was her laughter) which coincides with an inappropriate "Bambi's mother getting shot" kind of moment in the movie, where Andy's the only one in the theater laughing – a scene involving the death of Brad Pitt's dog. With a date who's dog-obsessed.

At the Chinese restaurant...

Lori: I'm very good at what I do... Some of the people I deal with are such jerks. This one whose desk is right next to mine. She's talking about her old boyfriend. Really great guy. (Adapting Janet's blather from Howie:) And she goes, he never listens. And I go, I've seen him listen. And she goes, how can you see somebody listening? So I go, that's ridiculous. You can see somebody listening. And she goes, what are you, taking his side? And I go, it has nothing to do with sides. And then she dredges up all the times she's listened to me. And I go, so, I've listened to you plenty of times too. And she goes, my listening to her has nothing to do with her listening to me...

Finally, on Andy feigning interest.

Andy: (glassy-eyed) Huh.

A beat as they chew away.

Lori: You oughta try chopsticks.

Andy: I'm no good with sticks. Can't eat with a stick. Can't drive a stick.

Lori doesn't get the humor. Another awkward beat.

Andy: How's your chicken?

Lori: Good. Want some?

Andy: No thanks.

Lori: How's your shrimp?

Andy: Good.

A beat.

Andy: Want some?

Lori: No thanks... Okay, maybe just a bite.

She takes a healthy-sized bite. Andy reacts.

Lori: (mouth full) Mmm.

A beat.

Andy: Maybe I will try your chicken.

Lori: Oh. Okay.

Andy: Do you mind?

Lori: No. Go ahead.

Andy takes a medium-sized bite.

Andy: (mouth full) Good.

Lori: ... Want some more?

Andy: No thanks.

A beat.

Andy: (still chewing, feeling obliged) Want some more shrimp?

Lori: No thanks...

Then Lori reaches for...

Lori: Just one more bite.

Andy reacts to how little is left.

Lori: (chewing) This is awesome.

Andy: I can't say that word for some reason.

Lori: What do you mean?

Andy: It's everywhere. I don't know.

Lori: You can't say "awesome?"

Andy: I'm not putting it down... It's like... (re: like) I hate using that word now too... (re: awesome) It implies something is really special. But when it's used all the time, <u>everything</u> becomes special. Hence, nothing is special.

Lori: (a beat) Say it.

Andy: (a beat) I don't think so.

Lori: Say it.

Andy: (V.O.) Do the opposite!

Andy (barely) Awesome.

Lori: That... was not awesome.

Lori's mood lifts as her dog, Chelsea, approaches her. From Chelsea's POV, we see Lori petting her.

Lori: What do you want, Chelsea? What do you want, Chelsea? Are you my girl? Are you my girl?

Improv: Up couple notices proud "mom" and her dog, and quizzes a beaming Lori with anthropomorphic questions: i.e.) "What's her name? ... Chelsea? What a cute girl she is! Hi, Chelsea... How old is she? ... Just turned three and a half... Oh, they're a real handful then, aren't they?"

Andy reacting.

Harp-like music. Pull out to reveal (as we hear Lori go on with the "Are you my girls?")...

Andy: Shoulda done the opposite of the opposite. Shouldn't have said "awesome." She doesn't get me.

Imaginary Dr. K: (echo effect) She's sharing her food with you? Comfortable opening up to you about her co-worker's old boyfriend? It's good!

Andy: She's gossiping with me, like I'm a neutered girlfriend.

Imaginary Dr. K: (echo effect) By the way, disclaimer: Imagining your therapist eavesdropping on your life doesn't necessarily mean what I'm saying here is accurate.

I'd figured out a different angle for Richard Rubin...

Another imaginary character in the series: Andy's "younger self," played by the thirty-year-old star of *Beauty and the Geek*. Their chemistry can tap into irony, humor and even pathos that can have a universal appeal.

In the second episode, "Lying Up," my character admits the truth to a Plenty of Fish online date who likes his voice ("Blind people find me very attractive") – that he'd also knocked five years off his dating profile age, making him five years over her "cut-off age" of 55. She isn't pleased.

Andy: My freshness date didn't expire at 55. I'm not better if used before 55. You can use me now!

Later he's surprised to talk to Angela, an attractive supposedly fifty-year-old woman he eventually learns is really forty (from the bouncer who'd carded her as a compliment and has the uncanny ability to remember driver's license birthdates). Returning home and thinking to himself in voiceover about the evening's events...

Andy: She's not proud of being 40, but she's proud of being fake 50?

In pops the introduction of Andy's thirty-year-old imaginary younger self...

Younger Andy: Remember when we didn't trust anybody over 30?

Andy: Now, they barely acknowledge anybody over 30.

Younger Andy: Why are you lying about your age?

Andy: I'm not gonna be lectured by my younger self.

Younger Andy: We used to be proud of our age.

Andy: You used to say you were almost 13 when you were 12, so the cool kids would talk to you. You were in such a rush. (displays five fingers) I'm five... (then a half) And a half!

Younger Andy: Sixty and a half would require a lot of fingers.

Andy: I could offer you <u>one</u>.

Younger Andy: That would be self-loathing of you.

Andy: You were a nervous guy overly concerned with what others thought of you. I don't care what others think of me.

Younger Andy: Then why are you lying about your age?

Jazzed about hooking up with Angela for a date, Doug later springs a surprise on Andy as Andy springs one on him:

Andy: She's 40! / Doug: She's 60! (Simultaneously) Andy/Doug: **What?!**

They connect the dots. She admitted to Doug she was lying about being fifty. After he asked her, in shock, if she was *sixty*, it would have been too depressing for her to admit she was *twenty* years younger than he guessed! Plus, she knew he'd tell her she looked even greater if she pretended she was even older! Flashing back to Dr. K's advice from the pilot to try the opposite, Andy decides to lie *up*, pretending he's a senior citizen for the perks.

As for recording yet another thirty second voiceover gig audition to send to his agent that asks for "young sounding voice, 20s-30s," he strains to "young up" his voice by raising the pitch. He then complains to his imaginary younger self, who pops up again, that when Andy was his age, "older sounding golden throats" were in. But that was before somebody decided kids were the only ones who bought stuff...

Andy: And you wonder why I have to lie about my age?

Younger Andy warns his older self not to get upset. He could have a heart attack or something. Andy insists he's healthier now than he was at younger Andy's age.

Andy: We didn't work out. We didn't read food labels. You thought you were invincible. That you'd live forever.

Younger Andy, pointing to older Andy: I was right.

Older Andy: Sixty isn't forever!

Younger Andy: It's twice my age. To you, 120 is forever.

Older Andy wonders if Younger Andy might be onto something.

Andy gets an email from his niece, Ashley, double checking that he's taking her to the airport tomorrow. The only time he hears from her is when she needs a favor. She also mass-emailed him a link to her latest YouTube video and an attachment of 30 more JPEGS of the baby. He opens one up, "still cute," and deletes the rest.

Younger Andy: Talk about overkill.

Andy: I know! When we were a baby, a couple dozen Kodak moments a year. Tops.

Younger Andy: They showed visible changes. Like the new cars did.

Andy: Now it's week five, week six...

Younger Andy: Invisible changes.

Andy: Like today's new cars!

And among future episodes...

To a Loving Mom & Great Dad

Big birthdays are coming up for Ruth and Harold – 85 and 90. Andy is extremely grateful that both his parents are still with him unlike most of his contemporaries' folks – and tries not to obsess over those big numbers. Still, every time the phone rings, he fears the worst (besides a creditor calling him). He also feels guilty about avoiding birthday cards that are *too* mushy and don't necessarily describe Ruth and Harold's qualities with total accuracy. (Resurrecting my Griffin show panel gag: Nobody he knows is as nice as Hallmark says they are.) While at the card counter, he discovers other birthday cards for sons with a lot more flowery sentiments than any of the ones he ever got, as younger Andy remembers, a reminder of all the descriptions his family apparently don't connect to him – *the cards left behind*. All of this is plenty of grist for the mill for Dr. K. Choosing cards for parents whose birthdays are just two days apart is especially challenging. The first card is still lying around the house when the second card gets there; still fresh in their minds, they could compare. Does "To a Loving Mom" sound less appreciative or more appreciative than "To a Great Dad"? And how does Andy compete with his twin sister's cards? Ultimately hoping they'll appreciate the joke, and that it makes them feel young again instead of pre-eulogized with mawkishness that fixates on their scary big numbers, Andy does THE OPPOSITE of sending his folks flowery cards and gives them gag cards – for 8 and 9-year-olds, with their second digits (a 5 for Mom, a 0 for Dad) scrawled in... "Hey 85-year-old, have a hop-hop-hoppy birthday!" They wind up not too hop-hop-hoppy about it. By episode's end, Andy's good intentions help relay his love better than a mushy card ever could.

Amazing Tattoo

Doug's latest too young girlfriend (in Andy's opinion, not Doug's) called the movie "amazing," the pizza "amazing," the gum "amazing" and Judaism "amazing." Either she thinks the latest superhero movie, thin crust, and

Cinnamint are replete with the wisdom of the ages, or thinks Andy's cultural identity is overhyped, cheesy and loses its flavor after chewing on it for a while! Meanwhile, Doug is picking up the "amazing" habit from being around her. Andy tries to get them to stop overusing "amazing" by calling things that are THE OPPOSITE of amazing "amazing," to hopefully wean them off the word. "That garbage is amazing." "That ingrown hair is amazing." Younger Andy pushes older Andy to reintroduce a glowing adjective from their youth – "groovy." Andy doesn't ever remember using that word and he certainly wouldn't feel 'groovy' using it now. Younger Andy: "Okay, how about 'neat'?" Remembering that one, Andy tries to sprinkle it back into public discourse with less than 'amazing' results. Meanwhile Doug's thinking of getting a tattoo to match his girlfriend's. Andy, never having warmed up to "body graffiti," tries to talk Doug out of it. But Andy warily decides to do THE OPPOSITE and go for a tattoo as well, thinking it might make Ashley and Zach connect with him more. Which tattoo captures a picky guy like Andy, who changes his screensaver after a week? Plus, he has good genes. He could be living with this thing for another forty years; this could be his longest relationship. Not if the tattoo "artist" decides Andy's not ready for this type of commitment.

Cell Mate

Andy is kidded by Doug and others for being the last person in L.A. without a smartphone. He only uses his dumb cell phone for emergencies, hasn't even memorized his cell number. He's embarrassed leaving "cell phone number" blank on applications. Embarrassed telling women his cell is "broken," that his social life and lack of going outside don't justify another monthly nut, what with his continuing underemployment. Taking a page from his niece and nephew in-law's slavishness to technology, he decides to do THE OPPOSITE, and not only buy the very latest model, but now flaunt his cell phone use in front of others – something he used to resent when others turned elevators into their own private phone booths while he stood there feeling like an eavesdropper. Now that his life is more centered on his phone, he realizes his smartphone isn't smart enough to come up with anybody to talk to! The numbers he transferred from his landline directory are of people he's long since lost touch with. That's the problem with getting older – not maintaining friendships as easily. His goal... to do THE OPPOSITE and make a new friend worthy of replacing with the number of a friend he hasn't talked to for over ten years. How does a sixty-year-old make a new friend? (Borrowing from an earlier *Seinfeld* story pitch:) He ultimately comes to prefer the audio portion of their relationship to in-person encounters. Over the phone, the "friend's" animated and friendly. In person, there's a disconnect. Could it be Andy sounds like an "Andy" but looks like... a "Todd?" Meanwhile, like the rest of society, he's becoming hooked on his cell, the tiny picture at the expense of the big picture – life and the world around him. Ashley and Zach, of all people, help Andy do THE OPPOSITE and break him of his new habit.

Honeymoon Photos

While visiting his folks, Andy stumbles upon some of their old honeymoon photos buried in a drawer which (we infer) show them naked in bed. Afterwards, the slightest display of affection between them makes him squirm, and he can't tell them why. For over fifty years he's done a very good job of not being able to picture his parents having sex. Now he can't picture anything else, which negatively impacts his own sex life, such as it is. (One other thing that gnaws at him. Who the heck took the pictures?) As Dr. K probes into why the photo discovery is causing Andy duress, he suggests talking to his folks about it. Andy ultimately realizes if they knew he saw their pictures, they'd be embarrassed. Then everything would be back to normal. Then when Andy thinks of his parents and sex, he won't picture them liking it. He'll picture them being humiliated by it. To know our parents are embarrassed by sex is what we all need to perpetuate the species, which is why he winds up doing THE OPPOSITE of feeling weird about it and goes out of his way to talk about the pictures, hopefully making *them* feel weird about it.

Not Miserable Enough

Andy realizes he's finally accepted a major component of his life and become less down about being alone. He's not thrilled. Not happy. Not miserable, like Younger Andy reminds him he was when his hormones were all the rage back in college. Basically, Andy's numb, but used to it. Ironically, he needs help from Dr. K to get him to do THE OPPOSITE of feeling okay, and again feel miserable enough about feeling alone to motivate himself to do something about it.

Ex Marks the Spot

Andy meets a beautiful divorcee he badly wants to impress. But in the course of getting to know her, he learns that the many character flaws her ex had (which led to her leaving him) are identical to those in Andy. Andy has a lot of faking to do. When he doesn't exactly feel all warm inside about the fact she's starting to like a guy he's making up, Andy decides to do THE OPPOSITE and play up all his faults, especially the ones that resemble her ex. The unexpected outcome – she falls for Andy more than ever. (Smart women, foolish choices – why she chose her first husband, flaws and all.) Fearing that he too could be a divorce waiting to happen, Andy now must figure out THE OPPOSITE of THE OPPOSITE to help wean her off him.

The Good Fight

Andy realizes he's never had a relationship last long enough to where it's survived a fight and grown stronger afterwards. It's usually more superficial and just peters out before the therapeutic cleansing/bloodletting begins. His goal: to do THE OPPOSITE and pick a fight with Ellie, a new woman he likes. And survive it.

The Good Woman

Andy meets a woman he fears is too good a person, opening a can of worms about his own relative self-worth, as far as Dr. K is concerned. Meanwhile, if Andy doesn't find some flaws in this woman soon, it'll be over sooner than later. To "help," taking a page from Andy's goal of doing THE OPPOSITE, Doug tries to show she's all too human by *temporarily* being THE OPPOSITE of a good friend – as he tries getting her to cheat on Andy and go out with *him*.

Other 180s...

- Doing the opposite of avoiding nepotism, Andy fosters fake nepotism and tries subtly guilt-tripping successful people named "Cowan" into throwing him work by making them think they're related to him, whether they are or not.

- Doing the opposite of dreaming big, Andy notices a career cashier laughing. Why is she so happy? She has no big dreams that can wind up biting her on the ass, that's why. Time for Andy to embrace the mundane too. If a summer job cashiering made him happy once, why not now?

And many more.

Lionsgate TV wrote back...

We loved the originality and the freshness of your voice. There were big laughs and it's pleasantly amusing throughout.

But didn't pull the trigger. Their digital wing (I pitched it as a half-hour and/or for shorter webisodes) wrote back...

It's a really sweet story and I think you're very smart to cast Taryn and George (the YouTubers) as the niece and nephew.

But didn't pull the trigger.

SyFy wrote back...

It was really cool and interesting, totally unique and a great way to explore relationships and people's neuroses.

. . . . .

SyFy was circling my other project at the time – an allegory on modern society at its most neurotic, *Down Under*. Four people meet in the afterlife in what's basically "Hell Lite," a place that resembles earth but is always slightly more annoying. Not constantly oppressive, no references to hell or devils. Just a wee bit worse than we have it here. One of the show's themes: We're all sinners. This was my opportunity to analyze society's ills in a magnified light. . . and the main characters' separate encounters with their own individualized hells, based on specific character flaws from their past lives they need to address and rise above down under in order to move up. Tonally I envisioned *Cheers* meets *Taxi* meets Albert Brooks' *Defending Your Life*. (complete with a Rip Torn type character, the devil's advocate). My own hell lite was generating lots of initial interest in *Down Under* over the years short of closing a deal. Why, I wondered, hadn't a comedy in this arena been snatched up already? In 2016, TV Land announced they would develop a half hour about purgatory that sounded thematically similar.[1] And NBC picked up *The Good Place*, starring Ted Danson and Kristen Bell, who accidentally arrives in a heavenly place and tries to figure out her path towards deserving to be there. The season one finale revealed this "good place" was really hell.

· · · · ·

Comedy Central "liked the writing" in *Opposite Andy* but didn't think it was in "their wheelhouse."

Showtime called it "funny and quite well-written" but was looking to do more "provocative" and "subversive" things for a paying audience.

TV Land passed, "moving in an edgier direction and no longer targeting boomers." I was unfortunately old enough to remember when TV viewers asked, "Anything good on?" Did TV Land's new target demo, "female Gen X'ers with a sweet spot of 35 to 40," wonder: "Anything *edgy* on?"

Steel Wool Entertainment CEO, Kevin Morrow (former president of Live Nation) "loved" and was willing to produce it, and couldn't believe I wasn't "on some island somewhere" after the dues I'd paid. He laughed at my calculation that I'd wandered the Southern California desert five years short of the time Moses wandered his desert. My Commandments should have warned: "Thou Shalt Not Kill Time." Let my people go? Showbiz people were let go all the time.

Kevin strategized about where else to take it and set up a meeting at Sony Pictures' digital platform, Crackle, then the home of Seinfeld's *Comedians in Cars Getting Coffee*. But *Opposite* would prove too challenging for them as far as generating international sales traction. Kevin also tried reconnecting with an old friend, Dan Aykroyd, about playing the sometimes-imaginary shrink, with whom Aykroyd's eccentric qualities as an actor could make a great fit. Short of his reaching him, I have yet to find out if he might remember that phony SNL meeting all those decades ago.

Thom Hinkle, former co-president of Steve Carell's TV production company, was now responsible for original scripted comedy at TBS, a cable network that ran plenty of *Seinfeld* reruns and was eager to cultivate their own watercooler shows. I sensed a refreshingly genuine quality to him in the announcement of his hiring, so I reached out to his office and sent *Opposite Andy*. After reading both the pilot script and second episode outline, it was rewarding to hear that he saw the series as a whole... "loved the writing and unique voice" ... and admired how subtly the opposite hook was applied. He'd stick a pin in it for possibly down the line. I was so eager to develop with a network executive who got it, a dolphin in a sea of sharks.

Not only did he appreciate my continuing to follow up with him, he admitted "the passion doesn't go unnoticed" and that it surprised him how often it was lacking in a lot of pitches he heard that boiled down to tossing out an idea to see what sticks before moving onto the next one. He "enjoyed" and stressed that he never got annoyed at the expression of such enthusiasm, a refreshing demonstration, I found, of the opposite.

Every day he was learning more about how to get things on the air. Equating the challenges as an executive with some of the same he'd had as a producer – he still had to sell "up," to the network president. Now he was at least down the hallway with easier access. The problem was that they didn't buy much, but when they did, they really got behind it. So, it was tricky breaking through, but if it happened, the hope was you'd stay on the air a while. In the end it was all about timing. As the months ticked away and I later met with him at his office, he awaited the freeing up of more development money as well as upper management changes, which left everybody in limbo. Under the new regime headed up by former Fox and NBC entertainment chief, Kevin Reilly, Thom would now report to a new executive VP of original programming. Cancelling all their original returning comedies, the goal was to double their slate of original programming over the next three years in a more "daring" "in-your-face" direction. They also wanted to "age it down" and try to grab the more elusive younger male audience. I thought about the younger characters on *Opposite Andy* they might connect with. Or the seemingly endless recent YouTube comments from younger viewers about "The Opposite" still being one of their favorite episodes. Or the young commenter who cited on the industry website, *Deadline Hollywood*, how *Seinfeld* reruns still connected with him more than many contemporary shows did. I was "daring" to think clever and funny and, yes, Seinfeldian, trumped "in-your-face."

Digging back into development, Thom asked to recirculate the script among the team, promising to get back to me soon on whether it could still work. A few months later he regretfully reported that it was a pass. He "loved its originality and point of view, but couldn't get the entire team behind it," adding that they bought so little.

Another Talk Show!

In 2010, I won myself a tiny victory for writers whose original words often go unheard, while scratching my own talk show itch. Castle Rock allowed me to perform excerpts from my first draft of "The Opposite" on a talk show pilot I hosted, *Another Talk Show! with Andy Cowan*. I played Jerry, and my lead guest played George, none other than Jason Alexander:

2010 – *Another Talk Show! with Andy Cowan*
http://bit.ly/andyandjason

http://bit.ly/andytalkshow

My choice for the title winked at the glut of talk shows, what was certainly on my mind when a young "manager" in Los Angeles suggested I host an hour talk show pilot and he'd help sell it.

His suggestion alone, coupled with his lack of connections, made me internally scoff. I'd found him through a Craigslist ad (red flag #1) in search of clients, and he'd asked to meet me in his Encino office, professing his passion for *Seinfeld*. After he explained how he'd secure the crew and venue, I figured what the hell; it couldn't hurt. He told me he could sell anything and here he was beginning to sell this grizzled guy. Maybe this was my chance to showcase a contemporary but comfortable throwback aimed at multiple generations... something gently hip without being too hip for the room... clever versus edgy... hosted by a self-deprecatingly amiable comedy writer who related with America's struggles, credit card debt, the search for love, and barely coped with the 21st century assault of technology (as his younger female sidekick texted).

I was no longer a kid nor was I a name. But what the hell, I understood talk. First and foremost, I needed some name guests and was thrilled to get Jason on board. He'd recently lost thirty pounds as a Jenny Craig weight loss spokesperson. He was a champion poker player and Magic Castle Best Parlor Magician. And he was willing to don the George glasses and read "The Opposite" first draft passages I sprang on him by "surprise" (which he knew about, but we hadn't rehearsed) after the McSweeney Half a Band, our top-notch four-piece jazz group, kicked in with a bit of the *Seinfeld* theme. In a camera reveal gag earlier in the show regarding the "other half" of the band, we showed we couldn't afford the other musicians, just their instruments lying on the floor.

While I watched the "manager" gather together and address the crew in the months leading up to the show, I began sensing his prior mild-mannered deference switch to slightly unhinged dictator. He became completely unhinged after I gently vetoed his very own metal band as the musical act. Heavy metal wasn't a fit for this show's sensibility; lousy heavy metal wasn't a fit for any show's sensibility! My choice of having Sheila Raye Charles ("Raye Charles" a nice reference to billboard) join her backup singers in a mini-medley of her father's hits was a no-brainer, and the seventy-some audience members cheered their performance.

I connected with shows from the past where the audience sounded respectfully receptive up front, not excessively juiced. At the risk of sounding like the obnoxious professor in *Annie Hall* waxing in the movie line about Marshall McLuhan, I still think TV, and especially late-night TV, is a cool medium. When a studio audience is whooping and hollering at a "party," this party of one in my living room wishes they'd cool it.

So, I advised the warm-up guy...

Let them know we appreciate a hearty response, without overkill to the point where the home viewer thinks electrodes have been attached to their seats.

Nicola McGillicuddy, a friend and my female sidekick, prerecorded the announce, which obliquely poked fun at how we didn't tape specifically in Hollywood, just as Ed McMahon's "From Hollywood!" should have actually been "From Burbank!" ...

From Hollywood, or close enough... It's Another Talk Show... with Andy Cowan!

After she announced the guests and introduced "Another Talk Show host... Andy Cowan!" I waited a beat or so behind the curtain before entering the spotlight, what Johnny used to do.

Swapping my nerves for simulated relaxation, I flew without a net, minus cue cards, into an opening evergreen monologue that wouldn't date the show, leading to the pledge that this talk show would be cutting edge, because I was a cutting-edge guy – the cutting edge of a butter knife. Illustrating my point, I closed with live vocals of an original show theme song, *20th Century Man...*

http://bit.ly/20thcenturyman

I'm a 20th century man
20th century fan
I walk down the street without a handheld device
Laugh out loud instead of typin' LOL twice
Visit a website versus a friend – no dice
I'm the past!

In the opening bit post-monologue, Nicola prepared me for a 21st century attempt at a "virtual date" with a potential Ms. Right who might be watching. Looking into the camera as the band played *Feelings* (to my later annoyance) I held a one-on-one conversation with a hopefully compatible home viewer, for whom we left space to react to my questions...

Andy: Hi ... Nice couch ... What's your name? ... Nice name ... Where are you from? ... Nice town ...

Graphic: IF "PACOIMA"

Andy: (snorting derisively) Nice town.

"IF CASHIER," in answer to my asking, "What do you do?" I tossed in an "interesting" as I nodded and listened a little too long before replying, "I didn't know so much went into rolling quarters." As the date later fell apart, I asked, "*You're* nervous? What do *you* have to be nervous about?" A graphic gave "her" three choices for a response...

A] Virtual Dating a Future Celebrity
B] Virtual Dating a Present Nobody
C] Letting it slip that I took money from the cash register. Whoops.

We couldn't afford a teleprompter, so my sweaty face (conveniently in-character) gaped into that super-close camera lens and luckily timed all the memorized responses without any slip-ups that would have been magnified in close-up. In the middle of the "date," she visited her rest room while I worried with Nicola that the date wasn't going well and moaned, "If only she liked me!" After she "returned" and the audience learned she now liked me enough to want to move in with me, I promised I'd call her sometime and muttered, "If only she didn't like me. There's gotta be something wrong with her... We'll be back with Jason Alexander after this!" My date with the audience seemed to be going reasonably well.

If I'd thought even more about the fact that Jason was waiting backstage during all of this, I would have been even sweatier. Our two long segments together, much of it free-form, thankfully clicked with the crowd. He poked fun at the desk being to the right of the guest, what I reminded him was "the opposite" of a normal talk show layout. I was impressed enough with his thirty-pound weight loss to have channeled my 21st century man and Googled other things that weigh thirty pounds (a young grizzly bear) offering perspective on the feat he'd accomplished. With a recent birthday behind him, I wondered if there were any wishes left unfulfilled when he blows out the candles...

Jason: Well. Angelina Jolie still hasn't gotten a taste of this guy.

Having no clue he'd say that, I told him we may make that happen later. In between his spot and Sheila Raye Charles, I'd planned on telling Nicola how I shoulda done a talk show years ago. How I'm always with the "shouldas." Shoulda invested in Google years ago instead of the Club Club...

Nicola: What's a Club Club?

Andy: An anti-theft device for the anti-theft device on your steering wheel. Seemed like a natural.

Nicola: Then you'd need a Club Club Club.

Andy: I know, it's endless.

I would then ask the audience if anyone else had a "shoulda" to get off their chest. If a non-plant raised his or her hand, I'd let them unload to make it seem off the cuff, and I could always come back with: "I shoulda asked somebody else." Then I went to the pre-chosen plant to gripe about a question once asked of me...

Plant: I was at this cocktail party the other night, and the hostess was this married woman I didn't know. And right away she asks me something I found a tad shallow and obnoxious. And I shoulda said something, but I didn't.

Andy: Okay. Give us the "tad."

Plant: "Do you rent or own?"

Andy: That's more than a tad. Well, to help you move on with your life and relive it the way you shoulda lived it in the first place, playing the part of your obnoxious hostess is our own Nicola McGillicuddy. And playing the part of you with what you shoulda said, welcome... Angelina Jolie!

Musical fanfare. Lights flash. Out comes an Angelina Jolie lookalike. And after my previous scouting of young Asian mothers on the streets of Santa Monica to see if $50 would allow us to borrow their little tykes for walk-ons, "Angie" brought two of her six kids with her.

Nicola: Rent or own?

Angelina: (lifting a kid) Rent.

And off they walked.

It read better on paper than it played. (I shoulda known.) So, I left the "I shoulda" bit on the cutting room floor, save for Angie and the kids' entrance, which dissolved (after post-production) out from my "we may make that happen later" to Jason's Jolie mention, with the graphic...

Show runs long, so we're bumping Angelina Jolie. Impressive, huh?

Jason later zinged my attempt at making a poker face, remarking that I had a small tremble even when nothing's at stake, but that it could work for me. If I didn't at least come back with some kind of retort, I'd risk losing control.

Andy: Hey, it didn't hurt Katharine Hepburn.

His generous reaction was worth it. And in a magic trick segment audience members thought was rehearsed (it wasn't), he asked me to privately calculate a series of numbers before magically guessing the ultimate number. He guessed wrong. As laughter started building, he grabbed my scribblings, retraced my computations, approached the camera against my plea not to show my mistakes, and explained why *I'd* screwed up...

Jason: He wrote 1571. Then I said rearrange the numbers. He writes 7511. That's correct. Then I said subtract the lesser number from the greater number. He gets 211. This is why America is going to shit!

As the audience laughed and applauded, he tore up and tossed my figures into the air while I silently followed the pieces of paper with my eyes as they floated to the floor. After back-and-forth wisecracks, we went to commercial while the audience cheered. Though my mistake felt like a derailing at the time, it injected a little edge into what would have otherwise been a conventional magic spot. It looked like our goal had been to poke fun at the convention.

A decent math student back in school, I tried in post-production to *absolve* America by legitimately explaining the method to my madness, as the letters in this chalk-written lesson unfurled onto a chalkboard into commercial...

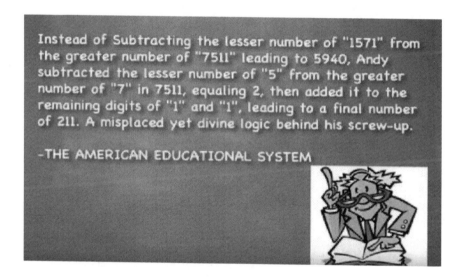

Instead of Subtracting the lesser number of "1571" from the greater number of "7511" leading to 5940, Andy subtracted the lesser number of "5" from the greater number of "7" in 7511, equaling 2, then added it to the remaining digits of "1" and "1", leading to a final number of 211. A misplaced yet divine logic behind his screw-up.

-THE AMERICAN EDUCATIONAL SYSTEM

Hosting, trying to look cool and performing math don't necessarily add up!

Leading into the *Seinfeld* reenactment segment, and calling back to the earlier subject of weight, I asked Jason how much his mailbox weighed *before* the residual checks got there compared to *after*. He conceded that "some people" have bigger residual checks, not being a partner in the show (as was also the case with Julia and Michael).

Andy: Still you've reached a level of success whereby... when you're in the shower with the soap, do you wait till it gets tiny before you throw it away? Or do you just throw it away when it's mid-size and say the hell with it?

Jason: Well, I'm strange. I like to tuck it away under my testicles and just walk away with it.

He poked fun at my initial impression of Jerry. With his own George he pondered, "Is this the voice?" guessing he was doing Woody Allen, whom he's admitted aping back in the early *Seinfeld* episodes. My favorite editing trick in post was undetectable, the best kind. After asking if he could try one of the lukewarm French Fries Jerry had been complaining about at Monk's, Jason grabbed and munched on an imaginary one, then said, "Yeah, I'd send them back." The script called for him to grab and feed himself one imaginary fry, then another, then several at once before telling Jerry he'd send them back. I ultimately cut from the close, to the wide, to the close shot of the same move, importing audience laughs from elsewhere in the show for the second and third manufactured grabs the audience never witnessed.

Following George's opposite epiphany, back at his folks' place (on the couch) the audience laughed after Nicola asked how long he'd been living with them...

Jason: Just... years. And years. This... isn't just temporary.

The closer she edged towards him, the farther he edged away. When she asked him to do something about the lights, he turned them *up*, spotlighting his imagined five o'clock shadow and how she loves it when a man doesn't bother to shave.

Sharing the stage with him was extremely gratifying. I made sure to draw our reenactment to a close on a laugh he earned, thanked him and was doubly honored to watch him point to his script, then me and mouth my name as the band played off to commercial.

With Sheila Raye Charles, I purposely avoided the "that was great" closing musical guest kiss-off that didn't include at least some conversation. After *Hit the Road Jack* and her suggestion I add more swag to my next "virtual date," I resolved to improve my math *and* social skills. She was instantly forthright about the addiction struggles she shared with her father, and how they were the hurdles she needed to jump through to become the woman she was today. Before her rousing *Georgia* finish, I thanked everyone and finally called the audience a word Nicola couldn't possibly get me to utter earlier in the show, the one whose use I reserved, per my vocal lament in 20th *Century Man*, for "awesome" events... *awesome!* Following the credits, as I'd done for the show's opening tease, the closing button returned to a brief video snippet on the phone from '09, attempting flirtatious dialogues with the computerized voices of the automated directory assistance and Sears service tech ladies (four years before Joaquin Phoenix's affair with his operating system in *Her*). The production vanity card below wrapped things up with the signoff, "So short!" the opposite of "So long!" not to mention the length of time it was held before cutting to black.

Alex Schumacher

The challenges in organizing and hosting this monumental undertaking weren't made easier by the steeliness of the young "manager" and his previously chipper girlfriend's cold glares prior to taping. At an especially vulnerable moment, when any show of support for the "star" of the show is vital, it seemed like the guy who was supposed to have my back could have thrown a knife in it. He was either still stewing over his band not making the cut or – as I had already begun to suspect – not of sound mind. The oddly obsequious puppy dog who'd initially requested my "autograph" on his *Seinfeld* book had slowly but surely come down with rabies. His brother, whom he'd chosen as "director," seemed a bit off too – which was also his reaction to my delicately posed question about his inexplicably off-center camera shots of the opening monologue. After later uncovering online a fifteen-year-old news report about a San Fernando Valley father's arrest for allegedly threatening a coach with physical harm for heaping verbal abuse on his teenaged son, I connected the dots in utter disbelief. The son grew up to be my "manager!" I'd hit the lunatic lottery. Maybe they were all chips off the old block/shoulder?

Apprehensive about setting them off in ways I couldn't predict, I stressed as respectfully as possible from day one how important it was for me to see all the footage and help supervise the editing, one of my strong suits. If the shoe were on the other foot, I certainly would have welcomed the experienced guy's contributions. After a slipshod initial pass by the director and his assistant, they suddenly stopped communicating with me altogether and held onto the original footage. How could it have come to this? How did I allow myself to be victimized by miscreants? With my finances less than secure at a time when the great recession was still taking its toll, I was so beholden to the young crew supposedly willing and eager for the experience that I unfortunately let them take advantage of me. One of my monologue jokes about past (but still present) credit card debt hinted at my lack of F.U. money...

Do you see in the credit card bills now – the government basically makes them spell out how old you'll be by the time you pay off the entire balance, if you just pay off the minimums every month? I was so happy about that. I had no idea I'd live to 140.

I would awaken in the middle of the night, literally catching my breath, reliving the horror behind all this effort now possibly being for naught. Even tracking down the director's co-worker at their day job workplace intercom and threatening to go to their boss didn't work. Until Brad Shairson, an investment banker/good guy who'd welcomed a dip in the showbiz pool and helped finance other parts of the show, offered up another thousand-dollar life raft. The thugs hadn't ever implied it was a matter of money before, but they grabbed it. And so, as if on a late-night drug run, a menacing enough looking buddy and I met them on a dark San Fernando Valley street corner, exchanged the dough for the show, and never laid eyes on them again. I then started from scratch on post-production my way. The easiest creative decision was axing their names from the credits.

Ray Richmond, then with *Deadline Hollywood*, kindly emailed me after attending the taping...

Much more when you have a chance to talk. But it was hugely impressive, wonderful, well-done all around. Jason was unbelievably generous and funny and charming and energetic. Sheila Raye Charles was stirring and magnificent. You were quick and endearing and funny and slick. Oh my God, was I impressed. Call me for more.

I incorporated some of his later comments into the pitch package...

It wasn't traditionally edgy. In its own way, it mocked edgy shows in a very clever way, which actually made it edgy. It was self-deprecatingly Seinfeldian and retro, hip without being smug and full of itself. It was also genuinely funny. The opposite of a talk show that hits all the typical comedy targets the others do, helmed by an obvious pro and broadcaster with a classic talk as well as classic comedy background. This is an untraditional 'everything old is new again' kind of show that can wear well over the long haul.

Part of the pitch also culled from this unexpected and much appreciated email from Michael Harrison, publisher of the trade publication for talk media industries, *Talkers*...

Just watched the whole thing (in a hotel room on a Saturday night so it kept me company). Congratulations on creating a really cool hour of TV. I am most impressed with the show and especially with YOU! Let's catch up on the phone next week. The show gave me a number of ideas regarding this 20th century man concept that you pull off so well. Again, congrats on a helluva production. I know how difficult it is to pull off a thing like that from scratch. And thank you for sending it to me. It made my night!

As the show developed, I could try to learn a little from my 21st century sidekick's generation, while hoping she'd learn a tidbit from mine. I did hope at least one exec would figure entertainment talk shows didn't all have to lust for the same young eyeballs (who weren't watching TV as much as older demos anyway). NBC had recently researched the "alpha boomers," 55-64, and found them still open to trying new products. Wouldn't programmers want to reach this sizable audience with huge discretionary incomes, who might connect with a kind of talk show they grew up with and classic guest stars who had something to talk about?

I peddled it on my own, forwarding the links through whichever agent was "representing" me at the time. Lionsgate thought it was "really funny," but talk formats weren't in their wheelhouse. The TV Guide Channel "really liked it" and kept the carrot dangling over multiple years before changing their focus and name. An exec at 20th Television, the syndication arm of 20th Century Fox Television, wrote back...

It's funny and has great energy (and as much as I REALLY enjoyed what I saw, being a fan) it unfortunately isn't quite what we're in the market for right now, so we're respectfully passing. Let me check and see if your talk show is something that the head of alternative would be interested in. Do you mind sending me material for that?

Did I mind laying more pipe for the pipe dream? Hell no! Though their alternative wing was no longer seeking talk shows, they dangled another carrot...

They think you'd maybe be great on a comedy panel for one of their shows in development and will keep you in mind as they move forward.

I had my doubts as to anyone ever being kept in mind for anything an executive said they'd keep him in mind for, but it beat the undeservedly cheery, "Thanks for thinking of us!" I followed up to illustrate I was still thinking of them. VH1 wrote, "It is so funny but unfortunately not a fit for VH1 at this time." Upon their Jenny McCarthy talk show pickup two months later, they explained...

We've been searching for our Chelsea Handler and finally struck gold with Jenny. Now we're focusing all our efforts on her and don't want to dilute the brand with another talk show before it has a chance to get proper traction on-air.

Fifteen episodes in, the gold rush ended, and Jenny left for a short stint with *The View*, after which VH1 invited me to send over more female-oriented programming if I had anything.

I sent the show to my contact at Comedy Central with this caveat...

No, I'm not a kid. Yes, it's aimed at multiple generations. Setting aside that it may not scream Comedy Central, take a page from "the opposite" (as Jason Alexander and I do on the show) do the opposite of instantly pass, and take a peek, or not – the opposite of taking a peek – so either way you're covered. Enough people who aren't related to me say the show's funny. As for those who are related, they were never comfortable expressing their emotions. No wonder I need approval from strangers.

They wrote back...

Cool stuff, Andy. Talk genre is something we're not looking for. Hope all is well.

When he was CBS VP of Late Night during my stint with *The Pat Sajak Show*, Rod Perth responded to my projects with a note that included: "You have an interesting style on camera and one that I would encourage you to pursue. Who knows, there may be a fit with us in the future." Twenty years later as NATPE (National Association of Television Program Executives) CEO, he expressed similar sentiments about *Another Talk Show!* ...

You've got a real sort of interesting television presence. I don't know how to advise you; I almost feel like you should do some cool thing on NPR. There's a kind of NPRish sensibility to it and to you as well, and that's a compliment. There's some amazing talent on NPR.

Associated Television International (producers of Marie Osmond's talk show) volunteered...

I'm gonna think of ideas for you. I think you're interesting. I like what you're doing. I just can't advance it here.

The executive producer of *Cops* said it was "different" and "interesting," but that he'd have a tough time selling it. Maybe it was because I couldn't get arrested in this town?

Like *Talker* publisher Michael Harrison, I wish NBC's longtime late-night executive (and early *Seinfeld* champion when it needed one) had been stuck in a hotel with nothing better to do. Maybe then he might have watched the whole show. Rick Ludwin struck me in interviews as the adult in the room, one of the reasons I thought he might connect with it somehow...

With your having granted life to Seinfeld [on which I was a staff writer] and your long imprint on the talk universe, I couldn't think of anyone I'd rather ask, for no other end goal than your giving it a peek. [Also thought you might appreciate the reenactment of scenes from my first draft of "The Opposite" with Jason as George and yours truly as Jerry.] Talk has been in my DNA ever since my first Hollywood job as a segment producer/writer/ performer on The Merv Griffin Show during the '80s and growing up glued to Carson.

I added this post-script about something I'd later stop referencing after a producer friend suggested I was better off making them think the "quirk" was a stylistic choice...

The "director" shot the monologue from the side rather than center stage, a quirk in a pilot not meant for broadcast. Nevertheless, I've been pleased with the responses so far.

Best wishes,

Andy Cowan

As in the blogosphere of endless opinions (Neil Armstrong's one big step on YouTube is replete with thumbs down. Landing on the moon wasn't enough for these people) our phone conversation two weeks later reinforced how verdicts can run the gamut...

RL: I didn't see every minute of your show, but I saw some of it. And I'm gonna be candid with you, because I don't know any other way to be. Obviously, you're a talented person and a witty person and a funny person, but there is, to borrow a phrase from Simon Cowell, an X factor, and it's tougher than it appears, even for industry veterans. Obviously, many have tried. This is a steep mountain to try to climb. I'm sorry to be blunt, but you asked me to take a look. You know (Seinfeld writer) Spike Feresten, I know Spike Feresten. Spike tried this, and it's tougher than it looks.

Apart from Rick's doing anything with it, I had deep down only hoped for a little validation. Disappointed if not deflated, I calmly replied I'd worked on talk shows for many years (ABC's *Into the Night* as well as Sajak's and Merv's) and was aware of the challenges, thanked him for taking a look and wished him luck in his transition to consulting for NBC. In 2006, I'd been interviewed as a potential writer for Feresten's new Fox Network weekly talk show. Its tone seemed to replicate a hip detached vibe that ran counter to my goal on *Another Talk Show.* Re: the eventually cancelled *X Factor,* I guess that too was missing an X factor!

I'm still proud of what we accomplished in one show, and the remarks from other execs and the audience who'd been there. Had an opportunity presented itself to further settle in, who knows what we could have achieved under saner circumstances? Factoring in the care, sweat, energy, music, star power, new light on *Seinfeld,* traumas and angst, as of this writing it's still millions short of going viral. Next time I'll let a young Swedish guy playing video games host.[1] In the meantime, I'll let this comment from a complete stranger on YouTube make Rick's a wash...

Loved every minute! Great show!

•   •   •   •   •

Long before my talk show, I was a staff writer on *My Talk Show.* A stripped five night a week comedy/talk hybrid from SCTV Productions and Imagine Entertainment (on which *Sex and the City* writer and producer/director of the film adaptations, Michael Patrick King, was also on staff) it first starred the reliably relatable Cynthia Stephenson (later Bob Newhart's daughter on *George & Leo*) as Jennifer Bass, a small-town hostess whose public access show led to a syndicated talk show out of her living room. This was 1990-'91, foreshadowing when YouTube would double down on Shakespeare's idiom that all the world's a stage. She'd interact, largely scripted, with the neighborhood characters. Partially off script, she'd interview genuine celebrities who showed up in the fictitious Wisconsin town and awaited their segments in her bedroom "greenroom," while a real audience in her "garage" took it all in and occasionally participated in the show. Cynthia's earnest approach to the role was both offbeat and endearing.

In '86, my own public access comedy talk show (about single life) led to an ad in the showbiz bible, *Variety.* Okay, my manager, Tracy Columbus, and I placed it there. But we were pleased enough with this particular episode to figure it was worth it. Jay Leno called to congratulate me after spotting the mention. My featured guest was someone I'd helped land on the Griffin show who later became a friend, *Cathy* comic strip cartoonist Cathy Guisewite.

Tonight, the comedy talk show that's too good for public access. Boy, how's that for cocky? Andy Cowan's L.A. Singles, with special guest, Cathy Guisewite. And CATHY'S first TV interview! 9 to 9:30 P.M. Group W Cable. Channel 3.

Before I interviewed her onstage, she provided her life-sized comic alter ego's voice offstage when I asked whether she ever felt like having a fling with another comic strip character...

Cathy: Opus, the penguin in Bloom County.

Who knew Cathy was so kinky?

Tooning In

Cathy encouraged my own comic strip pursuit (*Howie*) at the time, what had been my earliest creative outlet as a kid. I've more recently partially scratched that itch in nearly 300 panels I've written for the ingenious Dan Piraro and his strip, *Bizarro*, the winner of three consecutive National Cartoonists Society "Best Cartoon Panel" awards, syndicated in over 350 newspapers worldwide through King Features. (Pittsburgh cartoonist, Wayno, took over the weekday panels in January 2018.)

Dan Piraro / Andy Cowan

When pitching Dan, I relayed the gag along with the imagined characters, motivation and "staging." In a way, I'm the writer/casting director/producer. He's the art/ casting director/ writer-executive producer/ director/ actor. And magician.

Dan Piraro / Andy Cowan

I was a magician as a kid. My final trick made a toddler cry at a birthday party from the blood-red paint-drenched saw I used to separate the broom-handles-for-legs from my female assistant scrunched into a box. Caring more about her kid than my illusion, his mother leaped up, ripped apart and destroyed my gear, and pacified the squirt with the realization I hadn't impaled anybody after all.

With my mom his astute sounding board, my dad scratched his own itches penning freelance articles and cartoons, a creative respite from my grandfather's luggage manufacturing business he and his brother would eventually oversee. As a young soldier during World War II, he drew panels for the military newspaper, *Stars and Stripes.*

Ray Cowan

"Mom says trim it light on top. Pop says you're all wet about Truman."

He even translated French and Spanish for the FBI. But he could never quite understand why the interpreters of what America should watch didn't buy his game show idea I'd occasionally dust off and pitch around town to parties periodically interested enough to take a meeting. Showbiz – the never-ending battle!

My father's timeless mugshot notwithstanding, styles inevitably move on. In a '95 *Seinfeld* episode, "The Kiss Hello," written by Peter Mehlman, a guest character played by Wendie Malick sported a passé hairstyle the others mocked. I submitted this potential Jerry stand-up bit for the show opening, thematically borrowing from my George story about poking fun at his lady friend's childhood pictures...

In the present day here and now, we're all under the illusion that we couldn't possibly be cooler. That's what contemporary society is all about. Whereas you spot old pictures of yourself from '75 – "Check out those goofy clothes, that goofy hair. I look like an idiot!" The scary thing is – we're idiots now, but it won't be till 2015 when we find out.

Eight years short of 2015, I resuscitated the joke while occasionally ghostwriting for Brian Crane's Washington Post Writers Group comic strip, *Pickles*...

Pickles © Brian Crane, dist. by The Washington Post Writers Group. Used with permission

Three years later, I reworked it for this *Bizarro*...

Dan Piraro / Andy Cowan

In "The Cartoon," a *Seinfeld* final season episode written by *The New Yorker* cartoonist, Bruce Eric Kaplan, Elaine tries in vain to understand why a cartoon in the magazine renowned for its cartoons was funny. Short of planting our flag there as of this writing, I and versatile artist Dan McConnell have attempted the trek up that Mount Everest dozens of times.

Accounting Today / Dan McConnell / Andy Cowan

"If there's one thing I won't tolerate, it's a yes man. Understood?"

Dan McConnell / Andy Cowan

"Should we celebrate the 4th of July together, or Independence Day apart?"

Dan McConnell / Andy Cowan

"It's your wife. She wants to know when you're coming back to the table."

Amish-ish

Dan McConnell / Andy Cowan

"We may not worry about dying, but they don't worry about thunder."

The opposite:

Dan McConnell / Andy Cowan

"Is this worse? Or is this worse?"

"I see our time is up."

Dan McConnell / Andy Cowan

"Not till we clear the mistletoe."

"I dreamt of you last night. Playing your part was Scarlett Johansson."

I realized the dream of landing a gag in their 2012 election issue, this one illustrated by their frequent contributing artist, Harry Bliss. (The magazine added "face it," which I thought was unnecessary.)

The New Yorker / Harry Bliss / Andy Cowan

"Face it – Nothing gets done in an election year."

My election year pitch followed initial election material they requested as an "audition," some of which wound up accompanying an illustrated feature in their annual cartoon issue, for which I was thanked for my "advice" but not credited nor compensated. (Even Craigslist "no-pay gigs" offer credit!) Still it was a kick to penetrate their inner sanctum and later milk the sacred cow in this *Bizarro* gag...

Dan Piraro / Andy Cowan

Getting turned down by *The New Yorker* happens to the best of them, including Harry Bliss. But at least he can run the also-rans in his own Tribune Media Services syndicated comic panel, *Bliss,* as he did with about a dozen of mine. As the blind date who overused the below pet expression told me more than once, it's all good!

Harry Bliss / Andy Cowan

Harry Bliss / Andy Cowan

"Your '94 Nissan wants you to know she's fine."

Harry Bliss / Andy Cowan

"I used to dream of owning a pool. Now I dream of marginal friends not showing up uninvited."

The opposite snuck its way into these...

"Pride is my middle name – which, ironically, makes me ashamed."

Harry Bliss / Andy Cowan

"Are you suggesting that the rest of the menu isn't special?"

Obama's the opposite – a lefty. (*Left-underlined handed!*)

Some two dozen *Bizarro* panels also tapped into the opposite, whether it was the reminiscing grandmother of the peeved incredible shrinking man, raising her hand high above his tiny body: "I can remember when you were THIS tall!" Or the "seeing eye man" correcting a dog wearing sunglasses as the pooch sniffed another dog's face: "Other end." Or the housewife explaining how her voodoo doll screamed every time her ex went to the acupuncturist. Or the gift-giving officemate thanking his co-worker for not breeding on Never-Gonna-Be-A-Father's-Day. Or the wife admitting to her miffed husband that yes, she cheated on him with his twin brother, but she *thought* she was cheating on his twin brother with *him*. Or a briefcase-toting lion coming home from a hard day's work moaning to his wife, "It's a city out there." Or the rhino wife complaining to her rhino husband near the den wall featuring a mounted hunter's head: "*He* didn't have a horn. You call that fair?" Or the kid carrying his alligator science project informing his teacher, "My homework ate my dog." Or the woman spelling out that her date was the opposite of what she was looking for – "His car was old, and his wine was new."

Dan Piraro / Andy Cowan

. . . . .

I first played with "the opposite" theme in "High on Nothing," a late '70s stand-up routine during the waning hippy days about two bored druggies...

Hippy 1: What do you feel like doin' tonight? Pot?

Hippy 2: Nah.

H1: Hash?

H2: Nah.

H1: Ludes?

H2: Nah.

H1: Ripple?

H2: Nothing! Tonight... we're doing <u>nothing</u>!

H1: (Beat) Cool. Haven't done that in years. (Giggling) This is light-duty, man.

H2: I'm not quite... misunderstanding what you're saying.

H1: How long has it been since we decided to do nothing?

H2: Two minutes.

H1: Wow! It <u>seems</u> like two minutes.

H2: Far in... I'm starting to see ... single.

. . . . .

In 2013, Dan McConnell and I hoped 30 *Opposites* would attract, a comic strip single panel package we developed for Amy Lago at the Washington Post Writers Group, previously a long-serving editor for Charles Schulz' *Peanuts* at United Features. Another package we sent her was called *Head Trips*, in which you'd "hear" at least one of the characters' private thoughts. She cited the gags she liked most in each, and we eventually focused on *Head Trips*, adapting such *Opposites* as...

Dan McConnell / Andy Cowan

Dan McConnell / Andy Cowan

Dan McConnell / Andy Cowan

Dan McConnell / Andy Cowan

Dan McConnell / Andy Cowan

Dan McConnell / Andy Cowan

Dan McConnell / Andy Cowan

Liking everything from our latest batch, Amy kept her door open with continued encouragement, while acknowledging that newspapers are struggling, and editors rarely want to change their lineups of comics.

Sometimes the art needs changing. With *Reader's Digest* in need of military cartoons, Dan McConnell sent me this initial sample off a gag pitch of mine...

"Welcome to basic training."

I'd pictured the *opposite* of a gentle approach to potty training, a commanding uniformed guy towering over a slightly bewildered kid.

Reader's Digest / Dan McConnell / Andy Cowan

"Welcome to basic training."

Attention! ... to details landed Dan's fixes in our first of multiple *Reader's Digest* cartoons in 2016. All's wel [sic]!

"That's an order!"

The same year, our work periodically returned across the pond to *Prospect*, what they declare is "Britain's leading monthly current affairs magazine, featuring the best writing by some of the deepest and most influential thinkers in Britain and the world." In this country I can't even influence my neighbor's dog to stop yapping. Shared language aside, it's nice when your humor can translate to another culture and fun imagining readers processing the captions with British accents.

Prospect / Dan McConnell / Andy Cowan

"*Honey, the deal was 'til death us do part'.*"

"*If you let me change everything about you, I'll love you just the way you are.*"

Prospect / Dan McConnell / Andy Cowan

In 2007, I had a premonition that the late, great *Meet the Press* moderator, Tim Russert, might appreciate this *Bizarro* gag I pitched Dan Piraro...

Dan Piraro / Andy Cowan

After he drew it up, I emailed it to NBC in Washington, holding out hope that Russert might display it on the show. I soon received an email from his wife, award-winning journalist, Maureen Orth, requesting an original signed copy suitable for framing to give Tim for Christmas. With only one *MTP* left before the holiday break, his best friend reported that he loved it and would show it at the end of the broadcast the following morning, what turned out to be his final Christmas show.

TR: Well, you know, Meet the Press has not been spared this Christmas season by the funny papers...

After showing the cartoon and our names, future *Meet the Press* moderator Chuck Todd inquired...

CT: So you didn't get a red bike?

TR: No, I never got the red bike. But I put it up on the screen for fat boy to remind him. He better show this year.[1]

Another King Features comic I've had fun guest-writing (over forty panels as of this writing) is Hilary Price's whimsical *Rhymes with Orange*. As in *The New Yorker* Bliss cartoon, this one provided yet another rationale for not finishing the housework...

Hilary Price / Andy Cowan

Andy Cowan

The only time I wrote for Merv's *Jeopardy* ...

Hilary Price / Andy Cowan

337

Hilary Price / Andy Cowan

Hilary Price / Andy Cowan

Hilary Price / Andy Cowan

As the outside world grew more glued to their electronic devices, TV screens grew bigger and movie screens grew tinier, I wondered – why even go out? Nobody's kicking the back of my couch. *Inside Al*, yet another comic strip run up the flagpole in 2011, represented the ultimate cocooner and lover of the great *in*doors, hermetically sealed from human interaction... till his buddy, Benny, lover of mixing it up in the great *outdoors* – the opposite – once again surfaced to push Al out of his apartment. (My '07 narration of an Insight Media DVD comprehensive tour of Los Angeles was another case where the sound of my so-called expertise belied my own preferences... in this case, for the comforts of my inner sanctum![2])

Al tried to relate with the user-hostile outside world as it contrasted with his user-friendly inside one. Inside he had lasting relationships with (as in *Howie*) Sid, his equally housebound plant and lone dependent who knew him all too well... His family of visitors on his widescreen who offered their advice, solicited or not, after watching *him*... STiVo (his TiVo) who studied Al's viewing habits (before smart TVs began tracking them for advertisers) and drew strange conclusions as to what else he might enjoy watching... His fellow surfers on the web, whose handles in chat rooms and pictures on dating sites transformed Al's computer monitor into their alleged alter egos... His voicemail secretary and other virtual assistants in his life, who tended to his needs with efficiency (also pre-*Her*) minus the heart.

After able artist Brandon Fall "auditioned" the first Al and Benny, it was fun to don my "casting director" hat again and discover the right "actors," based on the characters I'd developed with initial artist, Alex Schumacher, who was no longer available.

I think Benny's eyebrows are too prominent. Between his sweatband and his eyebrows, it's very busy on that part of his face. Maybe simple lines vs. full brows? Al's eyebrows need trimming too. He looks angrier with bold eyebrows. There was an affable quality about him in the previous version that's harder to grasp here. Also, his reaction to Benny's "You need to get out" doesn't work for me. Instead of "What???!" or "Huhh?!" it should be subtler. He's heard Benny tell him this before, it's nothing new.

Brandon Fall / Andy Cowan

Tooning In

Brandon Fall / Andy Cowan

Brandon Fall / Andy Cowan

Before the Donald threw his cap into the ring...

Foreshadowing the online sales boom, if not the DVD decline!

Visiting a chain drugstore is a lot less efficient than shopping online. And I always wondered why callers got preferential treatment...

Brandon Fall / Andy Cowan

Al sacrificed a smartphone he could take outside for the computer he stayed anchored to at home...

Brandon Fall / Andy Cowan

I'd ventured outside enough to pitch *Inside Al* as an animated TV show years earlier. In 2002, the head of development at Film Roman, animators of *The Simpsons* and *The King of the Hill*, asked to hold onto it while she scoped out possibilities there. I later heard back...

> *Initially when you pitched this as an animated project, I responded positively, but I thought (and still think) that it's a stronger project as live action with CGI (computer-generated imagery). That said, if you feel strongly about it as an animated project, who am I to tell you as the creator how to sell this thing? Now, I actually AM developing live action, but since I haven't yet received my budget for this year, I really can't have an informed conversation about what I'm buying, animation or live action. I plan to have that conversation (pending the confirmation from my CEO!) in the next week or so. I'd like you to check back with me in a couple of weeks, but if you'd prefer to move on, please do so without hard feelings.*

Live action, animation, CGI, shadow puppets. I'd take anything! Several months later, she passed but, according to my agent, "loved" me and wanted to keep the door open.

Another executive at the Cartoon Network liked it "a lot," ran it by her supervisor twice but couldn't get him on board, speculating that he didn't respond to pitches about single guys because he was one. She also guessed it was probably too smart for their network. Eric Poticha at Jim Henson's company said it was a "terrific idea, very funny" but politically incorrect. He thought the TV show, *Monk*, was safer (in which Tony Shalhoub's character suffered from extreme OCD and the fear of crowds), while agoraphobes might get mad at this one and send letters. He laughed at my reaction: "Yeah, but they won't leave their houses to mail them."

Eric was "crazy about" another Seinfeldian half hour of mine, *Crumbs* (not to be confused with an ABC series picked up later bearing its name) and interested Brian and Lisa Henson in its tone for a potential animated project. Ultimately their costly new process, a la *The Polar Express* movie, was deemed too elaborate for *Crumbs'* minimalist and edgier sensibilities. Poticha also admitted their company wasn't enough to walk into a network and sell a half-hour prime time sitcom. It was about their hopefully connecting via their reps with showrunners who had their own concepts I liked – and bringing me on as a writer with Henson producing. Eric later asked me to adapt Lisa's notions about a well-known nursery rhyme into an irreverent *Family Guy* type project for young adults. Ultimately losing interest in pitching it, she told him mine was the best take she'd read and I'd be the go-to guy if they ever resuscitated the thing. Still later, I was in the running to help write their late night weekly puppet talk show pilot for TBS. Till they decided not to hire a writer and Brian, its creator, tackled what would ultimately become an improvisational web series.

Evening Stew

In a precursor to Kickstarter, a group of interested financiers coalesced around another passion project of mine in '96, the comedy magazine TV pilot, *Evening Stew*. It was spearheaded by suburban Philadelphia judge, Gary Silow, one of the cool kids back at Abington High School, to whom I'd regularly offered gum in hopes of a little coolness by association. During a break from *Seinfeld* a quarter century later at our high school reunion, Gary gave *me* something to chew on – an offer to help fund a creative project of my choosing, what turned into a jam-packed "stew" of departments, written and hosted by yours truly and produced with Arthur Insana.

Each week *Stew* would be based at a "world-class arena" previously closed to comedy. In the pilot, it was the White House lawn, where the fence slid open to layers of grass strips and fake trees (gently swaying courtesy of off-camera interns) seamlessly blending into the White House. That iconic image was captured from a then cutting-edge upside-down camera that somehow spit back the right-side up White House in a more faithful simulation than green screen. Visual layers included a waving flag, flying bird, and our own roaming secret service agents scouting activity from the ground and balconies. We even had a security agent tackle an intruder trespassing onto the lawn behind me mid-show, which I was too oblivious to notice. Throw in a delivery boy riding his bike by the front fence, heaving a ton of newspapers my way. (When you're the president, you read a lot of papers.) Finally, in front of a beautifully lit nighttime virtual White House at the end of the show and an actual band, I thank the president for allowing us on his lawn, prompting a lawn sprinkler to drench me with real water before my turn and reaction to the post-production window light effect: "All right, all right, we're goin'!"

Future episodes would gather at the Great Wall of China, Buckingham Palace, Red Square in Moscow, or even the Pope's antechamber at the Vatican. We pictured a weekly half-hour comedy magazine show that was smart, silly, odd and surreal, conjuring up a comedic *Twilight Zone*, with over a dozen, repeatable weekly departments.

With a jazzy original theme song Steve Crum created off my goal to replicate the feel of Nelson Riddle's classic theme from *Route 66*, and a wooden ladle diving into a world globe that swirled into a kettle of stew (a then cutting-edge computer effect) vegetable letters would form the names of each department as they slid off a cutting board (speaking of cutting edge) into the stew...

Front Burner – In this week's weekly exposé I confront a nodding shrink (another nod to therapy, and *60 Minutes*) who admits the nodding is a "crock" and he doesn't listen to his patients, who still think he's helping them.

Guy vs. Guy – Siskel & Ebert-type critics review everything but movies (twenty years before the Comedy Central Show, *Review*). Here they weigh in on restroom door symbols.

Celebrity Perks – Normal activities that nobodies experience – choosing between paper or plastic (the latter now outlawed in many supermarkets) – contrast with the special treatment celebrities enjoy. Among the "celebs" for the pilot, we hired a Michael Jackson impersonator as eccentric as his role model, arriving in full makeup with his own entourage before deciding upon silk vs. satin at the VIP checkout aisle we dummied up in a small supermarket afterhours.

Never-interviewed-guest – In a world exclusive, I interview the perfect woman. In another first, some half a dozen girl-next-door types who conjured up perfection to my eyes and ears read for the part in my apartment! The neighbors next door who watched them come and go might wonder what happened to my social life in the decades since. Among those we liked was one whose brief bio included "belching on cue" among her "special talents" and my hand-scrawled note sizing up her audition: "Interesting comedy instincts." Less than five years later, Cheryl Hines would go on to star as Larry David's wife on *Curb Your Enthusiasm*. As good as Cheryl was, actress Sandy Plute invoked the innocence I'd imagined for "Ms. Kathy Wright," someone the camera wound up loving even more than I did. I would toss her questions and react to thin air, before later merging her separately shot replies on a monitor we'd insert onto a giant steaming (stew) kettle effect on the White House lawn.

Andy: Well, Ms. Wright... it's nice to finally meet you.

KW: It's nice to finally meet you, Andy.

Andy: So. You're the "perfect woman." I'm not sure someone who thinks so highly of herself that she calls herself the perfect woman would necessarily be the perfect woman in my book... (falling under her spell) ... Mind you, I'm not sure.

KW: You're absolutely right, Andy. I apologize for being so full of myself. Maybe she was perfect!

Andy: That's OK. If you were full of somebody else, they wouldn't fit.

KW: (laughing endlessly) That is so clever.

Andy: (starting to melt) So what's your story?

KW: Well, I'm 35, I graduated from the University of Wisconsin. But enough about me, Andy, I'm much more interested in you.

Andy: I appreciate your interest, but I don't want to waste this segment jabbering about me.

KW: OK, let's waste it jabbering about me.

Andy: (fully melting now) You're... whimsical! Like Meg Ryan. Or Sandra Bullock.

KW: Oh, I could never be like them.

Andy: And mildly insecure. I like that.

KW: I like that you like that.

Andy: What do you do? Besides being Ms. Right?

KW: I'm a call girl.

Andy: (crushed) Ohhh... At least you work for a living.

KW: Actually, I don't have to work for a living. Last year, I won the lottery.

Andy: (intrigued) Oh?

KW: 'Course, most of the money I've already given to charity.

Andy: (semi-bummed) Oh.

KW: But I did invest a portion of the remaining $20 million in a state-of-the-art nursing home, where I call out numbers at the seniors' bingo tournaments.

Andy: (relieved over her true "calling" and wealth) Thank God.

I later looped in "Thank God" in a slightly higher pitch than my original take, a lesson I'd learned years earlier in a comedy workshop from comedian Phil Foster (Frank De Fazio on *Laverne & Shirley*) about how a naturally deep voice could sometimes lessen a line's comedic energy.

Andy: That's really admirable. A little too admirable. What are you, some goody-two-shoes workaholic?

KW: Oh no, I love to have fun! And I really love to eat.

Andy: (disappointed) Oh.

KW: I could just eat and eat, and never put on any weight.

Andy: (relieved) Ah!

KW: It's really fun riding in a limo to an expensive restaurant.

Andy: (disappointed) Oh.

KW: But I could have just as much fun sitting home in a lump watching TV.

Andy: Ah!

KW: As long as someone else controls the remote.

Andy: Ah!

KW: I'm sorry, I don't usually talk this much.

Andy: (repeating previous take for added comic effect) Ah!

After she admitted, "I really value romance in a relationship, but I feel uncomfortable when it comes to. . ." we dialed in a pink hue effect to her cheeks as she blushed, "*you know...*" And we lost it in time for her coquettish 180 into: "Till I get into the bedroom." By interview's end, playing devil's advocate, I asked if she thought there was such a thing as being too perfect. As she scratched her head, pondering this "good question," she swept aside her perfect bangs to reveal an offensive tattoo on her forehead (see closing medley) reinforcing Joe E. Brown's final words in *Some Like It Hot* (see **Tony Curtis**) as I muttered, "Nobody's perfect."

Debunking a Cliché – In the pilot, a poor victim steps on a shell at the beach, to which our intrepid female reporter added a (phony) razor blade, so she can catch the "blood" (ketchup) spewing from his off-camera foot into a jar and compare it with another jar of ocean water/ "sludge" /"condoms"/ "hypodermic needles," proving *the opposite*: "water is thicker than blood." (And that our oceans still needed protecting.) Carefully sneaking shots on the Malibu beach sans permit, we ran into cops who had caught porn filmmakers there! At least we weren't sans clothes.

Things Could be Worse – An already annoying phenomenon is made even more annoying, giving us a newfound appreciation for how well off we were to begin with. Call waiting, the indignity of waiting on hold while your caller takes a more important call, gives way to *lover*-waiting, where a beep prompts your partner in bed to interrupt the make-out session (with me in my first on-screen kiss!) and push the bedpost button to take a more important lover. In a cool sight gag we rigged up on the White House lawn, I and my half of the bed slid away in defeat, as another lover/bed conjoined and enabled the woman we cast to pick up where she left off and now make out with guy #2. Considering how the technical world distracts people from all sorts of human encounters these days, we may have seen it coming.

In my earliest comedic tie-in to polio...

If the World Made Sense (through rose-colored glasses) – Rosy tint is added to re-edited archival footage (Beatlemania fan reaction, Dr. Jonas Salk after announcing the polio vaccine) to convey a new message: Salk attracting groupies.

Timesaver – Where our hostess combines two time-consuming daily chores (cursing out your boss after a hard day's work, and making a dinner salad) into one easy step with *dinner salad therapy.* "Draw a reasonably accurate likeness of your boss on your head of lettuce with a non-toxic marking pen, rinse and squeeze the head under water as you simultaneously curse, 'You low life, son of a...' You feel better, and your lettuce was never crisper!"

Vanguard Theater – In "Birth of a Notion," a prehistoric cave setting was created with a real fire pit as a moving jib camera tracked our two cavemen tapping their sticks to the rhythms of rain drops, before their silhouettes on the rocks dovetailed into other silhouettes of people and instruments we constructed out of cardboard. We fashioned audio renditions of earliest music into classical, ragtime, big band, bop, Elvis, rock and roll, Motown, disco, hard rock, and intentionally cacophonous rap. Ultimately, we rejoin the cavemen tapping their sticks as they eye each other and decide to toss them in a "why bother" move, before digging into their fresh kill (ginormous turkey legs). It was our way of communicating that we didn't get rap, still working its way into the mainstream then. Like the cavemen, maybe we hadn't evolved yet.

What are the Odds? – The statistical likelihood certain quirky events will take place, announced by our resident bookie...

The odds are currently 97 to 1 that you or someone you know will suffer a debilitating back injury picking up a renewal card that fell out of magazine in a chiropractor's waiting room.

Take This Job – We profiled a guy who wore a cow suit and waves down customers at a rib joint, embellishing his thoughts in the suit, including how cannibal-like he felt eating lunch there.

Vox Populi – Man-on-the-street quick take on a cultural issue of the day. In '96, he was predicting that someday, we'd be ordering so many things online from the comfort of our homes that we wouldn't need shoes.

And finally, the BIG FINISH combined the lessons digested from that night's evening stew into one visual, fireworks-laden musical extravaganza, with a formally attired eight-piece band on the now nighttime White House lawn, and a tux-clad yours truly singing an original tune, live, that appropriately opened with a hint of *Hail to the Chief*...

If he doesn't listen, he could be your shrink! (Nodding shrink head flies in and out.)

If you crave a restroom, you may need to think. (Previously reviewed ambiguously confusing ladybug restroom symbol BUZZES in and out.)

Unless you're a celebrity and someone else reads you the paper. (Still of our William Shatner lookalike in his Star Trek outfit beams in, who'd enjoyed the celebrity perk of my off-camera David Brinkley impression announcing, "Here's a little news since the morning papers" [Brinkley's catchphrase at the time] – as we see the back of "Brinkley's" head prepare to read the news over Shatner's VIP public bathroom stall – versus the nobody who'd brought his own newspaper into a regular stall.)

How's this for a caper? The preventer of poli<u>o</u> had more groupies than Ring<u>o</u>! (Black and white still of Jonas Salk slides in, groupies shriek, Salk blushes like Ms. Wright had.)

If your head of lettuce resembles your boss... (Hands gripping lettuce with non-toxic likeness of boss slides in) You'll squeeze out the water, and not hit the sauce! (Hands squeeze lettuce till lettuce cuts in half and slides away.)

And you know that water can be thicker than blood my friend! (Hands holding bottles of blood and ocean water/sludge/hypodermic needles slide in.)

And call waiting is really a high, next to watching your chick tongue some guy! (Valentine's heart framing a still of second guy making out with my former bedmate slides in, then breaks apart.)

If a dame gives you the hots she...

My most challenging rhyme, as a still of beaming Ms. Wright glides in nearly full frame, revealing her offensive tattoo ...

Could be a Nazi!

Orchestra crescendos. Camera tilts up atop the White House to fireworks bursting in the night sky, as now multiple Secret Service men dance on the balconies.

• • • • •

In a 2003 *Los Angeles Times* Sunday magazine article in *West* originally entitled "Just Following Pecking Orders," I reported about my 14-day trial run on IMDbPro.com, the performance-enhanced version of the Internet Movie Database... "one of the mirrors that we in Hollywood peer into to see if there's a reflection staring back." Their STARmeter gauged "the popularity of people over time, and determines which events affect public awareness." My STARmeter ranking was 130,285. Another "star" I unexpectedly landed upon before my jaw dropped... *Adolf Hitler*, at 4,108! (A more recent look indicated he'd shot up.) Why, I wondered, was I 126,177 notches below der Führer?

> *As "writer" he's credited with "Mein Kampf," the 1994 TV movie.*
> *And four documentaries from the '40s, all adapted from "Mein Kampf."*
> *You call that range?*[1]

· · · · ·

Indebted to the financial backers' faith and hundred grand they'd placed in it, I've never pounded the pavements harder than for *Evening Stew*.

Merv passed it along to Ernie Chambers, my first encounter with the veteran producer and Griffin Enterprises executive, who was "intrigued," thought much of it was "really funny" and said I had a "million-dollar face" for situation comedy (making it blush minus special effects). He also had no idea where to sell it.

Comedy Central development exec, Debbie Liebling, called it "very, very well done, really clever, silly, funny and smart," while conceding their broadcasting landscape was tiny then with two launches per year. One was a new potential sketch show "people seemed to like," *Upright Citizens Brigade* (with future star, Amy Poehler) so they wouldn't launch two.

> *DL: It's hard to pass on things that are cool. Let me have a conversation with*
> *our weekly person before I give you a definitive pass, but I wouldn't count on*
> *getting the nod during this window.*

Her suspicions proved correct. The window could "possibly" open up a year down the road, although – debunking another cliché – absence generally didn't make a creative executive's heart grow fonder.

On the streets of New York, the drug-busting activities of former NYPD detective and producer, Sonny Grosso, were portrayed by actor Roy Scheider in

The French Connection. His nickname on the job was "Cloudy," a byproduct of Grosso's pessimism and the opposite of "Sonny." In an early '98 conversation with him about *Stew*, I was happy to glean a hint of optimism from this no-nonsense character...

SG: It was very creative; funny stuff I laughed out loud at. When the fuck do you laugh out loud at stuff? You've gotta have balls to attempt something different. I'm the kind of guy who pulls for actors and writers. Gave Richie Gere his first break in the movies. Got a chance to work with geniuses like Coppola at a time when people were second-guessing them. So, when you find somebody like you who can write, who's not afraid to take a chance, who can do something like Evening Stew, you say, "Man, that's a guy I want to work with."

Although that never directly came to pass, unlike those in Hollywood who blow enough smoke to give posteriors emphysema, I sensed that Sonny was a straight shooter, no pun intended. In the end, *Stew* received overwhelmingly positive reactions but couldn't find a buyer who would pull the trigger. At least the investors who took a shot liked it!

In the fall of '96, *Variety*'s 91st anniversary edition included me on their "50 Creatives to Watch" list, citing *Evening Stew* and another new high-concept scripted half-hour pilot project of mine with "significant buzz." Over a decade later, a revamped version generated some new buzz.

The Evolution of Stan

In 2009, Sonny-Jacobson's development head, Keith Johnson, responded to *The Evolution of Stan*, calling it "really funny and different."

The pitch...

At the head of the line on the evolutionary chart, a lean young man with better posture than ours holds "the club" – which attaches to his steering wheel, so lesser humans don't steal his car. Stan Ingram, circa now, is the very first member of the next evolution of mankind, Homo sapiens 2, the rare case where the sequel is better (in subtle ways not readily visible) than the original. His inherent sweetness and decency, with hints of Forest Gump and Chauncey Gardner (Peter Sellers' character in one of my favorite films, *Being There*) will endear audiences to him, and even leave some feeling they must be evolved too. But unlike the *Being There* character's tendency to say simplistic things that sound profound to others, Stan sometimes says profound things that sound simplistic to mere Homo sapiens. He thinks it's natural to enjoy your job, because bees like feeding on pollen and that's their job, so why do we deserve less than a bee? No superhero (which I was sick of), average looking Stan's evolutionarily less hairy body/face and super-erect posture are the only things that immediately distinguish him from your average Joe, and what got him picked on as a kid. Little does the rest of the world know they're the horses and buggies; Stan's the Model T. Not even Stan knows it. The only ones who do – the audience (given the catbird seat) and professor from hundreds of years in the future, who sparingly lectures to his futuristic anthropology class in the beginning of each episode about the very first Hs2 back in the early 21st century, before we return there to present day and Stan's story. Stan struggles to belong in a world one evolutionary leap below him, a chance to point out where our present-day society could stand to evolve. But when it comes to women, his less evolved Homo sapiens adopted brother, Louie (who also has no idea about Stan's true significance) thinks *he's* Mr. Evolved.

In following the theory of evolution, Stan would offer a preview of how the species of mankind adapts to his changing environment by spawning a select few who can thrive in the new environment. Might modern man's weakening language skills (for one example) hasten his eventual demise as compared to the new man who could more ably communicate matters of life and death, or minutiae, with ultraprecision? Stan might ask, "Is everything all right" with the qualification, "Not that it's possible for everything to be all right, which is a good thing, because otherwise everyone would lose his-slash-her drive and ambition to make everything all right, which would be all right because everything wouldn't be all right." Stan might have a unique ability to recognize (in a non-preachy way) individual contributors to the de-evolution of society. He could try to eliminate the overused "like" and "y'know" from the English language, except when the former is meant as a synonym for "appreciate" or "a la."

He can remember corruptive downloads of information all the way back to the womb, and like a computer hard drive, return his brain back to the moment before it became corrupted.

Along with improvements that had more to do with creative license than evolution, I could riff on how what doesn't get used enough in one evolution might get tossed out in the next. Our earliest ancestors climbed down from the trees and walked, long before muscle movement was overshadowed by crankshaft and piston movement. Global automation begat less defined muscle tone in Stan, who'll be even less inclined to physically exert himself when a self-driving car can do it for him. Though he no longer has an appendix or tonsils, his lungs developed a pollution filter. Less carnivorous, he grew smaller teeth. Unable to figure out the tip at a vegetarian restaurant, Stan is unequipped to calculate anything mathematical since computers upstaged human brains. (In answer to the age-old students' question, "why do we need math," evolution's answer: You don't.) Though he failed in eventually discontinued subjects like calculus and wasn't great at reading long passages (my first evolution of the Stan concept evolved before Twitter) school officials who thought he was an idiot were too dumb to realize he was more evolved than anyone else. He shined in "watching" and "contemplating," topics that were hundreds of years away from being taught. At what we called "physical education," he was the only student with the innate desire not to slam others with a (dodge)ball.

He not only stops and smells the roses... but everything else too.

Stan has a superior B.S. detector. To survive in an increasingly duplicitous world, he knows when others are lying. He's more aware than we are of lurking danger, a byproduct of our growingly perilous planet. Even *third*-hand smoke – the barely decipherable toxic vapor a nearby offender unknowingly exhales after breathing in the second-hand smoke exhaled from another nearby offender dumb enough to breathe in firsthand smoke. Outside of when the Sistine Chapel announces a new pope, Stan knows smoke doesn't belong on earth the other 36,491 days of the century.

He never holds a grudge. Never feels jealousy... envy... prejudice. He's the first human to fully understand racial equality. He understands people are like M&Ms. On the outside, they're different colors; on the inside, they're all the same. Except some are nuts.

With his evolved ability to know who would make a compatible friend, Stan would have no qualms about bonding with a complete stranger in an elevator – even if the "friend" is put off by Stan's intimacy and thinks he's patronizing him because he's black.

A byproduct of future increased lifespans, Stan rejects present humanity's tendency to scoff at anything "old." He enjoys connecting with the relative youngsters at a nursing home and disabusing them of the unevolved notion that money is crucial to happiness – before they stop caring about leaving their kids an inheritance, up their wagers on bingo and develop angina from the stress of losing their nest eggs.

He fully understands empathy and mirroring behavior and is the first human to fully embrace sexual equality – and how to be friends with a woman. Understanding that men also have hormonal ups and downs, Stan would threaten his cranky and disbelieving brother's masculinity after asserting that Louie's having his "period."

If future man is to survive, he ironically needs to procreate *less* in an already overpopulated world. So Stan is less into sex and more into nurturing talk and companionship. He could be the only man on earth on the same sexual wavelength as women. (Homo sapiens women. Homo sapiens 2 women will need even more nurturing, more talking and more gradual arousal than her predecessor to keep the relations between the sexes off balance.)

Homo sapiens women could find themselves strangely drawn to Stan without fully understanding why.

His cheek could be an erogenous zone – cleaner, less germ-ridden than the lips, which are no longer an erogenous zone. (The ultimate survivor, he instinctively recoils from touching a door handle a flu-ridden Homo sapiens touched five entrances ago.)

He has a new, improved unbreakable heart, not that it's made of ice. He can hurt over a woman as intensely as any mere man. But he gets over it a lot faster.

He's incapable of murder and can't even kill time.

Waiter: Baby back ribs, onion rings?

He places it near Louie. Stan recoils.

Stan: That meat doesn't belong there.

Waiter: Oh, did you order the ribs?

Louie: It belongs here. Don't listen to him.

Stan: It belongs on the steer.

He's learned how to recycle even more stuff than we do – like mouthwash. (He gargles and spits it back in the bottle. Not that his breath isn't always naturally fresh.)

An evolved multi-tasker, he can watch TV<u>s</u>.

He always understands his dreams, and preprograms them, like pay-per-view, based on ingesting certain food groups. Unlike a Homo sapiens, whose crazy nightmare last night makes him wonder what strange food he might have eaten to provoke it, Stan knows precisely what he ate.

To compensate for a world where free time is harder to come by, he needs less sleep, unlocking more time for other pursuits. He doesn't snore, thanks to his new soft palate suspension system. He wakes up fully recharged, un-groggy, taking less time to warm up.

He's incapable of addiction. Whenever he experiences too much of anything... booze... drugs... caffeine... food... chocolate... TV... sex... a built-in natural circuit breaker kicks in and makes him nauseous.

He no longer belches.

He no longer curses, a byproduct of all the other curse words becoming overused enough to lose their meaning and originally intended shock value. (Or he might express brand new curse words.) Should a mere Homo sapiens call Stan an asshole, Stan's enlightened reaction would be: "I respect the anus as much as I do any body part."

In the way our ancestors discovered fire or invented the wheel, Stan could unveil his own discoveries we don't yet know we need – like an invention that finally prevents us from closing our eyes when we sneeze, affording us that extra nanosecond to observe what's going on around us. Stan excels at observing and taking in what we mere Homo sapiens miss. His purer goals may leave him striving for things we don't even know we want. Rather than aspiring to be rich, he covets being 50% right-brained, 50% left-brained. Stan's hyper-awareness also allows him to recognize the relative unimportance of so-called vital trends (the internet, Starbucks) he considers ephemeral.

Stan might have evolved to where he realizes even more than we do that worrying is a useless exercise. But being around lower forms of humans who worry all the time might sometimes make him come down to their level and worry that he doesn't worry enough – an offshoot of wanting to fit in. (Until later in the series when he grows instinctively more at one with his own unique place in the universe.) Stan could also be more in touch with his problems and more acutely aware than we are of what truly deserves worrying about – akin to when young Alvy Singer in *Annie Hall* fretted about the universe expanding and breaking apart someday.

· · · · ·

My original mid-nineties *Evolution* script *Variety* referenced was a multicam half hour that juxtaposed Stan's more evolved goals with his less than evolved workplace, a PR firm, and was optioned by Kelsey Grammar's Paramount Studios-based production company, Grammnet. This version sparingly employed voiceover by the professor from the future, only when Stan's present-day behavior might warrant contextual justification. After Stan breathed heavily from channel-hopping, we might learn the Homo sapiens 2 is the first human to be aerobically conditioned from operating a remote. The Grammnet execs stressed it was tough to find a unique project like this. They loved the "cerebral writing" and use of voiceover. I told them I was sensitive to how it should be used sparingly, unlike how *The Wonder Years* overused V.O. in the later years as if the guy remembered every second of his life (which made them laugh).

They kicked around potential actors and wanted to get Paramount on board, who later called the script very funny, told me my time could have arrived, and awaited Grammnet's decision about when to pitch it to the networks. As time passed, the studio reported that they wouldn't be able to pursue it unless Grammnet made a move soon. Grammnet's senior exec, who'd initially loved the narration, now considered it a stumbling block, while the other repeatedly maintained she saw the show. Twice, she promised me that someday ("say in two years") when she was running things, she'd call me back in with the project.

An NBC comedy executive six years later, she didn't return my agent's calls. Another three years hence, now a partner in a production company with an overall deal at CBS, she responded to my email with...

So great to hear from you! I still have very fond memories of you and The Evolution of Stan and would love to read the new version – though I must admit, I think on our end, Grammnet's that is, we way overthought the V.O. and as a result, I'd be open to having that in there.

As for the new version I now preferred, I'd rewritten it into a more cinematic single-camera show with a cable sensibility, ironically minus any V.O.

The logline was: "Stan wants to be accepted by his peers... but there are none." Or are there? The noble female TV news anchor, Audrey, Stan's eyes zone in on... Or Eve, the highly idiosyncratic therapist (there's that topic again!) who seems to connect with him like no others... Could they be more evolved too?

Stan enters Eve's office.

Eve: Welcome. Have a seat.

Eve is lying down on a couch. With some reluctance, Stan sits on the chair next to a nearby second couch.

Eve: Try the couch. It's very relaxing.

Another beat. Stan lies down. Their heads face each other.

Eve: Thank you for coming.

Stan: You're welcome.

A few beats of silence.

Eve: Do you know why you're here?

Stan: You gave me your card.

Eve: Do you always visit people who give you their cards?

Stan: No.

Eve: How does that make you feel?

Stan: Sorry for the trees.

Eve: That produced the business cards that served no useful purpose?

Stan: Yes.

Eve: What else does Stan Ingram feel sorry about?

Stan focuses trance-like.

Stan: When I haven't accomplished enough.

We watch Action News co-anchor, Leonard Vince, beaming as he wraps up his newscast.

Stan: (V.O.) And the Action News team wishes me a great weekend. I doubt their sincerity. I'm sorry that I doubt their sincerity. I'm sorry when I didn't accomplish enough to deserve a great weekend.

We see Stan gazing downward, zigzagging back and forth across the street to avoid stepping on bugs. A bus approaches and flattens him.

Stan: (V.O.) What if I were hit by a bus?

We watch Leonard beam as he wraps up next week's newscast.

Stan: (V.O.) Seven days later, they'd be wishing my next of kin a great weekend. I'm sorry there isn't a mourning period.

Eve focuses ahead.

Eve: If people were as aware of their brains as their bodies, there would be more brain-builders. Are you a brain-builder, Stan?

Stan: Yes.

Eve: Good.

Stan: Why do I feel bad?

Eve: You tell me.

Stan: I'm tired of not fitting in.

Eve: With whom?

Stan: Everyone I've ever encountered.

Eve: Everyone?

Stan thinks long and hard. Then nods.

Eve: Let me dangle this prep-slash-proposition. Maybe they're not worth fitting in with.

.　　.　　.　　.　　.

In future episodes, Stan would try to nurture glimmers of what he perceives to be Audrey's evolved side and orchestrate situations in which her news director and fiancé, Todd, displays his less than evolved side. Stan will hope it awakens her to how she'll never "meld" with Todd like she would with Stan. How can Stan be so sure? Forget the sixth sense. Stan has a seventh sense – he sees dead relationships. Meanwhile Todd maintains his contempt for Stan and illusion of superiority over him.

After Todd and Audrey experience their first big fight, Stan is there to console her. She'll be reluctant to open up to him at first. But his advanced mirroring of her behavior helps draw her in, as does his evolved ability to empathize with exactly how she's feeling at any given moment, acting on her subconscious enough to keep her interested without precisely knowing why. And let's not forget Stan is more into nurturing than sex, which could make her wonder why he isn't interested in her in other ways.

Is Audrey a truly evolved creature? Maybe, maybe not. When all too human acts of misplaced values, self-absorption, gossip or jealousy (for starters) make brief pit stops, Stan wonders if Audrey's world is yet another in which he doesn't fit. But he'll sense enough promise to continue wooing her and subtly teaching her to rise to his level.

Brother Louie, who thinks he's an expert with the ladies, will still try to teach Stan, the real expert, a thing or two.

Louie and Stan walk ahead of their dates to Louie's car down the street. Stan gazes downward as he monitors his steps, weaving back and forth.

Louie: I'm tired of fixing you up.

Stan: I can't communicate with her.

Louie: The twin peaks on that chest of hers communicated plenty. Do you know how many guys would kill to nuzzle up to those?

Stan: Kill? Zero? I hope.

Louie: Where do you get off being so picky?

Stan: I can't picture myself melding with her, Louie.

Louie: Melding?

Stan: I need to find someone who sees the world the way I do.

Louie: Nobody else is that nuts.

Passersby shoot Stan looks.

Louie: (re: zigzagging) Stop doing that. She'll notice.

Stan: There are insects down there.

Stan pauses. He's a bit winded.

Stan: Shouldn't you have parked closer?

Louie: It's like three blocks.

Stan: Exactly like them. Driving three would conserve our energy.

Louie continues walking. Stan continues zigging and zagging.

Louie: You sit on your ass too much.

Stan: My system has low mileage. Why isn't that a good thing?

Louie: You want to save energy?

Louie stomps his feet all around them.

Louie: Killed the bugs. Kill the zigzagging!

Louie may be all about bedding a lot of less than evolved partners, making money and others jealous of his success. But deep down he might wonder if Stan sometimes knows what he's talking about. He'll also be torn between being embarrassed by him and defending his adopted brother if somebody else starts dumping on him.

Stan's evolved nature will help him recognize value in all sorts of jobs, as long as they help enlighten the world – whether it's encouraging vegetarianism at Meat Patty's, where he dresses as a burger to convince others he's no good, or landing a bottom rung job at Audrey's news station to try to change the landscape of TV news to reflect truly newsworthy events like kindness, not that Homo sapiens would be evolved enough to watch. (Usurping news director Todd's professional terrain would be another reason he'd be out to get Stan.)

Eve will continue pushing Stan to act upon his unique instincts. (Like hitting fertilizer balls into holes, not golf balls, to help fill up the golf courses turning the planet into Swiss cheese.) Is Eve another square peg in a round hole who identifies with Stan's disenfranchisement, or could it mean more? Might she be the new future Eve to his new future Adam? Or maybe she's just one very quirky lady.

Whether it's Eve, Audrey or someone else, by series' end, Stan will finally strike the evolutionary motherlode, melding and connecting with a woman on all levels. It's the first earthshaking step in the eventual worldwide repopulation of Hs2's, a future world we glimpse at the top of each episode when the future professor lectures his Hs2 anthropology students about their origins. Forget (the entirely different animal that launched six years after the first *Stan* multicam) *How I Met Your Mother.* This was *How the New Adam Met the New Eve.*

I sent the former Grammnet and NBC comedy exec, now with a deal at CBS, the new script, reminding her that I still had the multicam version in case she wanted to revisit that down the line. She confirmed receipt...

I'll take a look at this first since I'm dying to know how man has evolved since Stan. Thanks for sending.

I never heard back.

One day, an HBO executive called, intrigued and evidently surprised by the script and how "really good" the writing was. She wanted to know how it evolved (as it were) and to be kept apprised of anyplace I might pitch it. Months later, she told me...

We're gearing up on the comedy side with a lot of things in production now, so we've slowed down as far as buying. I think the writing's really good, so I want to stay in the loop as far as what you're doing. But I think as far as buying it on spec right now, it doesn't really make sense for us? But if you're putting together a full-fledged series pitch, definitely let us know.

A bit confused, I told her the script she'd read included several pages that spell out the arc of the series. She replied...

Why don't you send me those pages, and then I'll talk to the team and we'll go from there?

I asked if I could have my representative follow up in the fall.

Yes! By that point, at least two of our series will be off the ground and it'll be less crazy then. So, I think just send the pages and we'll talk about it, and I'll try to get you an answer as quick as I can.

Three weeks later...

Thank you for submitting this additional material. We took a look, and unfortunately the project does not make sense for us right now, as we are about to launch several series that thematically explore men in different stages of "finding themselves" and are hoping each one will find a long life here on the network. Thank you for continuously thinking of us – we wish you the best in setting up your project!

Faster than I can find Waldo in a crowd, I can find "unfortunately" in an email. Either a project isn't compatible with a network's programming, or in this instance it was too compatible? In the former case, SyFy called it "an enjoyable read, smart, very well written, like an intellectual play" but definitely not a fit for their action-oriented, edgy dramas. (Might their viewers sit up and take notice of something that didn't "fit" with those other shows, especially if it was enjoyable, smart, and very well written?) As for the latter case with HBO, I knew this much: It wasn't at all like their other shows in waiting.

Grosso-Jacobson further shopped it around, short of a sale.

Trading Up

Some years earlier, while the former Grammnet executive was still determining NBC's comedies, Andrew Singer (Lorne Michaels' Broadway Video) sent her my half-hour multicam pilot script, *Trading Up*. It featured Suzanne and Louie, a newly married couple on their fifth collective marriage who reinvent the rules of matrimony based on hard-learned lessons from the past – seen in periodic brief flashbacks with their four exes – as they compete with Suzanne's folks' inexplicably compatible relationship.

For better or worse sure as hell didn't work. This time, they'll aim for the "for better" parts. One example: Keeping the mystery alive. Less *is* more. Why does sleeping together have to mean *sleeping* together? Sleeping is a selfish, solitary experience, followed by waking up and adjusting to being awake, another selfish, solitary experience. Why not spend just the best moments together... when they feel the best... look the best? Why not keep their separate apartments? Suzanne's mother doesn't call that a marriage. Meanwhile Dad has always treated the tough-as-nails mother like a queen (the opposite of Peter Boyle's usual treatment of Doris Roberts on *Everybody Loves Raymond*).

Hal, the picture, and then some, of a doting, happily married older man, is whistling as he sets dining room table for Suzanne and Louie's arrival.

Hal: Is my whistling bothering you, dear?

Helene: (O.S.) Yes.

Hal: I'm sorry! Who needs a teakettle for a husband?

We hear Helene laugh heartily offstage.

Hal: Shall I fill the water glasses, dear?

Helene: (O.S.) If you fill them now, they'll get warm by the time we eat. You know how I feel about warm water.

Hal: You detest warm water! How could I forget?

Helene: (O.S.) Except...

Hal: In the ocean.

Helene: (O.S.) Unless...

Hal: There are children nearby.

Hal/Helene: (O.S.) And a bathroom wasn't nearby.

Helene: (O.S.) You know how I feel about your talking over me.

Hal "zips" his mouth closed. Helene arrives from the other room, with dress unhooked.

Helene: Hook me?

Hal hooks her dress up in the back, twirls her around, leans her back, kisses her passionately. Then:

Helene: (matter-of-factly) Herring.

Hal: I'll put it out.

He leaves for the kitchen. Doorbell rings.

Hal: (O.S.) Would you like me to get that, dear?

Helene: Ordinarily. Tell you what? Since I'm closer, I will this time.

Hal: (O.S.) You're so thoughtful.

Helene opens the door and greets Suzanne and Louie.

Suzanne/Louie: Hi.

Helene: Come in. Let me take your coats. (calling out) Hal, take their coats!

This earlier exchange between Suzanne and Riva, her relationship-challenged sister (think Julie Kavner in *Rhoda*) points to her challenge...

Suzanne: Wish I knew somebody to fix you up with.

Riva: Why bother? Nobody will ever be as good as dad. Not that I deserve a guy as good as dad.

Suzanne: Riva!

Riva: Not that mom deserves a guy as good as dad.

Ultimately the show was a testament to Suzanne's and Louie's creative attempts to connect with their last marital swing of the bat (including the challenge of working together at Suzanne's family's car dealership, where customers also "trade up"). I tried to mix a little Sam/Diane *Cheers* dynamic with a little *Everybody Loves Raymond*. After Louie's amorous attempt at work in the backseat of a new sports car, an embarrassed Suzanne explains the rocking car to a newly arrived customer watching: "Inspecting the shocks. They're fine."

Suzanne: Happy now?

Louie: Happier.

Suzanne: Well I'm not.

Louie's "I'm really trying here" conjures up brief flashbacks to Suzanne's memories of each of her previous two exes uttering the same remark. Then back in present day...

Suzanne: "I'm really trying here." That was a signal, wasn't it? You were signaling that you were angry at me, because you were just trying to do something nice, and I didn't recognize or acknowledge it.

Louie: ... Okay.

Suzanne: Well, I'm acknowledging it right now. Thanks for doing something nice.

Louie: ... You're welcome.

Suzanne: (a beat) That something nice. Can you give me... just the teeniest hint... what it was?

Louie: (needing tiny hint, himself) Well... if you don't know what it was, then... if I tell you what it was, I'll be recognizing what it was. Not you.

A beat.

Suzanne: We had a little fun. While you lost sight of the fact that this is a place of business. My family's business. Where we both happen to have reputations to protect. You placed your needs above mine. You embarrassed me. And you embarrassed us.

Louie: You're welcome.

Suzanne: Why?

Louie: Because I love you, Suzanne. And I don't want to lose you.

Suzanne: What are you talking about?

Louie: There was never an excuse not to make love. Ever. And then one day, there was. And before you knew it, there were a million excuses.

Suzanne: That doesn't sound like us.

Louie: I'm talking about my ex-wives. I can't have history repeat itself, Suzanne. Not with you. (doing the math) Re...repeat itself.

Another customer enters the showroom.

Louie: Can I help you?

Customer: Yeah. I'm thinking of trading up to a hybrid.

Louie: Sure. I can show you something.

As Louie and customer make their way to the hybrid, Suzanne approaches the sports car in which Louie had put the moves on her.

Suzanne: (to Louie) Get in.

Louie: 'Scuse me?

Suzanne: You heard me, mister.

Louie: Suzanne. I'm kinda busy right now.

Suzanne: Car. You. Now.

Louie: (to customer) I'll just be a minute.

Louie meets up with her. She pushes him into the car. They fall to the floor out of sight. Customer awkwardly directs his attention elsewhere a few beats as car starts rocking.

Casting director Ronnie Yeskel "loved" the script, wanted to cast it and would entertain names that included Albert Brooks and Alec Baldwin. After we met for the first time, she volunteered out of the blue...

RY: Just love that face. Gotta put you in something.

Did the woman who cast *Reservoir Dogs*, *Pulp Fiction* and the first three seasons of *Curb Your Enthusiasm* just tell me she loved my face? What about after it turned beet red? Though nothing came of it, I figured I had to at least send her a DVD and/or link to my latest performance pieces. During a later dry spell long before I landed a commercial agent for a while, I sheepishly reminded her of her remark in an email about a world I'd never been driven to pursue (outside of voiceovers):

Painful though it is to admit in this town, gulp, I need work! Might you know of a commercial agent to whom I could conceivably mention your name? I notice commercial casting notices often ask for "interesting faces." Not sure I fall into that category although I do remember your "love to put that face in something" comment, however embarrassing it is to write out those words here.

She emailed me that she was gulping right along with me, with two of her projects having gone belly up. And she didn't know anyone in the commercial world.

Keith Addis, the manager of Ted Danson (whom I'd originally had in mind for Louie) said the script was "very clever." He was happy to let Danson read it if someone from NBC supported the idea. Andrew Singer followed up with the current NBC executive and former Grammnet fan of *Stan*, who apologized for not yet reading *Trading Up*. But she was "excited" after learning I'd written it, reported that her own assistant really liked it, and promised to get to it over the weekend. Three weeks later: She "really enjoyed" it but didn't feel like it was right for them, adding that out of all the stuff she read, this was one that had serious consideration. Andrew was "proud" of it and thought there was time to hit up additional networks where Broadway Video had relationships. Though he had doubts that NBC Universal Studios, where Broadway Video had their deal, would finance a CBS show. Fox thought it was a "good concept" but "wasn't right for them." ABC "enjoyed the read" and echoed it "wasn't right for them right now." The defunct UPN didn't feel the concept would work, because they were targeting family comedies like *Everyone Hates Chris*. As a viewer, I didn't care whether a show allegedly fit the network's preconceived notions of their brand or not. I just cared if a program was well executed and original (*Cheers* and

Raymond influences aside) unto itself – the happy accidents networks seemed to cannibalize for future lineups.

· · · · ·

The following year, I emailed Ted Danson's manager about the new ABC pilot, *Help Me Help You*. Danson was set to star as a shrink who had more problems than the patients in his group therapy sessions. I'd written for *Cheers*. Addis liked *Trading Up*. I'd been addressing psychology in multiple projects over the years. Maybe all of that would help *me* help *him* to help *me* get a crack at writing on the show. He asked me to call him after the upfronts (when networks announce their fall lineups). ABC picked up the show, but as for me, it was all about getting picked by the showrunners, who would have their own people in line for ever smaller writing staffs. After watching a few episodes, I wasn't sorry I didn't land there. After nine, it was cancelled.

Outer Child

Among the four pilots I had been commissioned to write for various networks, one originated as a pitch in late '99 to what was then a new cable wing of Fox, Fox Family. I often wondered about nature versus nurture, and how our environment and upbringings compared to genetics with respect to impacting our behavior. *Outer Child* was the high concept way in.

The pitch...

What if you could be a kid again, knowing what you know now? Plus, *you* were the kid's guardian? After a mother's lifelong passive-aggressiveness has impacted her young son Gene's self-confidence, he grows up to ask his geneticist friend, Perry, to secretly clone him, so he can raise himself as a child (the same nine-year-old actor is the clone and father as a child in occasional flashbacks) undo his mother's mistakes, and prove that if it weren't for the wrath of Ruth (his mother), he would have grown into a normal, functioning, non-neurotic adult. His other goal: to meet an encouraging woman, the opposite of Ruth, and a supportive presence in his clone's life.

Gene's a writer who also dabbles in cartoons, but any resemblance to real persons, living or dead, is purely coincidental! We may write what we know, but not necessarily *who* we know. I'm done protesting too much now.

It's a very human story where the audience gets a heightened ability to know their inner personalities. Gene, the "father," and Eugene, his clone, were all about their characters and unique relationship with one another (reflective of a lifetime of behavior patterns), a secret the audience gets to share with them and Perry. Throw in the cool sci-fi concept and built-in empathy factor. With the right casting, how could an audience not root for the identifiable nine-year-old actor who would at least try to win life's tiny victories as Gene gets his second chance, vicariously, to do the same? This didn't clone other concepts associated with cloning over the years. This was a fresh spin on a "family" and the relatable dream of reliving one's life towards the goal of nurture winning out over nature. I could already visualize the billboard, with father and his spittin' image young "son" warily eyeing each other. High concept twist on living your life over again notwithstanding, I was aiming for a character-driven comedy with humor and a little heart.

I initially imagined Perry as an eccentric geneticist with a hint of Kramer. His face was orange from the orange gene in a carrot – which he'd cloned from another carrot. His big plans were to someday clone an entire salad. After an opening flashback of little Gene's childhood dynamic with his mother and a later young adult example of insecurity with women, childhood friend Perry notes Ruth has "pureed" Gene's ego into "a fine paste." Gene admits he still sometimes feels like a pathetic, defenseless little kid trapped in a big kid's body. When he learns how to love "little Gene," concludes Perry, he'll learn how to love big Gene – which propels big Gene to convince Perry to set his sights on a bigger cloning target than salads and, crazy as it sounds, help give Gene the second childhood he could have had. "Uncle Perry" would also serve as a clinical observer of nature vs. nurture. In the script's first incarnation, after Gene dubs his clone "Gene Jr." ...

Perry: Eugene! He'll be YouGene. You're MeGene.

Gene: Shouldn't I be the one who names my own... you know?

Perry: You did, you did. I opened the ketchup. But you loosened it.

Gene: Nobody can know. The press. My mother.

Perry: What are you gonna tell Eugene when he sees your old snapshots?

Gene: I know this – I'll make sure he gets a better haircut. I just want him to grow up like a normal kid.

Perry: (scoffing) He's you!

Gene's new girlfriend, Audrey (another borrowing of my mother's name I didn't hear often on TV) could be drawn to him after thinking he's been raising his "lovechild" ever since his "ex-girlfriend" died during the birth. (The same never seen "girlfriend" story he fed his mom too.) 1) He wants Audrey and the rest of the world to treat Eugene like a normal kid, and for clinical reasons, so does Perry. 2) Gene's afraid of how Audrey would react if she discovered the truth. Would it change her image of him as a loving and caring dad? Audrey could represent a grounding, less negative influence on both Eugene's and Gene's self-images. Not that she'd always agree with Gene's parenting choices. And in her positive, together, non-confrontational way, she might have an occasional suggestion for Ruth too. Ruth could suspect she's being sarcastic or biting when there isn't a biting bone in Audrey's body.

Or the opposite...

As in "I want a girl just like the girl that married dear old dad," Audrey could slowly turn into a younger version of Gene's mother, to Eugene and Gene's chagrin. The negative effects of nurture all over again with Gene's clone! Gene will also try to keep Mom from screwing up her "grandson" the way she screwed up him although Ruth can still hold sway over them both.

Gene would relive various rites of passage via Eugene and make sure that this time, his younger self has more confidence and fun out of life, less fear and insecurity, succeeds at sports... music... girls. Maybe he eventually even pursues show business. What could be worse than a stage father of a clone? A stage father who blames the fact he never made it on the insecurity his mother instilled in him. But darn it, he could've made it as a child actor, and by golly, he will this time!

Unless that was too showbiz-centric.

·　·　·　·　·

It took me till late in life to realize – you spend your first childhood as an *actor*. You start off thinking the world revolves around you. Everybody lavishes attention your way. It's all about how cute you are. Tantrums are really performance pieces. Later you try to *act* cool in school! Upon your second childhood, you become a director. Directing your kids; spouse, if you have one; underlings, if you have them. Actors naturally grow into directors.

·　·　·　·　·

No matter how hard he tries to fix things, Gene finds that Eugene repeats some of Gene's childhood mistakes – minimizing nurture's influence over nature (and Ruth's influence over Gene's upbringing). Other times nature and Eugene will prevail! And Gene will feel vindicated, realizing he wasn't crazy, that his environment indeed hadn't made it easy for him. Eugene's successes can make Gene appreciate that these same successes must be imbedded in him too. But even when the kid fails, "father" will now have a more adult, nurturing perspective about stumbling along the way... in a way, making it easier to accept and forgive himself... as the audience continues to root for father and clone's success next week.

Through Fox Television Studios executive, Lou Wallach, I delivered the treatment to the new Fox Family network. They flipped, calling it their potential signature show in prime time, "the most original family comedy conceivable," and agreed it should be through the father's perspective. They even loved the double meaning of his name, "Gene." This would be the first Fox TV Studios pilot script deal under Fox Family's new regime. I was psyched.

Setting up Gene's backstory...

Proverbial suburbia twenty-five years ago. One or two fast food restaurants.

Ruth, 35, and little Gene, 9 and typically disheveled, are in the front seat of Ruth's car. Gene reads his Cracked comic book.

Jackie DeShannon's "Put a Little Love in Your Heart" softly plays on the oldies station. Gene cracks his knuckles.

Ruth: What do you think I'd rather listen to. Music? Or your knuckles?

Gene gets in one more crack as a nervous reaction. Their eyes meet.

Little Gene: I'm sorry.

He continues reading, occasionally blowing bubblegum. Then laughs.

Ruth: Don't read in the car. How many times do I have to tell you?

Little Gene: Sorry.

Ruth: It would be nice if you read a book for a change.

Little Gene: In the car?

Ruth: Don't get smart with me.

Little Gene: I'm sorry. I read books.

Ruth: Comic books aren't books.

Little Gene: Then why are they... books?

Close on Ruth. From little Gene's POV:

Ruth: (echo-effect, speeded down) That isn't "clever." That isn't "wit."

Little Gene: (a beat) Ma?

Ruth: What?

Little Gene: What are we having for dinner?

Ruth: I don't know. What do you feel like?

Little Gene: I don't care.

Ruth: Then why did you ask me what we're having for dinner?

Little Gene shrugs his shoulders and pops his bubblegum.

Ruth: Could you not do that? And sit up straight. You're gonna be all hunched over when you grow up.

She grabs the comic book out of his hands.

Ruth: IF you ever grow up.

Little Gene: Spaghetti?

Ruth: (a beat, sacrificially) All right.

A few beats as Ruth makes a turn. Then:

Little Gene: It doesn't have to be spaghetti.

Ruth: (sighs) Then why am I driving to the store to pick up spaghetti?

Later, on the street, Ruth, carrying packages, hurries with little Gene, as he runs awkwardly.

Ruth: Look at the time.

Little Gene: I'm sorry.

Ruth: Could you stop saying "I'm sorry?"

Little Gene: I'm...

He catches himself. They walk by a storefront window. Ruth stops to take a gander, as little Gene keeps walking. She calls after him.

Ruth: Gene! Come over here.

He does. She points him to a well-dressed, erect mannequin we don't yet notice in the window.

Ruth: See that? Now that's the way a young man should look. Why can't you look like that?

Close on a diminutive and dapper mannequin with a smooth, featureless knob for a head. An identical mannequin looks on from behind it.

In the window reflection, a slightly spooked little Gene gazes ahead, then at his mother, then back to the faceless dummy.

As the months ticked away after delivering the script with no word, I learned Jason Alexander had sold them a show the previous September they'd also been excited about. It was due to premiere in July and they still hadn't closed the deal.

In April, Fox Family passed on *Outer Child*, citing that "it came a long way" and was a "great concept" but "didn't get to where it needed to be." "At the end of the day," the cliché that was already worming its way into the vernacular, their president "kind of felt sorry" for Gene. Probably feeling sorry for me, Lou offered, "Chin up. Good ideas make it on the air somehow." About a year later, Fox Family was sold to Disney and renamed ABC Family, which was renamed Freeform in 2016, focusing even more on teens and young adults.

This was another project I couldn't let go of. One person's "pass," the less risky reaction in development hell, was no more objective than another's "yes." And whether or not the industry tended to sour on a project previously shopped, this wasn't better if used before the sell-by date; the slightly tweaked script was still fresh fourteen years later. Sundance film director Ben Wolfinsohn reached out in 2014 about shooting a sample from a pilot of mine after reading my *Splitsider* interview about the origins of "The Opposite."[1] He felt it was easier for the gatekeepers to watch something than read something, and *Outer Child* was the script to which he felt he could bring the most. Who would play Gene? One popular comic we thought had potential was Dov Davidoff, who wrote back...

Very cool script – funny/interesting/fresh. I'm not sure how I'd fit into things right now as I've partnered with (TV writer and producer) Bruce Helford, and am headed out soon with a scripted idea, but if there's a way to be involved I'd be interested.

In checking out comedians on YouTube, Ben and I both responded to Gregg Rogell, a New York comic I'd first admired on Carson twenty years earlier. He had the "it" factor I felt could marry well with the humor and slight pathos of characters I tended to write. After tracking him down on Facebook, he wrote me that he'd have a few weeks off before his two-month world tour he was about to continue, opening for Russell Peters, one of the most successful touring comedians in the world and a judge on *Last Comic Standing*. A day after I emailed Gregg the script, he emailed me back...

This is a great script! I would be honored to be associated with this project. I need to be upfront about a few things. I'm 47, a lot older than Gene. Also, I've spent the last decade doing stand-up, not acting, so I've been out of the industry loop for some time. Not sure if I'm the best sell, as the lead... Could be my low self-esteem due to my bad upbringing talking. That being said, I am very grateful and would love to read for the role. Whatever I have to do to move forward with this, let me know. Thanks!

Gregg would meet up in Los Angeles. He could play 40ish, that was no problem. And we cared less about network actor wish lists than capturing the right tone of the characters. If the clone who looked enough like Gregg was as endearingly charming as he appeared on a child actor's video link we reviewed, *my* wish would be granted. We'd also try a visual cue or two that implied they weren't just father and son. Maybe even a tiny ketchup stain on each of their sleeves. (I'd earlier shown Gene's propensity for spilling condiments.) As for Perry, Gregg mentioned Russell Peters could be interested down the line were we to land this somewhere.

The plan was to show the dynamics between "father" and clone in a scene where Gene picks Eugene up from school. Rather than the tight confines of a car, Ben suggested that maybe we could shoot it as a walking scene. If only we'd stuck with that plan. Behind the wheel of Ben's Volvo, Gregg's focus on spouting off his lines competed with his slow drive down an unfamiliar neighborhood street.

We shot him prior to meeting up with the child actor to capture his portion separately. We never met the kid. The next thing I knew, a stranger offering me a blanket and water kindly advised me to remain seated on the ground, what struck me as overprotective in my confused state (till the pain later kicked in).

Though we were unable to complete the task at hand, seeing just a part of it come to life strengthened my resolve to pitch *Outer Child* again later that very day. Recounting our saga in an email to an executive I knew at TV Land, I figured, might at least provoke her to read it...

I and a production team started shooting a sample driving scene today with Gregg Rogell and his child "clone." Gregg is in from New York on his world tour with comedian Russell Peters and connected strongly with the script. He is such a great fit for this lead character, something I saw in action today... before a car slammed into the back where I was seated, and the director's car was totaled! I'm still in shock from the whole experience, and thankful to be alive. I write this in pain just to relay our strong conviction that this thing has a lot of potential.

Her reply...

How are you? I read the script. You are insane! Unfortunately, we don't do shows about parenting. We don't mind kids who are seen and not heard but we decidedly stay away from parenting stories. It has been the way in the past we differentiated ourselves from our sister company Nick at Nite who does lots of parents and kids stories. You are still an innovative thinker. Wow.

Along with the elbow abrasion, an X-ray at the urgent care center the next morning revealed hip and shoulder contusions but thankfully no broken bones. Gregg tried massage therapy and acupuncture after his shoulder and arm pain kicked in three days later. I felt bad. I also thought he'd shown real promise in revealing the layers behind reliving his life through his clone. Though he was open to trying it again, our roles as human crash test dummies seemed to lessen everyone's urges to reconvene before his clone's voice changed. And Gregg was resuming his world tour in January.

An Amazon Studios exec, expressing interest in the world, "enjoyed" the script and "saw potential." But the rest of his team was in limbo until I addressed changes that would make it a more cinematic dramedy along the lines of their new industry darling, *Transparent.* By now I'd become so invested in this project that I welcomed edging it up and heightening the reasons to binge on the many opportunities to explore an adult trying to come to terms with his childhood and adulthood.

In the original script, a quick montage showed the initial steps, from cloning celery stalks, to water bugs, to dogs, before leading up to the reveal of Eugene nine years later. Amazon thought the montage wasn't grounded enough. They gravitated toward the original age I'd had in mind for Gene, thirty-four, and still liked introducing Eugene at the impressionable age of nine. But Perry needed to already be up to speed on cloning, and part of a larger organization or secret experiment. Keep the mystery alive. And find some way of setting up Gene and Eugene before we're even sure he's a clone. That seemed interesting to me. Grounded with a hint of sci-fi. A bit strange and not without humor. You sense something is a little off between the father and kid.

As we peel away the layers, we piece together who he is as the backstory sheds light on how he wound up there and sets the stage for the series to come. Gene also needed to be a little more successful to warrant a friendship with Perry – now less like Kramer in my mind than a younger Roger Sterling from *Mad Men.* If Gene were too established, would you deflate the rationale behind why he'd think he could have been more successful had he been more nurtured? Regardless, he could be unsuccessful at interpersonal communication and relationships. He could still be a freelance cartoonist but needed to interact more with the outside world. (I opened it up to his weekly regimen pitching cartoons at *The New Yorker.*) They especially liked the relationship between mother and son. This passive-aggressive influence could have instilled in him deep down insecurities, no matter how successful. When they suggested he might simply feel there was something missing in his life, I thought that begged the question, so why not have a kid? That, they guessed, could be a good question to ask.

With thirty-four pages their sweet spot for a producible half hour, I needed to trim a little. As a guideline, they sent me a *Transparent* pilot script with my watermarked name on every page. A few days later, I suggested maybe I could open things up in the past with mother and little Gene, as in the original, but then go to present day with adult Gene waiting in his car at school (an update of the ill-fated scene we shot) before his "kid" arrives and, to our surprise, he looks exactly like the kid we just saw twenty-five years earlier. They immediately responded, "That could work!"

Present day or not too distant future. Even more fast food restaurants. Identical to one another.

Gene, now 34, is waiting in the car, reading a Kindle. The school bell rings. A swarm of kids run out. On Gene's face watching out the car window: wistful.

The object of Gene's wistfulness comes into view as he runs, uncoordinated, towards us...

Eugene, 9, who looks just like little Gene, the same kid we saw from a quarter century ago! With hair and clothes a tad more 2015.

Eugene climbs into the backseat.

Gene/Eugene: Hey.

Eugene holds out his hand for his daily gift. Gene hands him bubblegum. Eugene unwraps it and tosses it in his mouth.

Gene: Put on your seatbelt, please.

Eugene: What about you?

They hook their seat belts and drive off. Eugene reads his comic book and blows his bubblegum. It pops in unison with Gene's bubblegum.

Gene: How was school?

Eugene: Okay.

Gene: Gym class?

Eugene: Yeah.

Gene: Dodgeball?

Eugene: Yeah.

Gene: Stings, doesn't it?

Eugene: Yeah.

Gene reaches back to rub Eugene's shoulder a bit.

Gene: You know how hard it is to be a human target? You're like a bull's-eye – what everybody's aiming for. You should be very proud of that.

Eugene looks less than convinced.

Gene: Where's your backpack?

Eugene: I lent it to somebody.

Gene: You lent it to somebody? I just bought you that, Eugene. When are you getting it back?

Eugene: ... Soon.

Gene: How soon?

Eugene: I don't know.

Gene: I think you do.

Eugene: (beat) That big bully, Ralph Nattans, took it, Dad! He's always messin' with me!

Gene: How could you let somebody take advantage of you like that?

Eugene: I'm sorry.

Gene: You don't have to say you're sorry for my benefit. I know you're sorry.

Eugene: You do?

Gene: (beat, then) Don't feel bad about it, okay? Just ignore him. We'll get you another one.

A big guy in a sports car cuts in front of Gene's car. Guy flips Gene the finger and tears off.

Eugene: Why did that man do this (gives finger) to you?

Gene grabs Eugene's finger.

Gene: Eugene! Please don't use that finger.

Eugene: Ever?

Gene: (chuckles) I mean in that way.

Eugene: Why not?

Gene: It's not nice. And you're nice. You're a very nice young man.

Eugene: Did you do something wrong?

Gene: No.

Eugene: So he did something wrong?

Gene: He wanted to get ahead of me. I let him.

Gene makes the connection, looks at Eugene.

Gene: You've gotta let your fucking bully... I'm sorry... know he can't get away with crap! (then) Which you're totally capable of, Eugene.

For Eugene's benefit, Gene now attempts to follow his own credo... And softly beeps his horn at the long since gone guy:

Gene: Consider that a warning!

A week later I congratulated them on *Transparent*'s Golden Globe win, the first for a streaming series. As I continued digging in, I voiced my excitement, that I didn't want to get ahead of myself, but was thankful they'd sensed *Outer Child*'s potential. They sounded enthused after I promised I'd have something for them soon.

The birth mother was another wrinkle I introduced to Perry's now larger world. I tried to creatively sneak in exposition, a necessary evil in pilots, to fill in some but not all of the blanks...

In the background of a biotech lab, scientists peer through microscopes. Two others examine identical Dalmatians.

A geneticist, Perry, intense in an offbeat way, strolls the corridor en route to the receiving room.

Moments later, Brooke, a well-earned 40 with a bit too much makeup, confers with Perry.

Perry: Nine years. Goes by... (snaps) like that.

Brooke: Can I see him?

Perry shares an image on his smartphone we don't see.

Brooke: What's that clunky thing on his head?

Perry: Walkman. (off Brooke's look) Okay, it's the father. Looks exactly like him.

Brooke: Can I see him?

Perry: Ms. Harold...

Brooke: Brooke.

Perry: Your womb... was... how can I put this... like a timeshare. Need I remind you that you willingly put it on the market?

Brooke: So?

Perry: And for a pretty penny, I might add. We visited it AFTER the embryo was developed in a test tube to study the cloning process. (chuckles) Maybe Pyrex and you should share visitation rights.

Perry also informs her that the kid thinks the old man's wife died during childbirth. No trying to hunt down his birth mother when he's older or wondering if he's adopted and who his father was.

Another complication and ticking clock later in the script...

Close on Perry's face. He's addressing his supervisor, Raymond.

Perry: We can't make it public.

Raymond: If the government eases restrictions, we can.

Perry: The kid has to at least be of age. That was the deal.

Raymond: I don't recall any "deal."

Perry: The donor wants him to have as normal an upbringing as possible. How is that supposed to happen if the press catches wind of this? Not to mention it'll corrupt the results.

Raymond: The inventors of 3-D printing are fucking rolling in it. Throw in the five senses, this is 8-D printing!

Perry: Private investors have already helped us, Raymond. They'd prefer to stay private.

Raymond: That's chump change compared to what they expect to reap off it when Washington finally comes through. We've waited nearly a decade – It's working! How long should we make the world wait to learn they'll never again have to say goodbye to somebody they love?

Gene is taken aback upon learning of the "birth" mother's reappearance after nine years. She never wound up having any kids of her own: Time-released empty nest pangs. Not to worry, says Perry. She knows better than to complicate things. (Or does she?)

Other hopefully seamless exposition nuggets within the script included...

Gene: She had zero interest in seeing him after she... incubated him. It was like the new me getting dissed by my new mother.

Perry: Just like old times.

And...

Perry: As long as Ruth doesn't puree Eugene's ego into a fine paste, chances are he'll be the unencumbered you.

Gene: My mother meant well.

Perry: There's revisionism at work. After your dad died, her passive-aggressive bullshit had you by your prepubescent balls. And she never let up.

Which we first witnessed twenty-five years earlier, and in one of several flashbacks that compares little Gene's fear of performing in *The Wizard of Oz* class play and concocted excuse he's sick (after getting caught under the sheets here with the thermometer and Ruth's hairdryer) ...

Ruth: (reading thermometer) 109? You're going to school, mister!

Little Gene: I can't do it, Ma. I don't want to be in the play!

Ruth: The only one you're making SICK is me! I don't know what I did wrong, but I must have done something wrong. Because you are incapable of doing ANYTHING right, do you know that? You couldn't even figure out when to turn off the hair dryer!

Little Gene cracks his knuckles.

...with Eugene's public speaking phobia over the upcoming *The Blair Witch Project* class play. (An unsuccessful 2016 sequel [clone?] to that original film was still a year away.)

Ruth still induces knuckle-cracking in both Gene and Eugene...

Ruth: Look at that hair. It's so much thicker than your father's was. But why do you wear it like that?

Eugene cracks a knuckle.

Gene: It's fine. Eugene, sit. Mom, sit.

Gene goes to the table to sit next to Eugene, but Ruth manages to slip in and beat Gene to it.

Ruth: Your father tells me you're in the play tomorrow.

Gene: He's the shopkeeper interviewed about the legend of Blair Witch!

Ruth: Oh.

Gene: ... What?

Ruth: Nothing. Good for you, Eugene. (then) Why such a meager role?

Gene: It's not meager.

Ruth: It isn't called The Legend of the Shopkeeper.

Gene: Ma! It's an important role.

Eugene: I don't feel good.

Gene: Reasonably important. Not insanely important.

Ruth chuckles, brushing hair out of Eugene's eyes.

Ruth: (to Eugene) I hope you don't inherit your ability to make a point from your father.

Gene: (cracking a knuckle) What... is that supposed to mean?

Ruth: What? I'm just making conversation. Don't slouch.

Gene/Eugene sit up straighter.

Gene: I... I don't know what you...

He notices Eugene struggling to open the ketchup bottle.

Gene: You can do it, Eugene. You're as strong as any... bully.

A beat. Eugene finally gives up, and hands bottle to Gene.

Gene: Okay. When I open it, remember – you loosened it.

Gene struggles too. Before Ruth grabs it and opens it in a flash.

In another scene I hoped the reader could properly visualize – Gene tries pumping up Eugene's confidence (the opposite of Ruth's approach) during a Frisbee toss, a challenging task considering Eugene's throws are as genetically off the mark and unworthy of praise as are Gene's.

By pilot's end, I wanted to tip Gene's growing resolve to not always put up with Ruth's negativity. One way was by timing his profane unexpected outburst in reaction to a bully at Eugene's school play to coincide with one of Ruth's passive-aggressive comments from the audience. Could *she* have been the "bully" for whom some of Gene's antagonism was intended?

I also wanted to show somewhere in the script that Gene's unique bond with Eugene could sometimes cause a backlash...

Gene tucks Eugene into bed.

Gene: Did you finish your homework?

Eugene: Almost. I'll do it in homeroom.

Gene: No, you won't. It's not homeroom work. You'll be too tired.

Eugene: Nuh-uh.

Gene: Uh-huh.

Eugene: Nuh-uh.

Gene: Uhhhh-huhhh.

Eugene: You think you know everything!

Gene: What? No, I don't.

Eugene: Yes, you do. You think you know what I'm gonna do all the time!

A beat.

Gene: I wish I thought I knew everything. I don't, Eugene.

Gene isn't surprised their physical similarities he tries to downplay to Audrey, an undergrad professor fix-up, don't go unnoticed by her. How can *Ruth* not remember Gene when she looks at Eugene (different haircut aside) Perry would like to know? Ruth's more of a trip, reflects Gene, than a tripper down memory lane. As for Gene's wondering if he and Audrey are on enough of the same wavelength, his friend who knows him too well poses, "You mean the one where she likes you, but you don't like you?" Offering up another expository nugget that might spring from Gene's parental upbringing...

Perry: You know why your love life sucks? You don't love yourself. Women smell that.

Gene: Why, did Audrey say something?

Perry: Plus – you don't like the ones who do like you, because you don't respect their taste. (Memories of Howie.)

When he learns how to love little Gene, he'll learn how to love big Gene.

Gene: I do... love...

Perry: Eugene? ... <u>You</u> ... Gene. The little boy in you that Ruth forgot.

Maybe Gene loved himself too much? Maybe he was too selfish? Maybe he should have waited to fall in love – with *somebody else* and raise *their* kid? (The question Amazon thought it didn't hurt to ask) Maybe that can happen. Someday. After he forgives and embraces who he is enough to truly accept someone else's love. This experiment is for Gene, Eugene, and the scientific community. And the fully realized person Perry and Gene both know deep down he still can be.

A sign Gene may *not* be on Audrey's wavelength – her dinnertime revelation that her students in class represent a generation "overly rewarded for things," and how her goal is to awaken them to how tough life is, short of totally raining on their parade. Could her message have been a veiled reference to how often Gene overly rewarded Eugene at dinner, his overcorrection of Ruth's approach with him? One part of the wavelength Perry reports Audrey may indeed share with

Gene: She too likes edibles. They both self-medicate, theorizes Perry, to at least artificially feel better about themselves, something Gene calls presumptuous. Another edgy element I added: When a shocked Gene later stumbles upon Eugene secretly huffing model airplane glue the night before his big play to "feel better." Could this be nature trumping nurture?

In early March, I submitted the revised script, even including a sound clip of a stripped-down opening theme, just vocal and keyboard. With a full orchestra and visual effects, I could hear and see the foreboding sci-fi element in my head...

MORPH from somber looking little Gene to big Gene. (Via similar looking actors of increasing ages during transition) . . .

During which we hear MUSICAL THEME:

"What *if*... I could-do it over again? ... If... my mother didn't raise me? ... If... someone who nurtured me, praised me, *gets* me did... What if, what if, what if, what if, what if... that someone... were..."

Fully morphed big Gene calls little Gene into the picture, and we see the two of them together, each smiling for the first time.

"...Me!"

The Opposite of Holding Back

About a week later, the Amazon executive emailed me…

Had a chance to read the new draft over this weekend. Overall, I really liked the changes you made. The relationships between Eugene and Gene and Ruth is [sic] much more dynamic and compelling. The addition of Brooke also adds some interesting aspects of where the show could go. However, I still don't feel that this is right for us.

Best of luck with the new script.

The original script and world interested him enough to relay specific notes for a rewrite I wound up executing, gratis, so his team who'd been in limbo prior to such changes could at least take a look at the changes he now says he "really liked." And he was closing the door on that possibility? In answer to his "How are you," after I immediately called him back, I grunted, "*Not* great." After wondering why he couldn't show it to the team before sticking a fork in it, he said they didn't develop much, but he was sure this script would open doors elsewhere (with which I agreed). Much as Gene had unexpectedly exploded at Ruth, I was ready to diffuse my own pressure cooker…

(Calmly) I've been in this business for decades. (which elicited his chuckle) I guess I'll just have to chalk this up to another (pulling away receiver and yelling into mouthpiece) FUCKING!!!!!!!!!!!!!!!!!!!!!! (back to normal volume) inexplicable Hollywood chapter.

He had no response. There'd been no personal attack. No attachment of my expletive to any part of him, just the "Hollywood chapter" I would eventually go on to write and entitle "The Opposite of Holding Back." Sometimes it's more dangerous to keep diplomatically playing the game than it is to burn a bridge and build a new one to your sanity. I felt better. If the meek inherited the earth, menus wouldn't have lamb chops on them.

Also in 2015, Showtime wrote...

Outer Child is a smart and timely concept with a strong character voice. We appreciated the multiple conflicts introduced here as well as the Gene and Eugene relationship. It was a pleasure to read! Unfortunately, the humor is a little broader than what we're looking for in our comedy programming right now and isn't a good fit for Showtime.

Calling it a "really nice job" on the original script but too high concept for them, a junior executive at AMC nonetheless wanted to see the new version, liked the changes but still passed. This was a concept I'd also pitched online via Virtual Pitch Fest, a website that cracks open another window for conveying your TV, feature and web projects to industry agents, managers and producers. One was a young female former executive assistant at Sony Pictures. Responding that TV wasn't her domain, she added...

A man parenting himself is a funny idea, but I also don't love the roles women appear to be playing in this story. Female audiences are more lucrative than male audiences these days – you have to give them characters they want to identify with. Mean Mommy and Perfect Girlfriend just don't cut it. Best of luck, and feel free to pitch again in the future.

Taking her up on her offer, I prefaced the next pitch by thanking her and responding to her "perfect girlfriend" caveat...

The woman the male lead meets in episode one, the prospective woman in his life and the life of his clone, is a well-rounded, multi-layered individual. I wouldn't bother to write the other kind, especially for this character. It's not a show about his shopping around for the perfect girlfriend. It's about his sensitivity, borne out in the backstory leading up to his meeting this woman, about welcoming a prospective presence who'll be more emotionally supportive and positive in his (and clone's) life than his mother had been to him. This woman who'll become a part of his life, a college professor, is smart, and also happens to be sensitive to overly rewarding the younger generation when their accomplishments don't necessarily warrant a reward. She wants to prepare them for how tough it is out in the real world "without totally raining on their parade." Which is an interesting dynamic compared to the lead's having compensated by over-rewarding, in a way, his clone, to make up for how he felt under-rewarded by his own mother. The bottom line being – the woman could be the strongest and most relatable character in the piece, more than the neurotic male lead. As for the mother, yeah, she's a passive-aggressive piece of work. But she's an interesting character. The "mean mommy/perfect girlfriend" dynamic sounds to my ears like a high-concept film that could demean or overly caricature in a way I can picture all too well among past movies I've avoided like the plague.

I ended by pitching one of my comedy features, *The Seventy Year Itch*, about the old Hollywood generation at a famed motion picture retirement home grabbing one last shot in the spotlight to try to beat young Hollywood with a movie of their own. I'd first developed it off a one sentence pitch by Joe Bruggeman, the late husband of *The Joy Luck Club* executive producer, Janet Yang.

Sony Pictures' representative first addressed my reaction to her comments about *Outer Child...*

Hi again, Andy. The problem with "a prospective presence who'll be more emotionally supportive and positive in his (and clone's) life than his mother had been to him" is it still defines the female character entirely by what she can do for the man. It's distasteful to me and every other female development exec I know, and it alienates female audiences too. Women are now the primary consumers of filmed entertainment. You need to get this stuff right or you won't have much luck going forward. Honestly that literally made me wince. Get to know women better, read women's writing. Fix this.

As for *Seventy Year Itch...*

Sorry, this just doesn't feel like a studio movie, and it has issues with the female characters again. There definitely is an audience for senior-focused films, though, so I'd look into pitching it as an independent film. Best of luck.

The degree to which she drew inaccurate conclusions about my alleged depictions spoke to her own false depictions of me. It was time to build another bridge to my sanity. I emailed her one more response in the form of a new movie pitch entitled, "Keeping it In Perspective," in the hopes it wouldn't go unread...

Keeping it In Perspective

Logline: With All Due Respect

I definitely don't refute or discount what you report about the importance of female audiences. But with all due respect, over nearly four decades as a professional writer, countless female executives have connected with my writing, which has incorporated strong females, whether they're in established series, original pilots that feature female leads, or feature scripts. In the limited submissions so far of the Outer Child script, not just the pitch, most of the positive and even glowing responses have come from female executives, specifically about the writing and script's execution, irrespective of their not yet offering a home for it. As you know, things fall short of trigger-pulling on quality material in this town all the time.

There is nothing inherently demeaning about a man looking for a more emotionally supportive and positive female presence in his life, if circumstances are such that he hasn't had enough of that presence up till now. It doesn't mean that's all he's looking for in the woman, or that he entirely defines her in terms of what she can do for him, nor does it mean he isn't aiming to be just as compatible for her – something he communicates in the script. I would no sooner presume a woman looking for a more emotionally supportive and positive male presence in her life is subjugating men, or that her goal was (unfairly) defining the male character entirely by what he... can do for her!

I think both sexes benefit from getting to know the other sex better, something I continue to practice to this day, twenty years after writing on *Murphy Brown* creator Diane English's staff, thirty years after first writing for Shelley Long's character in the first of what became three classic *Cheers* episodes.

As for the "issues with the female characters" in *70 Year Itch*, the young female budding screenwriter who works with the seniors, an old soul and their champion, is strong, extremely bright, sensitive, isn't susceptible to the young male hotshot producer's simplistic dictates and calls him on it. If that's bashing or demeaning women somehow, I stand accused. As for the Marilyn Monroe body double, she's a multi-layered individual who grows, learns, teaches one of the male leads an important life lesson (a guy I clearly show has his own insecurities) and he comes to value and cherish her for who she really is. Monroe had a body double in real life. Why is it somehow anti-woman to depict such a character in her retired years with the artistic license that

Marilyn may still control a part of her self-image? If a script were to depict an Elvis impersonator who still obsesses on him, is that male-bashing?

Re: my earlier comment and logline: "with all due respect," your presumptions and directive that I need to "fix this" and learn more about women, and implication that my "issues" are basically sexist and demeaning, accords no due respect to someone with my long history of penning quality, sensitive, intelligent, well-rounded characters – the execution of which you haven't even laid eyes on yet.

I wish you well.

Her final response...

Best of luck to you.

Three decades earlier, the TV pioneer and relatively new film director, Garry Marshall, shared this tidbit with me before sitting down with Merv...

The key to pitching movies to bigwigs is cursing. If you preface every other word with a curse word, you'll get their attention. And the other thing – look in their eyes. Every time their eyes blink, you change subjects.

Changing the subject, maybe I would have received more attention from my less-than-bigwig if I'd transferred the expletives in my head to my computer screen! Changing the subject again, Jason Alexander, in Marshall's *Pretty Woman*, relayed to me the trick in doing the Bronx native's voice on *Another Talk Show!* "You always put the noun at the end of the sentence: 'That was good, the scene.'"

• • • • •

Business meetings are like blind dates. Sometimes the chemistry lays a sulfurous egg. In a meet and greet with a Fox executive in late 1992 about potential comedy writing prospects, I slipped in my CableACE win from the previous year and the fact I also occasionally performed – generating evident disdain on his part. As he coolly sampled the *6 Minutes* video, I was already mentally driving home, eager to erase this lousy fix-up from my memory. It would have stayed erased had I not caught *Townsend Television* ten months later, a short-lived Fox variety show hosted by comedian Robert Townsend. One of their ongoing segments: A *60 Minutes* parody entitled *6 Minutes*.[1] And one of their executives in the credits: *my bad blind date*. It wasn't as if I were the only one allowed to send up the news magazine institution. But considering this exec's initial condescending attitude, I had to figure out some way of at least reminding the powers that be (*if* they needed reminding) about the chronology of events. After my manager faxed them my refresher, the show renamed their next installment *6½ Minutes* with an execution I thought as uninspired as its title.

$$\bullet \quad \bullet \quad \bullet \quad \bullet \quad \bullet$$

When rewrite nights go into the wee hours as was often the case on *3rd Rock from the Sun* and most sitcoms, a writer's time for recharging brain cells is crucial. When a memo came our way that we were to show up early the following morning to laugh from the audience at a scene they'd be mounting, I told myself... not me. I'd be of no use. A) I'm not an out-loud laugher. B) At eight in the morning, after a late night staring at Styrofoam, cold food and dancing writers on tables, that goes double. I didn't completely hide my displeasure with this management of our time in front of other writers who'd shared a history with the showrunners on their earlier short-lived ABC sketch show, *She-TV*.[2] Maybe I subconsciously looked at it as my Get Out of Jail Free card and suspected they'd share my feelings with them. How I was later told I wasn't being renewed for the remainder of the season still stung, as I implied in my letter to the Turners...

Needless to say, the last week has been a rocky one. As you well know, the manner in which business affairs informed my agent that I wasn't being picked up (following their call the previous day telling her that I had been picked up) all in time for the official announcement of the show's scheduling, not to mention Thanksgiving, was certainly one for the books. Put it this way: It was the first time I experienced the Thanksgiving Twilight Zone marathon without it being on TV.

It was comforting to hear Linwood tell me that I'd been valuable to the show. And Joe (Fisch), who spent as much time with me in the room as anyone, volunteered that for a guy who wasn't a fan of room writing, I'd done a great job. He cited some of the many instances where I'd delivered jokes or specific setups that led to jokes. In the latter case, I believe the point guard is as essential as the guy who makes the basket. i.e. – My "What if Harry combines two colors to invent a new color" led to a fellow teammate's "red-yellow" punch.[3]

To a large degree, perhaps it was a matter of style. I was far from the loudest. I was the honorary loner. It was probably easiest for me to fall through the cracks. But I continue to take pride in my work, and I know I impacted each and every script, both in the planning and rewriting stages. In an ideal situation, I would have preferred the opportunity to rewrite passages on my own, much like the other teams did. They are separate entities. As a solo writer, I am a separate entity. That is how I do my best writing, and how I wrote many high-profile scripts, including the one on which you based your hiring of me.

I know these situations aren't easy for anyone. I'd intended to personally say goodbye on Monday. Thanks again for the opportunity to work with you. And best of luck in January. I'm sure 3rd Rock will be a winner.

Rob, Buddy and Sally may have had fun writing together on *The Dick Van Dyke Show*. But in the real world, at least the larger group writing situations where I was a cog in the showrunner's big wheel, conflicting personalities, motives and allegiances tended to stifle my creativity, as did the din that engulfed it. I would have had more fun tripping over an ottoman. In her 2012 non-fiction bestseller, *Quiet: The Power of Introverts in a World That Can't Stop Talking*, author Susan Cain reflects on how many notable creatives were introverts who worked more productively on their own...

Did (Stephen Wozniak) seek out a big, open office space full of cheerful pandemonium in which ideas would cross-pollinate? No. When you read his account of his work process on that first PC, the most striking thing is that he was always by himself.[4]

Perhaps future creative "families" can better accommodate the creative introverts among them and heed her caution not to undervalue them.

Our Time is Up?

A wide-eyed wannabe whose youth is but a speck in his rearview mirror finally sets out from the hinterland for iconic Hollywood to make his mark and his parents proud. Can Tommy Williger's (the last name of my former writing partner I thought had a nice ring to it) optimism withstand the reality of a town with enough lack-of-success stories to fill its latest entertainment news magazine show, *Unemployment Tonight?*

Pastoral farmland. No longer young son with his old backwoods parents. Patriotic music.

Tommy: I'll write you every day, Ma. I promise.

Ma: Tommy, don't leave. You know how dangerous that part of the world is.

Tommy: I'm a fighter, Ma. I've gotta go.

Ma: Stay here. And you can take over the farm in a few years. Your father ain't gettin' any younger.

Tommy: Neither am I, Ma. Look at me. I'm not a baby anymore. In fact, I'm starting to get arthritis. (END patriotic music.) I'm gonna conquer Hollywood, Ma. And when I land that first movie, I'm gonna send for you and Pop.

Pop: Remember to get a piece of the backend. I'm talkin' box office. (Spits into spittoon, boorish:) Not some fruity guy's ass.

My favorite line...

Ma: Gross. Not the net.

Such was the setup for *Knocked Down*, a Ted Collins-directed 22-minute film I wrote, Best Comedy Short Winner at the 2009 Southeast New England Film, Music & Arts Festival.

The ticked off, written off, dumped on and hung up on... Whether it's dining at the un-trendiest restaurants or hobnobbing with those on the F List, nobodies were out in force last night and UT was there to greet them!

I also sported a fake beard as a Leonard Maltin type, reporting on the death of "97-year young" unemployed actress Isadora Whitehead.

UT's "Leonard Siegel"
http://bit.ly/andyonUT

In 1998, former Poway mayor, California State Assemblyman and college buddy, Jan Goldsmith, invited me to speak at a campaign rally during his primary run for California State Treasurer, where I tacitly addressed my occupation's hazards to the crowd...

As a member of the entertainment community, I can promise you this: If you support Jan Goldsmith for state treasurer, one day we can all look forward to his name being on my unemployment checks!

He wound up unemployed too but not for long, later serving as a San Diego County judge and elected San Diego City Attorney. Politics – steady work next to the politics of Hollywood!

Tommy Williger's journey from gullible innocent to trampled-upon ticking time bomb in *Knocked Down* didn't *exactly* replicate mine. But Ted (with whom I shared story credit) understood his frustrations, as did I. *Hitchin' on the Highway of Life* was a song that poured out of me. The music and lyrics to this Americana departure from my usual jazz genre landed one of several humble songwriting nods in 2008.[1] With Toby Keith's manager among its fans, I grabbed an opportunity to lay down my vocal demo with busy L.A. session musician

Marty Rifkin (Bruce Springsteen, Tom Petty, Jewel) arranging and applying his multiple instruments and infectious steel guitar licks to my charts.

http://bit.ly/Cowanhitchin/

I keep hitchin' on the highway of life

And ain't nobody stoppin' today

I keep watchin' 'em slow to a crawl that's only a prelude to speedin' away

I keep lookin' in their eyes to see

How clear a window to a soul can be

Keep thumbin' as my foes keep a thumbin' their nose

Keep lurchin' on the sidelines

Searchin' for the guidelines

Twitchin' on the byways

Hitchin' on the highway of life

A portion of the song accompanied an animated endless highway behind *Knocked Down*'s closing credits.

Are my credits about to close? The longer the road, the more opportunities there are to absorb and learn from the bumps along the way as you navigate through to your ultimate capabilities. It is doubtful Hollywood sees it that way, even after 2010's historic class-action age discrimination settlement in favor of older television writers. Visiting a studio lot can be like returning to a college campus long after you graduated. The "undergrads" who do the hiring want to be with their own vintage, and powerbrokers wear their pursuit of youthful writers as a badge of honor. Production companies would never tout in entertainment trade journals how an executive has great relationships with "white" writers or "thin" writers; not the case with "young" writers. Something for them to think about: In ten or fifteen years, continued industry ageism may cut short their own creative lives and guarantee their own obsolescence.

Dan Piraro / Andy Cowan

Experience in this profession doesn't necessarily open doors that stay open over the long haul. In attempting to email the new president of Imagine Television in late 2017 – the company behind two comedies on which I'd been a staffer in the '80s and '90s – and a woman who'd "loved" my original writing when she was a Fox executive in the 2000s, my experience led Annie, her assistant, to put me on a list... to eventually receive this *assistant's* email address. After a week and no such email, I offered to save Annie time by my jotting it down as she recited her address over the phone. I'm still waiting for the email address. I have a hard time *imagin*ing that Imagine's co-founder, Ron Howard, would have supported such treatment.

The older you become, the more annoyed you become. The challenge is not becoming *crotchety*. I'm not at "Get off my lawn" yet. But is "Stop hocking loogies like the street is your personal toilet" safely <u>pre</u>-crotchety?

When lifespans keep growing, why should the years you're relevant keep receding? Maybe if I could humorously poke holes in ageism, my own "better if used by" date could expand a little before I turned sour. In *The Colbert Report*, Stephen Colbert used to play an extremist slamming Democrats, whose hidden agenda was slamming extremism. With the hidden agenda of slamming ageism, I could self-deprecatingly advise fellow boomers to embrace the fact their time was up, as boomer "psycho...therapist" host of...

Dan McConnell

Our Time
Is Up
with *Andy Cowan*

We're no longer cool. No longer hip. The millennials are our hip replacements. And if there's one thing boomers know about, it's hip replacements...

As we boomers prepare to pass the baton while clinging onto it for dear strife, the time is now for attracting both generations into the fold – our huge audience controlling trillions in purchasing power, weary of being marginalized in today's youth-obsessed culture. And the demo-friendly millennials, who I thought might appreciate the faux boomer-bashing and satiric groveling towards their generation and were smart enough to get the joke.

http://bit.ly/ourtimeup

In 2015, director Cindi Rice and I produced a five-and-a-half-minute pilot as a potential springboard into a web or half-hour TV series. The open/close made for an appropriate fit with a brisker version of the *20th Century Man* theme song, as my cartoon likeness floated out to sea on a block of ice courtesy of a millennial. In future episodes, I'd not only filter cultural issues and trends through boomer vs. millennial perspectives. I'd welcome an in-studio guest, an improv artist in character or an occasional celebrity millennial or boomer. Or even an alleged celebrity call-in who didn't want to put his or her voice on the air! Maybe Justin Bieber could help make us boomers feel less invisible. What are the smart boomer tattoo choices that can help prompt the rest of the world to look up from their handheld devices and admire *our* body graffiti? After you're run over by a car from gazing at a text instead of the VW headed your way, is there an app that can return your body to an earlier time? How do *I* focus on a handheld device at the exclusion of life around me? The heck with the big picture, teach me about the little picture!

We're too stubborn, slaves to precision and the specifics of communicating our exact thoughts. Millennials are free enough to communicate ideas "like" their exact thoughts. As a millennial slips "like" into his patter every other word, I could probe into what word "like" the one he just used he was reaching for...

Millennial: He, like, works out all the time. And I, like, go, that's awesome.

Andy: Wwoh, wwoh, wwoh. Help me out here. 'Cause I'm a boomer. My brain is atrophying as we speak. By "like" works out, are you saying he does something akin to working out that's "like" it, but not actually it?

Millennial (beat): He works out.

Andy: Ah! So it's "exactly like" works out. (taking notes) Okay, okay. (re: old-fashioned notepad) Boomer iPad. (continuing to take notes) Okay.

Now, when you "like" went "that's awesome" ... Oh, by the way, "go" or "went" means "said?"

After a beat, millennial nods.

Andy: Okay. So, you "like" went, "that's awesome." (thinking) Hmm. What's like "awesome?" Did you go ... "That's amazing?"

Millennial: Not really.

Andy: Okay, okay. What else is "like" going "that's awesome" or "amazing?" "That's ordinary?" (off millennial's confused look) You call just about everything awesome or amazing, right? And since just about everything is ordinary... never mind.

Rob Burnett, *Late Show with David Letterman* executive producer and CEO of *Worldwide Pants*, made me think I might have struck a chord...

RB: The pilot was really funny. I am sure there is an audience out there for this point of view.

A manager, former *SNL* producer and casting director called it "hilarious," sent it to her contact who "loved!" it and proposed we attend an AARP event to gauge interest. Labeling herself a bit more aggressive, the manager suggested shopping it to RLTV, the cable network targeted at fifty plus. I'd already pitched the Senior VP of Programming/Chief Content Officer there...

May 2015 – I think this is fun and you do an excellent job. That said, RLTV is in the middle of a transition right now and there won't be any programming decision made until that is complete. My prediction is mid-July. We'll keep

*this on our development slate and can revisit then. You should also check in
then if you have not placed it.*

*July 2015 – Thanks for checking in. This project is not going to be a fit yet. I
still like you and it, but it doesn't fit current direction.*

I needed more clarity...

*Am I to assume that RLTV has made the transition, per your previous email,
or is that situation still fluid and is it worth checking in again on this project
down the line?*

His response...

*July 2015 – Definitely still fluid but no change anticipated until October.
Definitely   check   in   and   be   sure   to   cc   my   assistant.*

*October 2015 – No change on our end. We should assume it's a pass at this
point as I don't anticipate a change for many months. Thanks for checking in.*

*April 2016 – Still no appetite or funding for original content like this
although I know it would do well.*

After disclosing to the former *SNL* producer other targets that I already hit
and had yet to hit, she stopped communicating, and also stopped short of passing
along contact information on the friend interested in taking it to AARP. So I
tried on my own. A contact in the California office called the pilot "great" and
would try to track down someone in the national office with the authority and
budget to move forward. I never heard back. Still later, an executive assistant in

media sales wrote, "Thanks for the laughs!! Great way to start the morning. Will find out the best person to send this to and cc you when I do."

I still think a project that addresses boomers and millennials could resonate beyond AARP and RLTV. Westwood One Executive VP Bart Tessler wrote, "Very clever, Andy. I think you're onto something. Wish we had a platform for it." The challenge in selling a show that acknowledges an older and still vibrant audience speaks to an irony expressed in the pilot...

Advertisers don't care about us. We have too much brand loyalty and aren't willing to embrace new things, because we've learned most of them are bullshit. The advertisers and programmers who have ageism loyalty and are unwilling to embrace old things say we're set in our ways!

. . . . .

Cartoon on the perpetual drawing board: New arrival in heaven tells God, "I'm adapting quite well to being a ghost." God replies, "That's why I made you invisible when you hit fifty."

. . . . .

When will I know I've hit the wall or it's time to stop banging my head against it? Will it be after another AARP exec finally gets the go-ahead from his boss, at one time a "big priority," for my writing and voicing multiple multi-platform animated shorts inspired by *Our Time is Up, Howie* and *Opposite Andy*? Will it be after TBS development exec Colin Davis (grandson of the late *I Love Lucy* writer, Madelyn Pugh Davis) determines with his development team the most advantageous moment to try to "upsell" *Outer Child* to their network head, Kevin Reilly? Davis ironically liked the script even more after I later added another wrinkle, pun intended, aging Gene up to fifty and lending more room for pathos. But as more "cooks" joined the layers of development and Reilly further drilled down on grabbing young eyeballs, I could see the writing (and my head) on the wall.

Will head-banging time end after I finally complete the second half of a spec comedy feature for Bradley Cooper's production company (after I'd heard the fellow Philadelphian tell Howard Stern he was open to new material) and ground it with a little more drama, their one note after informing my agent they "loved" the premise and thought the writing thus far was "great?"

Or will it be after knocking down the walls to peddle a brand-new project created and executive produced along with Emmy-winning comedy and reality veteran, Rich Ross, *The Lost Sessions with Andy Cowan*? If ever a TV vehicle seems like the right fit, it's this comedy/reality docuseries (whose title appears on a vintage Sinatra type album cover, following an animated opening of seventeen-year-old yours truly and a hidden *Playboy* to the melody of the *It Was a Very Good Year* parody) about an actual therapy session with a bright young marriage and family therapist.

2016 – *The Lost Sessions* – in the field

Highlighting snippets of comedic yet real and sometimes very personal reflections about life, a jazzy score, strategically placed visual thought bubbles, and comedy/reality field pieces that call back to moments broached in therapy, the twelve-and-a-half-minute demo reel made us think we were holding a winning lottery ticket the state didn't know about yet. In March of 2017, Rich tried reaching out to CNN contributor, radio and reality show host, Dr. Drew Pinsky, on Facebook. Maybe a grown-up humorous approach to an arena like this might intrigue him or his production company? The good doctor suggested calling his company's managing partner and veteran Hollywood jungle navigator, Howard Lapides. Focusing on talk and comedy, Lapides at one time managed Jimmy Kimmel, Adam Carolla and Carson Daly – before he found his *The Voice*. In April of 2017, one day after Rich sent Howard the video link and our carefully crafted pitch, including a potential CNN version that addressed news, political and cultural events psychologically impacting the audience and me, the "patient," Howard emailed back...

Rich,

Both Drew and I think there is more than just something here. Let's find a way to get Mr. Cowan on TV!

H

Whether the wall eventually needs to get plastered from all those bangs to the wall, or I do, I'll keep banging away. Because after all the headaches, heartaches, heartburn and harrowing near-victories/actual ones, in the end I'm a down *and* up guy. Thank you so much for scaling my walls with me. If and when you're knocked down scaling yours, do the opposite. Get back up!

Keep uppin' my chin till my ship comes in
I'm lurchin' on the sidelines
Searchin' for the guidelines
Strivin' for the entry
Jivin' for the gentry

Aimin' to please as I bend to my knees
And I ask, 'Goin' my way?'
Twitchin' on the byways
Hitchin' on the highway of life!

TAG:

Sound of car screeching to a halt; honks and female driver asks, "Need a lift?"

FADE OUT.

Epilogue

In March of 2017, I cold-called a contact number for David Steinberg, the veteran comedian and director of numerous comedies that included *Newhart, Mad About You, Friends* and *Seinfeld*. His 140 appearances on Carson, second only to Bob Hope, roots back to *The Smothers Brothers Comedy Hour* and ushering into prominence the stars behind SCTV, spoke to the continued respect he held as recent host of Showtime's *Inside Comedy* and returning guest director for the new season of *Curb Your Enthusiasm*. I had long wanted to be in this guy's orbit and wondered if an adult like him just might get *The Lost Sessions*.

Two days after I left a message, Robyn Todd, co-executive producer of the Discovery Channel's Emmy-winning *Cash Cab*, executive produced by Steinberg, returned the message. She said the pitch sounded "fantastic" and asked that I send along the demo link. David was in production but would watch and get back. This sure beat the proverbial "we don't take unsolicited material."

A month later I checked in to make sure she'd received it. Still friendly, she confirmed they had and were also still buried. (Cartoon note to self at the time – Agent's tombstone: "Still Buried")

In June she informed me they were headed back from New York to Los Angeles in the next week, and that I should resend the treatment and link. David would look at it soon. I mentioned we were getting interest elsewhere (Dr. Drew and international lecturer, reality show producer, casting veteran and CEO of The Conlin Company, Sheila Conlin, among them) but that we didn't want to commit until she and David took a look.

Following another meeting with Dr. Drew and Howard Lapides at KABC, Robyn (I belatedly realized she was Steinberg's wife) called with David on the line. The demo reel, he volunteered, was "very good, light, funny, charming." On the first of several occasions, he likened me to Woody Allen, but added I was "better looking" and "without the money." (From Seinfeld's *Jerry Before Seinfeld* Netflix 2017 special, I later sent him a screen grab of a vintage Manhattan poster touting the Everly Brothers and *The New York Times*' quote about their opening act, "the funniest comic since Woody Allen," David Steinberg.) He pictured *Sessions* as a series, threw in the cool query, "What coast are you on?" and asked if I minded coming to his Beverly Hills home to throw some ideas around to see what could help move it forward. I hadn't minded anything less in my life.

Although my lifetime of eccentricities was completely mine, David agreed we should hang a lantern on any Woody comparison to get it out of the way. Rich and I addressed it in a second show sample opening V.O., where the thoughts in my head are always heard in a long shot along Santa Monica Pier en route to a session...

Another one tells me I look like Woody Allen... I look like me! ... Maybe I should get different glasses... I couldn't write fifty movies... Who has that much to say? ... Last blind date did... At least she didn't make me write it down...

As for in session, the thoughts in my head would be sparingly and surreally visualized in still and moving image thought bubbles, a la our demo's retro film clip reveal of *The Fly* and a '50s actress screaming, while I bemoaned how people treat me like I have a disease because I don't have a smartphone.

David brought in Charlie Hartsock, former head of Steven Carell's production company, who told us, "You dropped off a very interesting mold of clay here." Over the next *seven* meetings at David's house, as we further honed in on the pitch, treatment and video links, we inched closer to the most opportune time David would set up pitch meetings – after the second *Curb* of the new season aired with his directing credit. He was open to directing some *Sessions* too. Rich and I both agreed this would be a reality show at its core, not scripted. We were rebranding what a "larger than life" lead character meant for reality television. Our version of the big tattooed biker guy who makes duck calls is the guy who taught George Costanza "the opposite," the guy to whom Larry David said, "You *are* George." Typical reality show leads may have been sold on their blue-collar working-class eccentricities. In selling an eccentric lead who represents the opposite, we wanted to tap into a whole other audience normally adverse to watching reality.

We would also play up the millennial angle, showcasing field pieces where I would mix it up with the growingly younger world around me and, unbeknownst to them, eke out extra therapy wherever I could find it. David said someone will want to buy that.

LOGLINE: The only comedy writer associated with *Cheers, Seinfeld* and *3rd Rock from the Sun*, boomer Andy Cowan, stuck in the 20th century, mentally disrobes for his therapist and the cameras in this trailblazing comedy docuseries, towards connecting with the 21st century and ultimately *finding* himself in... *The Lost Sessions.*

We reached out to other youthful, bright and appealing female therapists and arranged three shrink house calls shot back-to-back-to-back in David's living room with me as their patient! After witnessing Dr. Shirley Pakdaman's empathy and blissful unawareness of the camera, we all agreed we'd found our Scarlett.

2017 – In "session" in the Steinbergs' home

Off camera to the Steinbergs, I reflected on the weirdness in opening up about personal issues, labeling it mental nudism – stripping away my mask in public. If the public shed their "outerwear" in return, maybe we'd all be a little less uptight! Charlie recognized that this was an intimately introspective show, different from *Curb*, where viewers could share in the lead's vulnerabilities. Aiming for in-the-moment honesty and humor, I valued David's comment that my writing skills were helping to infuse the improv aspects to my therapy. Charlie could already imagine multiple field pieces springing from what was discussed.

Rich and I took it upon ourselves to send our demo editor, Henry Bolton, notes on Shirley's audition footage and the new opening V.O. segment, music, thought bubbles, and a close based on something David and Charlie were eager to include, to my delight, in each episode – singing at a jazz gig. That voice represented, in a way, the opposite of my nerdy exterior. And the song excerpt's lyrics could musically support one of that week's in-therapy thought bubble messages. We suggested David could even do a Hitchcockian pop-up in my group on his guitar. They wondered about shooting my upcoming jazz gig at a Sunset Strip venue not known for jazz, The Viper Room, and even how the arc over a first season could wind up with my landing in an iconic venue like The Hollywood Bowl!

Charlie thought David's growing engagement with a show he repeatedly called "completely original" would be "hugely valuable." As Robyn told Rich, "David loves this show. If we can find the right network for it, he thinks it'll be huge." She suggested their lawyer could represent all of us and introduced me in a conference call as the "star." We waited until David's *Curb* aired for him to dive into the sales attack. And waited. As in the phobia I'd relayed to Dr. Shirley about the other proverbial shoe always dropping, later supplemented with a thought bubble of President George W. Bush being pelted with a shoe by an Iraqi journalist in '08, it now appeared to be dropping yet again. By October 2017, David seemed to be second-guessing what his pedigree as a scripted director would bring to a non-scripted world he wasn't as familiar with.

Rich and I sent the latest package and links to Sheila Conlin, whose emailed reaction to the original six months earlier was: "I think you guys did an amazing job and Andy is very engaging." In November, Tim Crescenti, with whom I had mutual connections dating back to the Merv days, called me from London. He had decades of experience producing over 145 shows in some 61 countries, and a long history of seeking out unique reality projects for the worldwide marketplace, including one of my favorite aspirational shows, *Shark Tank*. He was also one of the executive producers of NBC's recently renewed comedy/reality fish-out-of-water show starring Henry Winkler, William Shatner, George Foreman and Terry Bradshaw, *Better Late Than Never*. Our show may have been aiming for a different sensibility, but I could certainly relate to their title! I also liked to believe our creatively analytical format could be adapted to other global platforms. (*Better Late* was adapted from a South Korean version.) The planet could use some therapy/smart humor right now. Tim viewed the latest package and emailed me November 29th...

Okay, this is friggin FANTASTIC! I was absolutely loving and laughing so much, I was literally – yes, really literally, not the millennial "literally" – laughing out loud! I have so many ideas but need to talk to Greg Phillips, our head of Kew-Content distribution. What are your next steps with US? With David Steinberg? Who is your agent/rep in US by the way? Thanks so much!

I no longer figured Steinberg would be part of the mix. The project was still free and clear, as was I agent-wise. Following Tim's return to the states, he spotted multiple opportunities from "hungry" buyers looking for something original, different and "relatable." I looked forward to digging down with him and his production consultant, both of whom thought *Sessions*, a show they "loved," could fit that bill.

In late 2017 I finally emailed my finished Bradley Cooper feature script to Weston Middleton at Joint Effort. In early 2018, The Producers Films, an independent production company in London, reported they "really liked" the script and that it had "sparked some great conversations within the office." Following our Skype meeting, company head Jeanna Polley emailed me script notes: "Refreshing and unique ...Engaging premise ... Would definitely fit in the American Indie category... Fast paced and witty dialogue throughout ... Well-developed and engaging central characters ... Interchanges between them are often slick and comedic whilst still remaining natural" ... They also saw great potential for it to be further explored as a "short-form TV serial." She closed by writing...

I think it will be very beneficial for us to continue chatting to see what we can do together. I look forward to hearing your thoughts on the above soon.

Along with Paris, maybe London was becoming my other European good luck charm?

Keep hopin'!

Contact Andy Cowan for speaking engagements:
contact@andycowan.net

Book Updates:
http://www.andycowan.net
http://bit.ly/BangingMyHead

Endnotes

Climbing the Walls

1 David Gates, "Johnny Carson, 1925-2005," *Newsweek*, February 6, 2005, www.newsweek.com/johnny-carson-1925-2005-122535

2 Perfectly Frank, Subliminal Messaging from Saturday Night Live, NBC.com, November 5, 1983, http://www.nbc.com/saturday-night-live/video/perfectly-frank/n9135

3 Mr. Subliminal, NBC.com, October 11, 1986, http://www.nbc.com/saturday-night-live/video/mr-subliminal/n9456?snl=1

4 *Tampa Bay Times*, "Kevin Nealon of 'Weeds' and 'Saturday Night Live' brings standup act to Treasure Island," May 16, 2012, http://www.tampabay.com/features/performingarts//kevin-nealon-of-weeds-and-saturday-night-live-brings-standup-act-to/1230278

5 *The Rich Eisen Show*, February 13, 2015, http://www.richeisenshow.com/2015/02/13/former-snl-cast-member-kevin-nealon-calls-res-21315/

6 *Classic SNL Review*: November 5, 1983: Betty Thomas / Stray Cats, August 3, 2015, http://www.bendouwsma.com/blog/2015/7/28/classic-snl-review-november-5-1983-betty-thomas-stray-cats-s09e04

The Opposite

1 *The Seinfeld Chronicles*, Pilot, Castle Rock Entertainment, July 5, 1989

2   *Meet the Writer with Larry David/Bryan Gordon*, Words Into Pictures, The 1999 Film and Television Writers Forum, Writers Guild Foundation, June 4-6, 1999

3   *Splitsider*, "Definitive Lists, The Episodes of *Seinfeld* in Order, July 12, 2011, http://splitsider.com/2011/07/the-episodes-of-seinfeld-in-order?

4   *Forbes*, "Do the Opposite: Seinfeldian Wisdom for a Brighter New Year," December 30, 2013, http://www.forbes.com/sites/robasghar/2013/12/30/do-the-opposite-seinfeldian-wisdom-for-a-brighter-new-year/

5   *The Wall Street Journal*, "What George Costanza Can Teach the C-Suite," February 23, 2025, http://blogs.wsj.com/experts/2015/020230what-george-costanza-can-teach-the-c-suite/

6   *The Wall Street Journal*, "George Costanza's Investment Tips," March 11, 2018, http://bit.ly/georgetips

7   *New York*, "Mitt Romney Increasingly Modeling Campaign on Life of George Costanza," May 3, 2012, http://nymag.com/daily/intelligencer/2012/05/romney-follows-costanza-does-the-opposite.html

8   Smerconish, CNN, March 26, 2016, https://archive.org/details/CNNW_20160326_130000_Smerconish

9   *Philadelphia Inquirer*, "The Pulse: Smerconish: Right Out Of 'Seinfeld,' The Opposite Candidate," March 13, 2016, http://www.philly.com/philly/opinion/20160313_The_Pulse__Smerconish__Right_out_of__Seinfeld___the_opposite_candidate.html

10 *The Michael Smerconish Program*, SiriusXM, "Donald Trump is George Costanza as The Opposite," March 14, 2016, https://soundcloud.com/smerconishshow/Donald-trump-is-george-costanza-as-the-opposite

11 *Seinfeld,* "The Mom & Pop Store," Castle Rock Entertainment, November 17, 1994

12 *Seinfeld,* "The Cartoon," Castle Rock Entertainment, January 29, 1998

13 *3rd Rock from the Sun,* "Post-Nasal Dick," YBYL Productions, January 16, 1996

14 *Entertainment Weekly,* "The Best Episode of 'Seinfeld'? Hollywood's Elite Weighs in with their Choices," May 4, 1998, http://www.ew.com/article/1998/05/04/best-episode-seinfeld-hollywoods-elite-weigh-their-choices

Cheers, 5 Mervs, 12 Icons, 6 Minutes

1 *Cheers,* "The Groom Wore Clearasil," Paramount Pictures Corporation, October 24, 1985

2 *The Hollywood Reporter,* "Oscars: Ellen DeGeneres' Hosting History," August 2, 2013, http://www.hollywoodreporter.com/news/oscars-ellen-degeneres-hosting-history-598767

3 *Cheers,* "The Cape Cad," Paramount Pictures Corporation, October 2, 1986

4 *The Free Lance-Star,* "Television," April 1, 1987, http://bit.ly/GeorgeSegalShow

5 *Time,* "Nancy Reagan 1921-2016," March 21, 2016, http://time.com/4248899/nancy-reagan-death-obituary/

6 *The Argonaut,* "Lindy Hopping through an Alternate Universe," September 2, 2015, http://argonautnews.com/lindy-hopping-through-an-alternate-universe/

7 *Los Angeles Times,* "A Net Loss for a Net Dating Bumbler," April 14, 2012, http://articles.latimes.com/2012/apr/14/home/la-hm-0414-affairs-20120414

What the Stars Told Me

1 *Variety*, "Fixing Oscar," March 9, 2004, http://variety.com/2004/biz/columns/fixing-oscar-1117901510/

2 *Deadline Hollywood*, "Oscar Nominees Luncheon: Contenders Told to Submit List of 'Thank Yous' in Advance As Event Draws Huge Crowd," February 28, 2016, http://deadline.com/2016/02/oscar-nominees-luncheon-brie-larson-sylvester-stallone-1201698767/

3 *TV Guide*, "TV Guide's 60 Greatest Talk Show Moments," December 4, 2013, http://www.tvguide.com/news/tv-guide-magazine-60-greatest-talk-show-moments-1074174/

Like an Alien

1 *3rd Rock from the Sun*, "Dick's First Birthday," YBYL Productions, January 23, 1996

2 *3rd Rock from the Sun*, "Angry Dick," YBYL Productions, April 2, 1996

Up & Down

1 *Larry King Live*, CNN, January 17, 2000, http://transcripts.cnn.com/TRANSCRIPTS/0001/17/lkl.00.html

More Up & Down

1 *Los Angeles Times*, "To Win with Defeatism," September 27, 2004, http://articles.latimes.com/2004/sep/27/entertainment/et-gottlieb27

Opposite Andy

1 *Deadline Hollywood*, "TV Land Developing Comedy Series Set in Purgatory," March 30, 2016, http://deadline.com/2016/03/tv-land-comedy-series-elsewhere-noelle-valdivia-corinne-kingsbury-1201728353/

Another Talk Show!

1   *Time*, "5 Things We Learned Talking to PewDiePie," May 26, 2016, http://time.com/4349086/pewdiepie/

Tooning In

1   *Meet the Press*, NBC, December 23, 2007, http://www.nbcnews.com/id/22342301/ns/meet_the_press/t/meet-press-transcript-dec/#.VujqDsywUzl

2   *Los Angeles & Southern California, Everywhere All at Once*, Insight Media DVD, January 1, 2007, https://www.amazon.com/Los-Angeles-Everywhere-Guides-Travel/dp/B000VUNUTM/ref=sr_1_2?ie=UTF8&s=dvd&qid=1299107527&sr=8-2

Evening Stew

1   *Los Angeles Times West Magazine*, "Always Know Your Place in the Pecking Order," September 3, 2006, http://articles.latimes.com/2006/sep/03/magazine/tm-rules36

Outer Child

1   *Splitsider*, "Sketch Anatomy: Andy Cowan Explains the Origins of Seinfeld's The Opposite," July 24, 2014, http://splitsider.com/2014/07/sketch-anatomy-andy-cowan-explains-the-origins-of-seinfelds-the-opposite/

The Opposite of Holding Back

1   *Chicago Tribune*, "Townsend Determined to Make Variety Work in Fox Show," Stereotypes with 'Meteor Man' and New TV Show," September 11, 1993, http://articles.chicagotribune.com/1993-09-11/entertainment/9309110061_1_love-lucy-red-skelton-fox-show

2   *Variety*, "Review: 'She-Tv'," August 16, 1984, http://variety.com/ 1994/tv/reviews/she-tv-1200438190/

3   *3rd Rock from the Sun*, "The Art of Dick," YBYL Productions, March 19, 1996

4   Susan Cain, *Quiet: The Power of Introverts in a World that Can't Stop Talking* (New York, The Crown Publishing Group, 2012), 73

Our Time is Up?

1   *The Great American Song Contest Honor Awards*, 2008 http://www.greatamericansong.com/honorary-2008.php

View other Black Rose Writing titles at www.blackrosewriting.com/books and use promo code **PRINT** to receive a **20% discount** when purchasing.

BLACK ROSE
writing™

Made in the USA
San Bernardino, CA
01 July 2018